Battles:

More Stories from The Mee Street Chronicles

Battles:
More Stories from The Mee Street Chronicles
By
Frankie Lennon

Battles: More Stories from The Mee Street Chronicles

Copyright © 2015 Frankie Lennon

Cover design by Frankie Lennon
Red Shoes Image by Nina Mathews

All rights reserved. No part of this book may be reproduced, duplicated, copied, or transmitted in any form or by any means without the express written consent and permission of the editor and publisher.

This work represents the recollections and point of view of the author. The names, characters, places, and incidents are used only in that context.

Published by
Dark Oak Press
Kerlak Enterprises, Inc.
Memphis, TN
www.darkoakpress.com

ISBN 13: 978-1-941754-60-3
Trade Paperback
Library of Congress Control Number: 2015959300
First Printing: 2015

This book is printed on acid free paper.

Printed in the United States of America

*This book is dedicated to my friend for life, Nancy D. Pate.
Your presence in my life inspires me to be better every day.*

Acknowledgements

Thank you to the writers of the International Black Writers of Los Angeles (IBWALA) whose feedback always provided me with unwavering support as an artist, and with the challenge to write the best story I could. Being in your company as you share your stories and screenplays is an experience I continue to treasure. It is a privilege to meet with you each month.

Thanks to my friend, Jair for taking the time from his own writing to read mine and give me feedback.

Thanks to Nancy for reading my writing and giving me her perceptive insights.

Thanks to my publisher, my friends, my students and colleagues. I'm grateful to all my supporters. Without you, I would not take the risks to do the work.

Frankie Lennon 2015

Table of Contents

Introduction ... 1
Prologue ... 5
Part One – Mojo Woman
Stalker ... 9
Fever ... 19
Unspoken Words ... 43
Masquerade ... 51
Part Two – Sleeper
Crossings ... 69
Legacies ... 81
Emerald City ... 95
The Sandman's Bag ... 117
Scotch on the Rocks ... 125
Trailblazer ... 145
Predators ... 159
Closing Acts ... 165
Part Three – Exotic
Where's Hollywood? ... 183
A Day in L.A. ... 191
Exotic ... 203
Tribes ... 211
Sanctuary ... 219
Skirmishes ... 229
Roger ... 243
The Throwaways ... 255
Pandora's Box ... 267

Introduction
Battles: More Stories from The Mee Street Chronicles

These new stories are the in-between narratives that I never expected to be published. They came out once I finished the first book, telling me that they wanted a voice, too. Although they narrated dramatic battles and challenges in my life, I didn't write them because I was afraid the first book would be too long, and, therefore, unpublishable. These other stories fill in gaps that you may have wondered about after finishing the first book. These stories begin after I move away from Knoxville, Tennessee to go to college in Bloomington, Indiana. In the stories of Part One, "Mojo Woman," you go on the journey with me—an in-the-closet Lesbian, desperate to hide that secret from prying eyes. The first story, "Stalker," dramatizes how speculative rumors about me and my secret served to put me in danger. The second story, "Fever," that won so many fans in the first *Mee Street* is retold here. This time, you get more with the aftermath in two, new stories: Stories about young girls being in love. And being in trouble because of that.

The stories of Part Two, in "Sleeper," are all new except for the two included from the first *Mee Street*, "Scotch on the Rocks" and "Predators." With these new stories, you get a clearer, fuller perspective of my life in Evansville, Indiana. By the time I got there, Mama had died and Daddy had remarried. I mention all this to say that by the time I stumbled out of graduate school, I was broken-hearted, grieving, rudderless, and entirely without focus or direction. My mother was no longer around to do the navigation I'd always depended on. Even worse, the love of my life—the woman whom I had desperately wished to skip down the road of life with—was nowhere around. I had gotten the requisite degrees and, now, something was supposed to happen. Something like living my life happily ever after. But how? Then,

Frankie Lennon

I visited Evansville, a college friend's hometown, and we passed by Evansville College, a postage-stamp sized campus on Lincoln Avenue. Somebody suggested that I apply at the college for a teaching position. I had never wanted to teach, but I was standing in the middle of a crossroads, clueless about what I was supposed to do next. The college had absolutely no faculty or staff of color, and the pressure was on to hire a Black face. When I applied, they hired mine, offering a year-to-year contract. I was in—the first Black, full-time instructor; this was one of many jobs where I would be "the first Black whatever." And so began my deep, long sleep, full of shadows and specters pale as death, hidden away in a cave called Evansville, Indiana... a sleep that went on for too many years.

It was in Evansville that I was introduced to Ron Glass, young, brash, and fiercely handsome, who would leave his hometown for the acting life and who would, years later, throw me a life raft that helped me change the course of my life. In the first book, I never wrote about the how and why of moving from Indiana to California. There were more battles involved in leaving Evansville, arriving, settling into, and exploring Los Angeles. I wrote about those things in Part Three, "Exotic." You'll find both the old and the new in Part Three. There are five stories from the first *Mee Street* and there are four new stories here.

I began this journey of writing the first *Mee Street Chronicles* because I needed to remember things; I needed to surf the images and smells and tastes and sounds, slipping and sliding across each other, shifting like a kaleidoscope... delicate, colored pieces of time gone by. Stories about my life that began, with the first book, in Knoxville, Tennessee. On the first street where I lived: Mee Street. As I wrote, those stories spilled over into the rest of my life, putting me on a path I'd never walked. And I had to trust that. Because the way was not lighted even though I was writing about my own life. Writing will tell you many things about yourself. Who you think you are. Why you believe what you believe. What you value and desire. When and by what you have been changed. The stories in this book did that for me.

Introduction

Sometimes, all too well. "And that is why I write," says Judith O. Cofer, "I write to know myself...." T.S. Eliot, an American poet, says it just as beautifully:

"We shall not cease from exploration
And the end of all our exploring
Will be to arrive where we started
And know the place for the first time." *Four Quartets*

I could not agree more.
Frankie Lennon, April 13, 2015

Prologue
Mee Street Is Memory

"Healing takes place within us as we speak the truth of our lives."
bell hooks, *Sisters of the Yam*

In one of my dreams, I am little and with Mama, uptown in Knoxville, Tennessee. We are on Gay Street and she is holding my hand as we walk through Kresge's five and dime. It is a hot Saturday morning and thirst blooms on my tongue like a red flower, but the tin sign over the water fountain warns: "Whites Only." Thirst binds my tongue as it spreads its roots. I lick my lips and swallow. Gay Street is a desert and its water is an oasis. But not for us. Not for Colored people.

A few steps away from the water fountain is a door to the ladies' bathroom. A sign that looks like the other one is over the door. I know what it says because Mama has told me. Has said that I can't drink water before we come uptown because there's nowhere we can use the bathroom. A White lady and a little White girl come out of the bathroom door. Quickly, I drop my eyes, like I was taught, and look away from them.

Once, Mama forgot to have me go at home like usual and before she was through with her shopping, the need-to-go feeling started pushing my belly out. By the time we got to the bus stop, I had to squeeze my legs together tight, so my pee wouldn't come down. And it didn't until I got to our front door; then, I couldn't hold on second longer. When I peed on myself, I wanted to cry cause I felt shamed of myself even though Mama said not to. It wasn't my fault, she said. And Mama never forgot, after that time, to have me go before we went uptown.

At the bank, while me and Mama stand in line, I peep around Mama's legs to look for the White lady with the big eyes and

Frankie Lennon

brown hair who sits in the corner at a desk, pushing and pulling wires that run out of a big desk. Every time we come, the snaky wires draw my eyes. I stare open-mouthed at them. There are so many. How does she know which ones to pull out and push in? This time, the White lady sees me looking at her and smiles. Before I can catch myself, I am grinning back until I remember that the others on Gay Street like her don't smile at me, and that I'm not supposed to stare in their direction. I stop grinning and hide my face in Mama's skirt. It's all so confusing that I forget the rules sometimes, and Mama fusses at me when I forget. She says, I must remember. Must.

And, I do.

Memory. It is the boat that takes me back to the past, so that I might move forward into the future.

Mojo Woman

Mojo: "*Personal magnetism, charm. A magic spell. Personal magic imbued with African flavor… powerful. Sex appeal that seems to come from the supernatural. A quality that attracts people to you.*"
Webster's Dictionary

"*Love does not begin and end the way we seem to think it does. Love is a battle, love is a war; love is growing up.*"
James Baldwin, author

"*Love takes off masks that we fear we cannot live without and know we cannot live within.*"
James Baldwin, author

Stalker

1. Rumors

"Frankie, sit down," Mama said.

We were standing in our living room, and Mama was holding a handwritten envelope. I was home from Indiana University for the winter semester break, so I'd been out all afternoon visiting friends. As soon as I'd walked in the door, Mama had stopped me. I glanced at the letter, about to ask her who it was from. But one look at her face kept me from opening my mouth. There was something in her expression that I'd never seen before: something very, very grim, very dark. I took off my coat. Whatever she had on her mind, it was going to be a bombshell. Unnerved, I flopped down on the piano bench and waited for the heavy artillery to fire.

"This letter is from the mother of one of your college friends, a Mrs. Powell. I'd like for you to read it."

What? Tori's mother? My mind raced around trying to figure out why my sorority sister's mother would be writing my mother a letter. I'd met Mrs. Powell once in Indianapolis two years ago when I was a freshman. Connie, another sorority sister, had taken me shopping in Nap town and we'd dropped in unannounced at Tori's to say hello. We regretted it almost immediately, sensing strangeness in the house. Tori crept around as if Mrs. Powell was going to kick her out into the street at any moment. Her mother was a woman made of glass shards, I'd thought. If you got too close, you'd end up bleeding from a million cuts. As I opened the letter, I could picture Tori's brown eyes, looking so sad and confused when she talked of Mrs. Powell. Fragments of what Tori had said floated round the edges of my memory, and I knew that this was going to be a very bad letter. I took a breath and opened it.

She informed Mama that there were "nasty" rumors about Tori and me circulating in Indianapolis. With sentences carefully woven together for maximum effect, her letter insinuated things about my behavior which she described as *unnatural* and *dirty*. Those two words stood out on the page as if she'd stamped them in red ink. With triple underlines punctuating the sentence, she emphasized how worried she was about my influence on her daughter. In fact, she was so worried, she would be taking Tori out of school this month to put her beyond my reach. And she swore that she would see to it that I never, *ever* communicated with her daughter again.

My face burned. When I looked up at my mother, fear and anger knotted up in my chest. I could hardly breathe.

"Do you know what she's implying about you and Tori?" Mama's eyes looked like lightning bolts. I'd never seen her so angry. Never.

"Yes," I whispered and gathered my courage. "What she implied… it's not true, Mama." And it wasn't. Tori and I were friends, nothing more than that. I handed the letter back to her.

Mama studied me, her jaw set. She nodded almost imperceptibly, then went into the breakfast room.

There, I heard her pick up the phone and tell the operator to find the phone number and then ring Mrs. Powell at a certain address in Indianapolis. "I'll speak to her person to person," Mama said.

While Mama waited for the operator to connect her, I wondered if my mother had somehow figured out my secret. But how could she? How could she know I'd always dreamed of being with girls, not boys? My woman dreams. I'd never let on about that. Not to anybody. Still, I was starting to feel guilty. Like I'd been caught with my hand in the cookie jar. But my hand hadn't been in anybody's cookie jar. Never. For as long as I could remember *those* feelings had slumbered deep inside me. Until I met Stacey. She'd woke them up. Now, there was a tug of war going on inside, pushing and pulling me this way and that. I kept trying to push them away, put them back to sleep—ignore them, but they kept sending me signals, pulling at me, making me aware of feelings—hot, wet, and deep. Stacey made me want to dive into them. *She* was the cookie jar I really wanted to get into. I admitted, feeling a twinge below my belly button, and Stacey's face promptly materialized in my brain. For so long, I'd fought not to let myself think about her like that. She hadn't been around for my junior year. Which made my struggle easier. Something to do with money had kept her out of school although she planned, I'd heard, to come back next year and finish her senior year.

Mama was on the phone talking to Tori's mother now. I crept closer to the breakfast room so I could clearly hear. Suddenly, Mama lit into the woman with barely contained fury, "I don't want to *ever* hear of you saying *these trashy things* about my daughter again!"

I was shocked that her tone was not the lady-like, soft voice she always used. Even when Mama got mad, she always kept her cool. What I'd heard just now was a different voice. Like a snake rattling. Urgent. Threatening. Dangerous. It was as if some raw, fierce soul had stolen into the breakfast room and taken Mama's place.

She saw my shocked face as I eavesdropped, and stepped into the kitchen, closing the swinging door behind her. The rest of the conversation was muffled, so I didn't get to hear anymore. A few minutes later, when she came out, her face was closed up tight. And I knew there'd be no more talk of the letter. And nothing about the phone call.

2. One Sunday

Spring was making itself known in Bloomington with the kind of afternoon that coaxes you to drift into a floating, lazy rhythm. Our sorority meeting had just ended and a group of us were standing outside the entrance to the The Commons.

"We're going to Fergie's for a burger, Frankie. Wanna come?" Asked Tweety.

"Naw. Got a test to study for. But you can bring me one back." I dug in my purse, pulled out fifty cents and gave it to her.

Frankie Lennon

On Sunday evenings, students had to buy their own meals because the cafeterias were closed.

We laughed together a while longer before they turned away, heading up the path that led through trees to the north side of Indiana University's campus. Tweety and the others disappeared through the heavy brush.

I didn't see anybody else nearby except for a dark green car ahead on my side of the street; it was coming slowly toward me. I glanced at the car. Normally, I didn't pay attention to the make of cars, but, for some reason, the Chevrolet insignia caught my eye. It was just moseying along as if the driver was looking for a turn or something. Was the driver lost? Had to be. There weren't any turns on this little street. You couldn't even get to a parking lot from here. You had to go in the other direction and turn left. Those thoughts vanished as I picked up my pace, heading in the direction of my dorm. Mentally, I began to run through the ten vocabulary definitions I'd already memorized. My Psych test was two days away and I didn't want to indulge in any distractions.

By the time I got to the third vocabulary definition, I'd noticed something. The green car seemed to be going slower... coming on toward me at a crawl. Was the driver waiting for someone to come out of The Commons? I glanced around. Nobody was about. Curiosity made me slow my pace to get a better look at the car. Without being obvious about it, I tried to peer through the windshield to see who was inside. Blinding rays from the sun bounced off the front windows, making it impossible to see clearly, and for some reason, uneasiness washed over me. I glanced around again. Still no one around. *This was silly*, I chided myself and took a deep breath to shake off my unease. Again, I picked up my pace, thinking of the test. Seconds later, the car braked a couple of feet away, coming to a startling stop almost beside me.

I hesitated, expecting a question from the car's occupants about how to get out of the cul-de-sac street they were on, but instead of the driver rolling down the window to ask directions, the back door swung out. Fast. The unexpected move left me momentarily confused, gaping at the well-dressed, a brown-skinned, middle-aged woman climbing out. At first, I didn't quite recognize her since I'd only seen her once before. But once I focused on the face, I could see that it was Tori's mother, the woman who'd kept her promise to take my friend out of school. Even though warning signals shot off behind my eyes, I looked to see if Tori was inside the car. She wasn't.

The only other person inside was the driver, and although he didn't turn around to acknowledge me, I could see it was Tori's father. Despite something deep inside telling me to back away, my home training kicked in then, telling me to fix my lips into a smile and say hello, like a well-brought up young lady. Before I could, Mrs. Powell, without a word, stepped toward me, and, quick as lightning, grabbed my both my wrists.

My confused brain went into overdrive, running this-a-way and that, trying to figure why this adult, this woman, Tori's mother, had her hands clamped on my wrists like handcuffs. Adults, my bewildered brain told me, just didn't act like this. Mothers I knew back in Knoxville *never* acted like this. What was going on? I opened my mouth to ask her, but my asking quickly dissolved away as she stepped closer, got a better grip, and then began dragging me toward her and the car. The high heels I was wearing worked against me. Off balance, I stumbled closer to her. Her fingers tightened on my wrists like a vise.

"Stop!" I whined, protesting weakly.

By now, her husband had rolled down his window. I threw a desperate glance at him, sitting there perfectly still, a small, slight man, wearing a bland expression, waiting patiently and silently, as his wife went about her grim task. He never turned my way. It was as if nothing at all were happening. As if he couldn't see or didn't care that his wife was trying to force me into their car. Kidnap me right off the street.

Lord, I wondered, *are they both crazy?*

Once my brain understood that there'd be no help from him, that I was on my own, my adrenaline surged and I pulled and jerked backwards, starting to really struggle. The woman proved stronger than I would have imagined. As I pulled back and away, I looked at her face and, as clear as day, I saw ugly hatred there, and that set my heart beating in a fast polka. It was her eyes, though, that thoroughly terrified me. Flames of a dark-bright madness danced there: hot and raging. I was scared witless... afraid she'd get me in that car and Lord knows what they'd do to me.

Desperation had ratcheted up my senses to animal sharpness. Traffic noises from the street below easily reached my ears. Random laughter floated languidly on late afternoon breezes. I twisted my head around for a moment, hoping to see a car, hoping to see somebody out here that might help me. Not a soul in sight.

A huge fear washed through and over me. *Your ass is grass*, said my mind.

I'd gained a few inches, by pulling back, but her sheer strength of will kept sucking me toward the car. Her hands were talons. Stronger than they looked. The more I pulled away, the more she tightened her hold on me. How was I going to get away?

"HEY!!" The loud shout came from behind me.

Startled, Tori's mother glanced in that direction, her eyes searching for the shouter, I felt her loosen her hold on my wrists for a moment. It was enough for me to jerk myself free.

Quickly, I staggered back from her, but the shift in balance was so sudden that I had to struggle to keep from falling. Pinwheeling my arms to find balance, I floundered desperately. My red high heels tangled up my feet so that I almost turned one of my ankles.

She swiped her talons at me, trying to hook me again. And she almost had me, but somebody upstairs threw some luck my way. Now, she momentarily lost her footing when she grabbed for me and her husband, seeing that, began to open his door. She half turned to him. And in those milliseconds, I saw my chance.

Run! Shouted my brain. I lunged forward, awkward and off-balance in shoes that were never made for that. Fear overrode everything. Pushed me forward, urged me to lift my feet, pump my legs. *Run!*

I ran.

With tears of fright running down my face, I gasped for breath, but somehow I kept my footing in those heels. And somehow, I got away.

3. Sneak Meeting

A couple of months later, Tori and I sat in an Indianapolis restaurant, smoking and talking. The restaurant was noisy with the clatter of dishes and humming chatter. Across the street a sign showed that early June was a sweltering 85 degrees. It happened that I was in summer school, so this was the first time Tori and I had managed to get together since her mother had forced Tori to drop out last January. Living at home with her mother made it all but impossible for us to keep up with each other, so I was pretty sure Tori was in the dark about what her parents had tried with me. That was one of the reasons I'd come down from Bloomington to see her for a sneak lunch. I wanted to find out if she had a clue that her parents had tried to kidnap me last April.

"Huh?" Confusion swam in her eyes. "Say what?"

"I said did you know they tried to kidnap me?"

Her mouth had dropped open and she shook her head, speechless. As I told her the story, disbelief, shock, then fear marched across her face. When I finished, her eyes were pools of dark water.

Finally, she pulled herself together and spoke. "I'm really sorry that happened to you, Frankie. I've never wanted to admit it out loud, but I've known for a long time that my mother is a very scary person. Very." The fear shined in her eyes.

"Damn straight she is. What I don't get is why they came after me when you weren't even on campus anymore. You're at home."

"I can't say." She puffed on her cigarette and looked out the window. "Knowing my mother though, I bet if I ever asked her about it, she'd probably say some shit about how she was trying to protect me."

"Well, from what? I'd like to know that!"

Tori smiled. As usual, there seemed to be a touch of irony in it. "You, I imagine." Tori peered out of the window again.

I squirmed in my seat to cover my discomfort at what she'd said. Someone came into the restaurant and I could hear cars honking and the hissing brakes of a bus.

"Seems like her taking you out of school would be enough if she thought I was such a threat."

Tori looked back at me. "You sell yourself short, you know." She flicked the ash off her cigarette and continued. "Frankie, I don't think you realize *the half* of what people see in you."

"Like what?" I didn't understand. "What do they see?"

She gazed at me in a way that unnerved me. "Something wild, I think. A femme fatale type. A boundary-crosser. Dangerous to the status quo. Somebody who will risk venturing onto forbidden ground." She took a last puff off her cigarette and ground it out.

"What are you, the gypsy woman reading my palm?" I blushed, then laughed to make light of it.

She joined in, turning her head to watch the street. My eyes followed hers. Men and women dressed for the office crowded the sidewalks, hurrying to lunch or wherever they needed to go. An older Black woman in the crowd caught my eye. Suddenly, I started to feel nervous about this sneak meet.

"Who are you looking for out there? Are you checking for your mother?" My voice had risen a couple of notches in alarm. "Does she follow you around, Tori?"

"I don't think so, but I wouldn't put it past her." Tori's face was set in anxious lines. She ran her hand through the dark strands of her baby-thin hair. "Don't worry. She wouldn't know where we are."

"What a mess this is!" I said, feeling stuck knee-deep in something that I didn't know how I got into. And poor Tori—she was in whatever this was up to her neck, too.

"Yes. A mess," she agreed. "I miss school; I was free from my mother there, and I miss all of my sorority sisters. Thank God my job helps keep me away from home as much as possible."

While she paused, I remembered some things Tori had said about her mother from time to time: *Acts jealous of me. Sometimes I think she doesn't like me. Maybe she hates me.*

"That's the worst part of all this... being at home with Mother." Her young face was a valley of shadows.

I wondered how Tori stood it. Frowning, I asked: "How is it at the phone company?"

A little smile peeped out. "I wouldn't want to do it for the rest of my life. But it's not that bad. When I get enough money saved up, I'm moving out for good and coming back to school."

I sipped coffee, wishing I had something stronger. The Monkeys who lived in my head started yammering at me, telling me all this was my fault, and trying to dump the whole mess into my lap. I fought them back. Why should I feel guilty? Or ashamed? It pissed me off that her mother had done this... taken her out of school, and had us sneaking around because she didn't want us talking to each other. Tori and I had been sorority pledges together, crossed "the burning sands" together to become sorority sisters. That was the bond between us. Not anything sexual.

"What are you thinking?" Tori asked. "You've got a weird look on your face."

"I'm not thinking about anything. Not really."

Tori looked at her watch. "I've got to get back soon." She caught the eye of the waitress and beckoned her. "Are you going to order something else, Frankie?"

I shook my head. "No, you go ahead."

When the waitress came over, Tori ordered, and I began to think about what she'd said earlier: *I don't think you realize the half of what people see in you... something wild, dangerous.*

What made people see me that way? Was I dangerous? Was I wild? When I looked at myself in the mirror, I couldn't see any of that. I looked common and ordinary. Not like the movie stars I'd fallen in love with so long ago. I was no dangerous Susan Hayward, who tossed her red mane and dared men to defy her. And who could ever think I was wild? Ava Gardner was wild and so beautiful that men fell at her feet. Wild? Dangerous? Me?

Why, that was just ridiculous! *Wasn't it?* Maybe not though. After all, Mrs. Powell *had* attacked me. Tried to hurt me. Maybe something in me *really did* attract other girls. But how was that possible? Where did this thing come from? Why did it live inside of me?

A thought skidded through my brain and dropped cold fear into my chest. Down the road this thing might cause me more trouble. I gnawed on my finger, worried. If I could see it coming, maybe I could try and stop that from happening. Sidestep it. Maybe. But who could see into the future? Nobody. So that only left one thing to do: I had to hide this thing somehow. *Had to.*

The waitress hurried to our table with a pot of coffee. "More?" She asked.

I nodded. As she poured, I looked down into my cup. And there, clear as day, I saw Stacey.

Her green eyes shot coded messages deep into my heart.

Fever

1. Green Eyes

As soon as I sat down beside her, Tweety Bird, squeaked, "Let's have a toast!" Her high-pitched voice had earned her the nickname when she was in elementary school and it stuck. Nobody called her Pat.

Motor-mouth Joann, as tall and skinny as Tweety was plump, jumped in, "Here's to us!"

"And to Christmas vacation!" Stacey added.

The four of us raised our glasses and I sent dagger thoughts at Stacey sitting across from me. *Where the hell had she been?* Her face was closed and there was a tightness around her mouth. Some people said Stacey looked like Lena Horne; others didn't see the resemblance because of Stacey's startling green eyes that just knocked you out when you looked directly into them. The effect, to me, was more pronounced because of the mole on the crest of her left eyebrow. It was like a punctuation mark, I sometimes thought, at other times, like a butterfly's wings.

We clinked our glasses and drank while I tried to catch Stacey's eye, but she and Joann had their heads together, giggling about something. That just served to stoke the coals of irritation simmering inside my gut. From the time we'd picked up Stacey at her dorm in Joann's ancient Plymouth up to now, I'd been maneuvering without success to get Stacey alone. To ask her what was up. Why she hadn't been in touch. Usually, she picked up on the signals I'd give her to go someplace where we could talk in private. Tonight, though, she acted like she was blind, deaf, and dumb to my cues. Frustrated, I took a deep breath through gritted teeth. Tweety bounced up, signaling me to watch her seat, and hopped away to another table.

Frankie Lennon

I plopped my purse in her chair to let the empty-seat searchers know this one was taken. This was the last Saturday night before Christmas break and it looked like all the Black students at Indiana University were here and ready to do some serious partying. People were leaning against walls, standing two rows deep at the bar, squatting on every chair. The place was packed out.

Years ago, Black students had christened this place "The Hole." You got in by going down a flight of concrete steps that disappeared under the ground. Legend said the Black Legionnaires ran out of money after putting in the basement of what was going to be their American Legion Hall. Instead of giving the whole thing up, they made do and turned the underground basement into a bar. It wasn't much for looks—an old, wooden bar at one end of the room, three or four dozen rickety chairs and tables scattered round, a pot-belly stove sitting near the bathrooms for heat in winter, ceiling fans that pushed hot air around in summer, and the essential jukebox in the corner—no, not much for looks, but we didn't complain since it served as somewhere we could dance to the latest James Brown, Ray Charles, or Temptations records.

As I watched people milling around "Ho-ho-ho-ing" each other, my mood blackened. I stole a glance at Stacey, my mind racing. Two whole weeks. And not a word from her. What was wrong? Why hadn't she called? What was up? My stomach lurched, a sure sign that things were amiss.

Over the hum of voices, Little Willie John's silky-smooth voice drifted up and out of the jukebox, singing "Fever," an ancient favorite of mine. The song's words were all about misery throbbing in your gut. Love misery. The kind that that settles into your bones. But it was really Little Willie John's voice—rough and smooth, like cayenne sprinkled on honey—that stitched the words into your soul. Stitched them, and then laced them with an aching so hot it boiled your blood. He shouted out a heat-soaked wail, and I turned up my glass to drink, glancing again at Stacey. The taste of scotch on my tongue was bitter and oily. Yeah, the man was singing about the love-fever: The kind that feels like blistering, summertime heat. The man was singin bout love-fever that has you searching for ice water to cool yourself down. His voice lit the fire of memory.

2. Heat

    I caught the fever the first time I ever laid eyes on Stacey. That was a couple of weeks after I came to Indiana University. She was in The Commons, the noisiest place on campus, where students swarmed between classes to gobble down doughnuts and coffee. I liked to study there; the music was surprisingly good for a place that White folks managed, and I could smoke and sip coffee. Which I was just learning to drink. The cigarettes and coffee conspired to make me feel all grown up. But the truth was, I was scared shitless to be on a huge college campus where I didn't know anybody, where I was hundreds of miles away from home, and expected by the folks back there to make the kind of grades that would do them proud. On top of all that, I was literally surrounded, for the first time in my life, by more White people than you could shake a stick at. The truth was: I was a wreck.

    That day I first saw Stacey, she was playing cards in The Commons, and I was between classes, sitting at a table alone. For some reason, I glanced up from reading about Odysseus fighting the one-eyed Cyclops, and that's when I saw Stacey gesture for me to come over. I was surprised, and thought she was motioning to someone else because we didn't know each other. Last week at a dance, somebody had pointed her out as a Greek and upperclassman. So I knew who she was, but I didn't think upperclassmen noticed freshmen. Feeling awkward and more than a bit flattered that she'd noticed me, I got up and tramped over to her table. Cigarette smoke curled around the heads of the four Bid Whist players, who studied their cards like they held the secrets of life. Two of the players were guys, signifying loudly as they slapped cards on the table with pleased exaggeration. That meant they were winning. Stacey—her auburn hair caught up in a ponytail—was doing some serious signifying herself. I was startled by the contrasting delicate curve of her neck and what was coming out of her mouth. She looked refined; her words were not. Obviously, she could handle herself and that impressed me.

I slid into a chair next to Stacey and stayed quiet. In between the card-slapping, she leaned over, smiling, and introduced herself. The moment she turned those dazzling green eyes on me, whatever else was going on in the place stopped and melted away. Though I tried not to gaze at her like an idiot, I found I could barely catch my breath. It was like one of those corny, Hollywood boy-meets-girl movies. Only this was girl-meets-girl. And, right then, I was lost. Lost. Or, maybe, found. Depends on how you look at it.

How I looked at it was this way. For a very long time, I'd known I didn't feel boys the way I did girls. In junior high, when other girls talked about liking boys, I'd used hook and crook to sidestep the subject. In a way, I was saved by Mama's rule of no dating until I finished ninth grade. But high school forced me to change my tactics. No more sidestepping. It was time for dates and boyfriends. Fear of being found out pushed me into conforming. So I made sure I got the boyfriends—Richard and Russell, to name two—and I blended in by dating Sammie, Merlton, Avon, and Bennell to keep up appearances. I even flirted a bit. Fear of the words, the accusations—*She's funny! She's a bulldagger! She's a dyke!*—fear of being severed, cut off from the pack, the crowd, the group taught me how to make myself fall in step, act in the conventional way, say the appropriate words. All in service of weaving an illusion, of building a camouflage so I wouldn't stand out as different. I blended in like a chameleon and the crowd bought my act.

It all went so well that I almost believed it myself. Almost. Until a willowy leg, a curve of hip, a swell of breast, or soft lips would bring to fore a distant longing in me, like tinkling bells from a far place. Like the smell of jasmine on evening wind. The ache inside me would start then—the ache to break free of the box I had put me in. Stacey's eyes that day I first met her—they were full of something that started that ache again. And I promptly slapped it down.

Black students at I. U. hung with other Blacks, so I saw Stacey a lot—at dances, at The Commons, in the cafeteria, between classes, at basketball and football games. Everywhere. By the time I was a sophomore, I had a serious ache, but I choked it off, never let it come up for air, hid it from myself in a secret vault, and buried the vault under boy-dates because I didn't want to admit the vault even existed. To do that I had to psych myself out. Not just act out the lie like I did in high school, but, this time, buy into and believe it.

Believing it was infinitely easier my junior year when something to do with family and finances kept Stacey at home the whole of what was supposed to be her senior year. That year, my pattern was set, and, had anyone bothered to notice, easy to predict. Always, I'd hook up with guys who were either engaged to the girl back home, or seniors on their way out, never to return. That I deliberately picked the unavailable ones, that my real motives were hidden deeper than the deep blue sea, never occurred to me because I'd buried the secrets in the vault under layers of double-dealings and deceit. And so, I went on living in Emerald City until the summer before my senior year when Stacey and I both ended up in summer school.

It had been muggy and humid-hot in Bloomington, so typical of Indiana summers. No air conditioning in the buildings. No ceiling fans. And the dorms were steaming. Girls moved about, in their rooms and down the halls, in panties and half-slips pulled up over bare breasts—the only way to cope with the weight of heat pressing down relentlessly. It made everybody edgy, the heat. You couldn't escape it. The television news added to the edgy feeling by telling us about the students pouring into Mississippi to register the Black people there as voters. They were calling it Mississippi Freedom Summer, and making, in their reports, fearful insinuations about White backlash. Everybody knew the reporters meant the Klan riding with their burning crosses. They'd torch a Black church in a minute—and do even worse. Seemed like everybody was living in the hot time.

Frankie Lennon

The friends Stacey and I usually hung with weren't there, and my summer roommate was a no-show, so Stacey started coming to my room a lot. Because neither of us had much money, at first, we'd go to all the freebie campus theater productions and musical concerts together; sometimes, we made library dates to study together. Occasionally, we'd have dates with boys, not many though because the fraternity brothers we dated weren't around. Mostly, we laughed a lot. When she laughed, the mole above her eyebrow looked, for all the world, to me like a gorgeous butterfly. She'd always thought the mole made her look ugly. I told her that I thought it made her look beautiful and she was touched, her eyes filling so that they looked like the crystal green waters of the ocean.

As the days wore on, I realized the more I was around Stacey, the more I wanted to be around her. She was like a magnet, always pulling me toward her. And when I saw that, I tried to back off, not spend quite as much time with her. For a while, I'd purposely leave my room at the time she usually dropped by, or I wouldn't answer the phone, just in case she was calling. I did it because I knew what the pull was and I fought against letting it slip into my consciousness. Each time it loomed up, I'd mentally tiptoe around it, or I'd try to quietly leave it in a room by itself. When it wouldn't stay gone, I locked it into the bottom drawer of my mind. But it—the feelings—wouldn't stay behind the barricade. What I'd done before, I realized, wasn't working: Because Stacey was golden fire to me, both frightening and inflaming me. The fear kept me in check, but the fire—the fever—drew me. And this time, I couldn't shake the fever loose. This time, my body was telling me things in hot-breathed whispers, in burning night dreams that I couldn't, and wouldn't push away.

And so came the Sunday afternoon of July fourth weekend. It was so humid that sweat popped out on your skin the moment you stepped out of the shower. With heat this intense, the dorm was near empty. Most people were out somewhere trying to find a cool spot. I was in the first floor lounge, watching television when Stacey came through, looking for me. She sat as close to me as she could without causing raised eyebrows if somebody walked in. We didn't talk much, just sat there, watching yet not watching the black and white pictures marching across the screen. We sat. Breathing in and out, drinking in each other's nearness. It was as if everything had conspired to bring us to this moment. I can't remember how long we sat that way. An hour, maybe. Or, perhaps, just ten or fifteen minutes. It seemed as if we were suspended in time. Held fast by a raging fever that had a life of its own. One that was palpable in the summer air. One that was full of sparks, like a tinderbox ready to go up in flames.

Without speaking, Stacey took my hand and we both got up. There were a few girls in their rooms on the first floor; we could hear them as we went up the stairs to the second floor where my room was. We went up, like sleepwalkers. And, without words, into my room. Neither of us knew what we were doing that first time, but it didn't matter.

Tenderness. Love. Joy. Release. That was what mattered.

That time, and the next, and the next.

3. Perfect Fit

Suddenly, somebody at the next table shrieked with laughter. It pulled me out of memory lane and back to The Hole. To get my bearings, I looked around. Joann was standing by the entrance, struggling to make herself heard on the public phone. Stacey's seat was empty; in the milling crowd, it took a few seconds to find her standing on the dance floor, laughing it up with Gene. Tweety, back at our table, asked me if I wanted a beer. Since beer was my drink of last resort, and I still had some money for another scotch, I shook my head.

"Frankie," she said before she headed for the bar, "Cheer up. You're a cute girl, but you're chasing the guys away with the gloom and doom face. Smile some, girl!"

My glum mood answered her silently as I watched her go. *Smile about what?*

I couldn't shake the down-in-the-dumps, blue devils. To cap it off, somebody dropped a nickel and Ray Charles came up singing

"Born to Lose." It was slow-drag time. On the floor, dancers draped themselves tightly around each other, hugging and clutching. Stacey, I saw, was dancing with Gene. One of his arms held her tightly at her shoulders, the other at her waist, his cheek pressing against her temple. Both of her arms were clasped around his back.

Perfect fit, I thought. *Dancing together, they're a perfect fit.*

Although I'd seen her dance with boys before, tonight, the sight of her body snuggled so close to Gene brought me close to tears. Why couldn't it be me out there with her? Why couldn't I nuzzle my face in her neck, fit my body close to hers, move slow and easy on the dance floor to Ray's heavy-hearted, country blues? The ache for Stacey was so clear and strong that I felt like running out on the floor, tearing her away from Gene, and screaming out our secret. Instead, I lowered my head to hide my face. Moments later, I saw an open palm under my nose and I lifted my eyes to Freddie's.

"Come on," he said, inviting me to join him on the floor.

Swallowing back the tears, I arranged a plastic smile on my lips and gave him my hand.

Put on the mask, girl, I told myself.

Out on the dance floor, my eyes searched for Stacey while I thought, once again, about the summer of 1964.

4. Secret Lives

For a few weeks, our secret life remained securely hidden. Then, there was that close call one afternoon in my room when Lynn, a student in one of my classes, barged in without knocking. Going by looks, nothing out of the ordinary was happening in that room, but if you went by gut feelings, the room was heavy with tingly, I-got-a-itch-for-you vibes. Stacey and I were sitting on the bottom bunk bed, books on our laps. Because my head was turned toward Stacey and away from the door, I didn't see Lynn coming in. But something in Stacey's expression scared me enough to make me jump to my feet, my book landing with a heavy thud on the floor.

Fever

It was a weird moment: Lynn at the door, wearing her usual dull-witted, sleepy look; Stacey seated on the bed with a startled, almost terrified expression, and me up and ready to take on whatever unknown bugaboo had darkened my door. When I saw it was only Lynn, my alarm drained away, and I asked her, with more roughness than I intended, what she wanted. As she told me, I noticed her dense expression changing. Into what? Curiosity? Slyness? While I hurriedly dug out my class notes for her, she stared, mouth half-opened, at me and then at Stacey. With guarded wariness, Stacey, I saw, was taking Lynn's measure herself. Everything seemed to be taking a long time, or, at least, it felt like forever before I found the notes and held them out to her. Lynn took them, nodding her thanks, and wearing a kind of smirking grin as she backed out of the room.

The door shut and I realized I couldn't breathe, was, in fact, holding my breath. I sucked in air as Stacey lit a cigarette.

"That," Stacey declared, "was way too close for comfort. We've got to be careful from now on. That girl was like a hound dog smelling a fresh trail."

I wrinkled my nose. "Lynn? She couldn't find her ass if you showed it to her in a mirror." I waved the idea away, moving close to Stacey again. "Does not play with a full deck, that one."

"No, baby!" Stacey snapped. "No. Pay attention. That one smelled our vibe. And we cannot afford to let that happen again." Stacey's voice had turned into an ice storm.

I still didn't see cause for alarm. "I don't think she suspected anything," I said, sitting again, putting my arms around her. "Lynn's too stupid to notice stuff like vibes."

"No!" She shook me off and drew back. "No! Don't do that! We'll get caught doing things like that!"

If the room had been feverish with steamy vibes before, now it was a below-zero blizzard. I backed off and got up, fumbling for my cigarettes. As usual, my hands trembled when I was scared. And Stacey's tone of voice had scared me. She'd never used it with me though I'd heard her use it before when she meant to cut somebody to the quick—slice em, dice em, and serve em up on a platter. She was known for her sharp tongue.

I could see Stacey trying to take a hold of herself and calm down. After a moment, she spoke. "Look, you're my girl, Frankie. But we're not like them. So let's don't act like *them*."

I was confused. What did she mean, let's don't act like them? Did she mean for me not to put my arms around her? Not to kiss her anymore? What was wrong with showing affection? And just who was them? "Who're you talking about Stacey?" I shot back, knowing the answer all along.

"You know. *Them*." Her voice was a cold wind. "Those freaks! Bulldaggers!"

The words made me flush with embarrassment; and, at the same time, I felt the sting of insult, of absolute put down. Why did she have to use those names? It was the same as calling us niggers. Or calling girls bitches. Anger rumbled in my chest, the kind that would usually goad me into starting an argument, but I didn't want to fight with Stacey. Besides, I could see she was already fighting, struggling with some invisible thing inside herself. A nerve at her temple moved up and down, throbbing. Her mouth was a tight slash. Whatever this thing was, it was a fearsome opponent. And it made her face ugly. Silence lay hard in the room, and I let it lay.

The thing to do right now, I told myself, *is keep quiet. Be cool.*

Stacey peered at me across the room. "I guess this is our first lover's quarrel, huh?"

I said nothing. Mostly because I didn't know what to say. Doubts about Stacey and me swirled round my head like fireflies. The undertone in Stacey's voice when she'd used the word *bulldaggers* was poisonous. Hateful. How could she feel that way about herself? About me? Anxiety wrapped its fingers around my heart, forcing me to take a long, hard drag on my cigarette. She was watching me, waiting for a reply. Still, I said nothing.

"Forgive me?"

I didn't want to make her madder, so I nodded, abandoning my feelings, ignoring my unease. I nodded because I was afraid to put my feelings into words. Afraid to pursue the threads of doubt setting up house in my head. Afraid of the doors doubt might open that couldn't be shut again. The meddling voice in my head was shouting a warning from a distance, but I turned the volume down on it. All the while, silently beating myself up for a coward. A chicken-hearted coward.

Our senior year, after that summer, started off badly. Lynn, the dumb bunny, had started rumors about me being a dyke. About me and any other females she saw in my company. Despite the rumors, we snuck around so we could be alone. It was hard because when we did manage it, desire radiated from us like a boiling desert, and we didn't have a place we could go to touch. To cool the fever.

And it got to be doubly hard because fear of being found out began running us. Just like those caged, white, lab rats in my Psychology class, running round and round on a wheel. Caught up on a course that was leading us into undiscovered country, we had no one to help us find our way. Nobody to talk to about where we were going. If only we could've talked to each other about what we were feeling. About what was happening between us.

But fear hung over us like a dark cloud, urging us into secrecy, and secrecy posted "No Talking" signs in our heads. The desire we felt was taboo. The feelings were taboo. So talking about it was taboo. If I tried, Stacey would make a shushing sign and cover my lips with her fingers. That bothered me, but I didn't want to do anything to make things harder for us, so I let it go.

September's Indian summer faded and I began to see Stacey struggling, more and more, with that invisible thing inside her. And I was afraid of it because I knew it had something to do with us. Sometimes she looked so hollow-eyed. So strained. I could see it was beating her down on the outside. But, Lord, what was it doing to her on the inside? Taunting her? Torturing her? Making her hate herself? What if, one day, she started to hate me, too?

I pushed the question away. Hard.

5. At the Cloister

Frankie Lennon

Two months later when Stacey and I walked across the campus, half-hidden in the shadows of the fading, evening light, dread was biting at my heart. A chilly, winter wind brushed against my bare legs and played with the hem of my skirt as we crossed the wooded campus: Two Black girls hurrying along, heads hunched forward, coat collars up, hands pushed deep into our pockets for warmth.

Faraway from the residence dorms now, we were passing Franklin Hall and several deserted classroom buildings, their darkened windows looking, to me, like watching eyes. A stand of trees—maple, maybe some oak and walnut, still holding on to most of their golden, red, and brown leaves—was just ahead. Stacey, a few steps ahead of me, moved swiftly into them. This was a secluded area so thick with ornamental shrubs, bush, and timber that students had dubbed it "The Cloister," a place as famous as "Kinsey Hollow," the make-out spot at Trees Center. I followed her in, glancing around to see if we'd ended up in the middle of couples sprawled on every bench, desperate for a place to make out. But nobody was here. She'd timed this just right. The deserted benches reminded me that our school was set, within an hour, to play our rival, Purdue, in a special nighttime football game. I looked around. Secret and cozy. That's the way this place felt. Or would have if I didn't have a queasy stomach about this meeting. I'd had one since Stacey had found me.

When she'd tracked me down an hour ago at The Commons and beckoned me out, there was a cloud of tightness on her face. Something was wrong and whatever it was had changed her face in a way I couldn't read. I'd come out into the hallway, and she'd put her hand on my wrist, pulling me into a darkened corner. Her grip on my wrist was a vise.

"You're hurting me, Stacey," I'd told her, but it was like she didn't hear me.

A fierce whisper leaped out of her throat. "We have to talk," she said. "Come on." And she'd said nothing more.

Now, here we were and I tried to get ready for whatever was coming. Stacey was standing deep inside The Cloister, partly in shadow, arms wrapped around herself for warmth, her face turned up to the night. My eyes swept in her profile, and I felt that something I always felt when I looked at her—a starburst of warmth, a surge of something electric pulling me to her. That electric current drew me close to her side.

"Frankie," she began, turning toward me, her voice earnest, too earnest, and low, "I want you to hear me out before you say anything. Okay?" She lifted her right hand and gently touched my cheek.

Somehow, that gesture which usually comforted me didn't, and I looked at her mole, my butterfly, at the crest of her left eyebrow for some sign of what she was going to say. When she was puzzled, or troubled, the butterfly's wings would lift as if it were ready to fly away. They had lifted.

"You know since Jimmy left and went to California, people, I mean... guys are asking me... Well, shit! I'm just gonna say it." Now, she took a deep breath. "I know you don't want to hear it, but we don't go out with boys enough. And it looks bad to people like Lynn. Just gives them ammunition to start shit, like she did." Barely concealed panic filled her eyes and she rushed on without looking at me. "I can't keep doing this." Her fist hammered the air as she finished, puffing for breath like she'd just run the 220.

Anger, deep and raw, flashed out of me so fast that my voice shook. It took me by surprise. "Why do you care what people like Lynn say? She's nobody! What are you so scared of?"

Stacey looked at me like she'd never see me before. "Well, hell, aren't you scared people will find out about us?"

I had to admit I was and I nodded. But then I realized I was tired of fear running us and I wasn't so scared that I'd give Stacey up for it. Which came as a revelation. I hadn't recognized before that I felt that way.

Stacey was reassured by my admission. "Okay, then. We don't want anybody to find out, so we've got to look normal. I've got to start dating somebody steady. You, too."

"Stacey, what the hell is 'normal' anyway?" I resented the word she'd used. It disrespected us, hissed that we ought to hang our heads in shame, slink away in disgrace.

A smile played on her lips. "Frankie, this is no time to be pulling out one of your technical arguments." She reached out and cupped my chin in the palm of her hand. "You know what I mean. We'll be graduating soon, and things with us will be different. We just have to do this a little while."

A dull pain crept into my throat. I wanted to say no. I wanted to plead with her. Beg if I had to. Whatever it took to avoid the sea change that was coming on. Instead, I heard myself saying, "If you've made up your mind, what can I say?"

The words tasted like gone-over milk in my mouth. The thought of her spending time with somebody else roused jealousy from its sleeping cave and forced it out into the night.

What if she leaves you? That meddling voice of mine whispered. The question dropped into my heart like a stone and I hung my head.

Stacey saw it and, in a rare gesture, she caressed my face. Impulsively, I grabbed her hand and kissed her palm tenderly. This time, she didn't draw away like she usually did. Instead, she sighed softly and murmured, "We'll be together, Frankie. But we've got to be careful. You're my girl; you know that. Don't you?"

"Yeah," I whispered, lifting my eyes to hers. They were shadowy pools of water, dark as the night that surrounded us.

"Ted's practically knocking down my door for me to date him steady, you know?" She turned away from me and sat on a nearby bench, beckoning me to come sit beside her. "Why not? He's a good guy, Frankie. Considerate. What do you think?"

Ted. My insides pained at the thought. "You're gonna date Ted? The puppy dog? He practically pants at your feet every time he sees you." I came over to her and sat down.

Stacey giggled. "Yeah. He's kind of like that, no lie. But he's manageable."

I made a face. I wanted Stacey all to myself, but if she had to date somebody, I told myself, Ted was the best bet. He was harmless. Better him than a few others I'd seen hanging around her. Like Lobo, or Honeybear. Cool, cute, and classy, the both of them. The kind of guys that girls fell over themselves to date.

Guys like Honeybear and Lobo made me nervous. Yeah, Ted was the best bet for Stacey. He was nowhere near the cool and classy league.

Stacey read the worry lines in my face. "Don't sweat. It'll work out okay, Frankie. You just be sure you don't let some guy get too close to you. Or I'll get jealous."

My heart started beating as fast as a hummingbird's wings when she said that. Could it be she *did* feel the same way about me as I did about her? I fished for her feelings indirectly. "Maybe I want you to be jealous," I teased, "to prove to me you care." I leaned close to her, intending to give her a kiss on the cheek, but, this time, she pulled back and away.

Her brow furrowed, and the butterfly wings lifted again. "Hey! Be careful. Somebody could come by." She looked around until she was satisfied nobody was lurking in the bushes. "Why should I prove it? You already know I care, Frankie."

But I didn't really, and that was the moment I knew I wanted a commitment from her. Wanted it desperately. But if I asked, she might laugh at me, or, worse, leave me. So I kept my mouth shut.

As we were walking home, the meddling voice tried to ask me something, but I smothered it, laughing at some joke Stacey was telling me. That was the night I started saying to myself that who Stacey dated didn't matter because things would turn out okay. That was the night I started telling myself that I should settle for what we had right now and that I could be happy later on.

Besides, I asked myself, *what did I want her to commit to?*

The answer came back so loud and clear that I couldn't deny hearing it: *To me,* the voice said unequivocally. *I want her to commit to me. Forever.*

6. Distant Thunder

Ray Charles howled one last time and the music ended. Back at my table, Freddie winked at me as I sat down. My mask was still firmly in place and I gave him a big grin, waving at his retreating back. Then I turned my attention to Stacey; she seemed preoccupied, staring into her drink, but I was determined, this time, to get some answers. Asking her straight out where she'd been wouldn't really sound weird if I kept my tone of voice light. Kept it playful.

"Stacey," I smiled, "where've you been keeping your butt for the last two weeks? I been tryin to catch you between classes cause I wanted to get you to quiz me for a test." The lie came out easily enough. I don't know what I expected her to answer: *My finals were kicking my ass...I've been pulling all-nighters in the library...My graduate professor laid a twenty page paper on us.* Something like that. But not what I got. Which was her looking at me with fear in those green eyes. Just for a moment, I saw it. Naked. Unmistakable. And then she did away with it. I blinked, startled, wondering if I'd imagined it. But I knew I hadn't. Before I could figure out what to say, Tweety pointed to the entrance.

"Hey," she chirped, "there's Ted."

At the entrance, Ted looked around, Jo lifted her hand and shouted, "Hey, Cuz, over here."

I could've snatched her bald. *Why did she have to go and do that?* Then I remembered that Joann and Ted were cousins.

I rolled my eyes and gritted my teeth. *Damn...Damn...Damn! Why'd he have to show up?* I knew he'd bring his raggedy-ass behind right over here when he saw Stacey. And, shit, we'd never get rid of him! Getting Stacey alone tonight was going to be almost impossible now.

I watched him make a beeline straight for our table. He was good looking enough with an open face the color of bronze. A friendly guy who wasn't stuck on himself, but it was all I could do to be polite to him when he pulled up a seat next to Stacey, looking like the big, brown Collie dog that he was. She'd been dating him steadily for the past year. Since after that time at The Cloister. He wasn't the only one she dated, but she was with him enough to keep me uneasy. Right now, he was whispering something in her ear and she was smiling like she was eating it up. I couldn't stand it. Jealousy gnawed at me with such ferociousness that I jumped up and headed for the jukebox.

Fever

I dropped some coins in and pushed some buttons. Martha and the Vandellas came up with that driving rhythm that speaks to your soul. I didn't want to dance so I pretended to look for more records to play. Tweety bounded up to dance with Gene. Somebody came by and got Joann. Then Ted pulled Stacey out on the floor. Everybody was having a ball, boogying back. That was the last thing I wanted to do. My mind was stumbling, tumbling from one thing to another: From the fear in Stacey's eyes, to her doing the ghost for two weeks without a word to me, to scheming about how to get her somewhere alone tonight so we could talk. Desperation settled on my shoulders and it was all I could do not to snatch her away from Ted and race out the door.

That we were leading double lives plagued me. It was nerve-racking. I hated what we'd been doing for the last year. Hated dating boys when I wanted to be with Stacey. Hated her and Ted being together more than she and I were. Hated the fact that this masquerade didn't stop after our senior year, but was going on still, now that we were in graduate school. The last time I'd seen Stacey alone, just after Thanksgiving, she'd talked me into being patient a little longer.

"Next semester," she'd said, "I'll have my own apartment and we can see each other whenever we want. For as long as we want. All night even."

I went along with her like I usually did, trying not to think too often about us being apart. Down the line, after we'd gotten our degrees and started living together, we wouldn't have to cover up—at least, that's the future I assumed. I'd tried to bring up the subject of us after grad school with Stacey two or three times, but somehow the conversation never took off, so we'd never really talked about it.

Lately, though, I'd been thinking about the future a lot. Never mind the meddling voice inside nagging me about the way Stacey acted that day Lynn almost caught us. Never mind the voice pointing out that Stacey couldn't even say the word *Lesbian*, couldn't fix her mouth to dignify us with the proper name, was always using the other lowdown words like *dyke, butch, bulldagger* to draw some kind of fine line, put up some kind of imaginary, protective wall. Never mind that Stacey had never really said she loved me, and had always cut me off from saying it to her. Never mind any of that. Because I had to believe that we had a future—had to believe that it wasn't crazy to think two Lesbians could have a future together. I had to believe it because...because, lately, when I thought about her, I was beginning to feel terrified of the future. Like now.

The Vandellas finished up and the dancers made their way to booths, or the bar, or stood in place waiting for the next jam to drop. James Brown had squealed the first lines of his latest hit by the time I got back to my seat. Jo's mouth was going nonstop, bending everybody's ear, but you really couldn't hear any conversation over the brass section of James Brown's band. I didn't pay attention to Jo and the rest of them for a while, that is, not until I noticed Stacey's eyes. Usually they were full of light; now, they looked flat and bottomless. I wondered about that, mulled it over until several words did manage to escape the noise and float my way: *Visit, Ted, Stacey's parents.* Now, I leaned forward hoping to catch what was being said. Only the music kept thumping and bumping, and I couldn't hear a thing.

I turned to Tweety, who was putting salt into her Schlitz and popping peanuts into her mouth. "What did Joann say?" I shouted.

Tweety put her lips close to my ear. "Ted's going to Gary for Christmas."

Ted lived in East Chicago, which was a hop, skip, and jump from Gary. Which was where Stacey lived. But so did Joann, and a zillion other folks. Even Tweety lived nearby in Hammond. Maybe, Ted was going to visit Jo and his relatives. Or, maybe, he was going to be in town partying. It wasn't unusual for somebody to throw a holiday party and have people from school showing up. Or maybe....

I stopped speculating, and asked: "Yeah, Tweety, so what?"

She shrugged, giving me that innocent, wide-eyed look that she was famous for. "I think Stacey invited him to meet her parents."

Fever

A cold blanket of dread spread itself on my heart. Stacey kept looking from Joann, to Tweety, to Ted, but was careful not to look at me. Something distant sounded in my head.

I opened my mouth to shout a question. The voice told me I didn't want to know, but I ignored it. Curiosity, after all, was my middle name, and I plunged ahead. "So, Ted," I hollered, "what's going on in Gary during Christmas?"

More than ever, he reminded me of Lassie. Any minute, I expected him to start panting. He leaned toward me, getting ready to shout out an answer when Stacey put her hand on his arm to stop him. Then, she slowly turned her eyes to me. They were deep and dark, like a drowning pool.

A few beats, and she said, clearly, her voice pitched over the music: "I've invited him."

"What for?"

You don't want to know, the voice warned me.

Smiling, Ted nudged Stacey. "Go on, you tell them."

A worm of fear uncurled at the bottom of my stomach. Stacey's eyes. They were so strange. Pulling me into their drowning pool. Maybe, it was a trick of the light; maybe, that was why they looked dark as a pit. And something was going on in her face.

"No, Ted. You say," she said so softly we all learned forward, straining to hear.

At that moment, James Brown's latest ended. Ted nodded and took a breath. "Stacey and me," he said, beaming at her, "we're engaged." He ducked his head and planted a firm kiss on her lips.

Jo whooped with glee. Tweety threw her hands up, screaming. Ted had a big, satisfied smile plastered across his face. There was no expression on Stacey's face, for a moment, and then it changed. She seemed to arrange it into a smile of sorts—one that didn't include her eyes. Eyes that held me tight. Eyes steadily pulling me under.

For a few moments, I could still hear them chattering and then I slipped inside the curve of time. Alone, inside that curve, Pain sat beside me, grinning, licking its lips in anticipation.

Later, it whispered.

I nodded, found a mask to hold my face together and tied it tightly in place.

"Congratulations," I managed to say, feeling like somebody had sucked the air out of my lungs. A tremor skipped through my body, and I steeled myself to be very still, balling my hands into fists, pushing the soles of my feet into the floor to anchor myself. I couldn't look at her. I wouldn't. "I never guessed," I added, keeping sarcasm just barely at bay.

"Me, neither," said Jo. "When did all this happen?"

"I'll tell you later. Let's celebrate," Ted said, "Who's ready for another round?"

"Me!" squealed Tweety, clapping her hands.

"You don't have to ask me twice." Jo declared, "I'll take a rum and coke. In fact, I'll go to the bar with you. I want to hear the whole story."

"I'll have one of the same, Ted. So will Frankie," Stacey said, moving to sit beside me in Jo's chair. "I thought about telling you in the car on the way over here." The butterfly's wings lifted high as the words streamed out of Stacey's mouth in a rush. "But I decided to wait; then Ted came and wanted to announce it, so...." There was a miserable bleakness in her voice though she tried to cover it with a shiny smile.

Tweety didn't notice anything out of the ordinary, and, by this time Jo and Ted had gone off to the bar. I said nothing in response.

"When's the wedding? Tweety gushed, thrilled at the prospect.

Their voices, too loud in my ears, pushed through the air until I heard something pop. And sound stopped. Everything had stopped. Everything except Pain, who leaned toward me and stuck its razor sharp tongue inside my chest, then licked its blistered lips, savoring the taste of the wound it had made. That's when I screamed, but nobody could hear me because my throat was paralyzed. And everything had stopped.

Stopped until I found myself outside alone on the street. A few houses stood sleeping among the trees and under icy stars on a clear, black night. Except for the music trailing after me and the

Fever

guffaws and shrieks of laughter drifting out of The Hole, it was quiet. I shivered, without a coat, in the frosty air. But the cold didn't matter. I needed to be out here. Needed to salve my wounds alone.

Didn't you know this would happen? The voice goaded me. Memories of that evening at The Cloister pricked at me. *Didn't you see where it would all lead?*

But I hadn't let myself think it. I'd dreamed of us growing old together.

Grief and anger and betrayal whipped me forward like a lash, pushing me along the sidewalk, pushing me to go somewhere, go nowhere, go anywhere. Agony sliced me up inside until, finally, a waterfall of tears tumbled down my face. I let them come. Covered my face and let them come.

The sound of footsteps behind me pushed my misery aside, temporarily, and I stopped crying, turning around, more than angry enough to jump down the throat of any would-be night bandit. But it was no bandit. At least, not that kind that takes your money. It was Stacey coming toward me, head bowed so I couldn't see her face, coatless shoulders hunched, and arms crossed against her chest to ward off the cold.

When she was within three or four steps of me, she stopped, without looking up, standing back a ways from me. I didn't think the distance was for the sake of appearance. Maybe she was afraid I'd haul off and hit her or something. In a way, I wanted to, yet I couldn't and I really wasn't up to that kind of drama. So, the both of us stood under the street light, hiding behind silence, waiting to see what the other would do or say. It took her a long time to look up at me, and when she raised her head at last, I saw something harsh and ruinous in her face.

"Don't hate me," she said softly, her green eyes looking like a brewing summer storm. "Please."

I didn't know what I was going to say until the words came: "Why didn't you tell me? Why like this, in front of all those people?" I hated lying. It made me crazy. And she'd done that. Lied by omission.

The mole on her eyebrow lifted and she shrugged. "I didn't plan it this way. I didn't know he was going to be here, let alone want to announce it tonight." She grimaced, and put the tips of her fingers to her head like somebody puzzling out the answer to a complex equation. "I wanted to tell you. A dozen times in the past few weeks. I just couldn't find a way." She stopped looking at me, glanced at the ground for a moment, and then shook her head again. "And...I guess. Well, I guess, really, I was scared to tell you."

"What were you scared of?"

Weariness weaved in and out of her words, as if she'd had a long, hard battle. "Of you. And of us. I know you, Frankie. You'd have tried to talk me out of getting engaged. And..." Something in her face worked mightily to force the words out of her mouth. "and I might have let you." I heard the fear in her voice. And, saw it again in her eyes.

Might have let me? What was she saying? She came close to me, lifted the fingers of my hand and touched them to her lips. The gesture startled me, startled me in its boldness, startled me in its obvious affection. It was a gesture she'd only done sometimes. And only in private. The Stacey I knew would never risk exposure by doing it in public. Someone could have seen us. Why was she doing it now? Did she love me after all? Maybe, there was still a chance. My head suddenly ached with confusion.

"Stacey just don't do it!" I blurted out. Silently, I had begun a supplication, a prayer—a bargaining with the gods. I would make a sacrifice, any sacrifice, to keep us together. "Don't marry him. We can be together. You don't have to be with him!" Tears stood in my eyes again.

She dropped my hand and smiled sadly. "Yes, I do. I have to be with him."

She sounded so sure. As if somebody had passed a sentence on her. "Are you pregnant?"

She threw her head back and laughed. It was a bitter sound. And full of despair. "I haven't even slept with him. Haven't been able to bring myself to do it."

Fever

"Then why?" My question sounded like a desperate plea—a cry in the wilderness. And it was.

When she touched her hand to my cheek, I had my answer. Because I saw the shadow of cold fear change her eyes in a heart-sinking way. I knew I had lost her before she said it. "You know the reason." Her voice was ragged, a thing torn and shredded. "Because I can't keep thinking about you. I can't! It's too *painful*. And—and so I *had* to do something to end it. Because, because you won't."

So that invisible thing inside had beaten her in the end. Made her give us up. With despair and grief surging up into my throat, I wanted to turn my face up to the night and howl. I wanted to shriek, bellow, scream, curse the gods. No, not the gods. The world. Curse what it had done to Stacey's insides. And what it made her do to us.

"Come back inside," she said, her hand on my shoulder. "You can't stay out here."

Raging anger clawed its way up from my belly and I shook her hand away from me. "What do you care?" I spit out at her.

I saw the pain washing over her face in waves. And though I hadn't planned it, I knew a second of bittersweet triumph because I had hurt her. But its taste turned my stomach. Still, the burning rainstorm inside me drove me to strike at her again.

"Get away from me!" I screamed. "Go back to your—your fiancé!" My voice shattered on the word and something broke inside me.

I looked into her green eyes once more. Those mesmerizing eyes that had always pulled me to her. I looked into them for some sign that she would change her mind. That there was still hope. But I only saw bewilderment there. Finally, I turned my back on her, a river of tears on my face.

Stacey hesitated, for a moment, and walked away.

It came to me then that nothing would ever be the same. That we wouldn't, as I had dreamed, grow old together. Realizing that made me tremble, suddenly, for I had no idea how I would navigate this new place where Stacey would not be. I was afraid then. Afraid of loneliness. Afraid of the path ahead. I looked up.

Frankie Lennon

The stars blazed like crystal fire against the black of night. In the stillness, I could hear Stacey's footsteps receding.

And her going away crackled in my ears like distant thunder.

Unspoken Words

"Love does not begin and end the way we seem to think it does. Love is a battle; love is a war; love is growing up.
James Baldwin, author

At eight p.m., there was a knock at my dorm door. Stacey was right on time. Ready or not, this was show time. I switched off the radio and took a deep, shaky breath. We needed to talk. That is, I needed to talk her out of marrying Ned.

Vee, the annoying voice in my head, got down to business: *How can you talk Stacey out of marrying him without breaking the rule?*

The rule. It said: No talking about us being lovers. No talking about the feelings flowing between us—feelings so powerful, they filled the sky. No talking because calling them by name would make us freaks... unnatural girls. But how could those feelings make us freaks of nature? That didn't make any sense to me. The problem was that Stacey thought it did. She was scared of the feelings. So I'd gone along with the rule because I didn't want to scare her off. But look at what had happened... she'd gone and gotten engaged. The feelings had scared her off anyway.

As I reached for the door knob, I asked Vee for the millionth time: *Vee, if I'd broken the rule... told Stacey I loved her, would she have gotten engaged?*

Vee said: *That's water under the bridge. If you want to stop her, you're you going to have to say how you feel. Tonight.*

A flutter of fear tickled my lips as I pulled the door open to see her, head down, standing there, almost lost in shadows. She was very still, but there was a movement—ever so slight—a trembling betrayed by the auburn curls of her hair. After a beat or two, she finally looked up at me. I ached to touch her. Longed to wrap myself around her. Snuggle into her arms. Find a balm inside her soft embrace for the bruised and battered place inside me. I didn't though. I just stood there gazing at her.

It had been weeks. Too long.

"Frank," she whispered. The sound of her voice was like coming home after a long, desperate journey. "I've missed you." She breathed the words out like a sigh.

Seeing her again, standing inches away from me, had my heart going like a runaway horse. It was hard for me to breathe when I was around Stacey. Always. Her mojo thing, I could feel it... reaching out, pulling me to her. The desperate, unspoken words wanted to gush out right then.

Not yet, something inside me whispered.

"Come on in," I told her.

And Stacey stepped out of the dark into the light. In that moment, it was as if she'd always been here, just out of my sight—been only just beyond it, at my very fingertips, waiting for me. I silently drank her in; she flowed through me like an eternal river.

"I brought us some Cold Duck," Stacey said, coming toward me, "to toast tonight's reunion."

She slipped out of her parka and dug into her purse, drawing out cups and a bottle. As she handed them to me, our fingers touched. And for a moment or two, we lingered in the touch. Lingered, remembering our desire... our heat. Remembering. I broke contact first and put the things down.

"How about some music?" She suggested, lighting a cigarette.

She switched the radio on herself, then stripped off her blue knit gloves—the ones I'd given her last year. Something flashed on her hand. As my eyes fixed on it, I pulled in a ragged breath. She heard me and followed my eyes. It was as if she'd forgotten the diamond solitaire on her third finger. In the background, the radio station's D.J. babbled as we both stared, transfixed, at the ring. Her face showed a cascade of feelings—distress, regret, sorrow. And then, as if on cue, the gospel-righteous voice of Ray Charles began to sing.

Unspoken Words

I can't stop loving you...

It took me back a month ago to that night at the club when Ned had announced their engagement to everybody at the table. I remembered—though I didn't want to—that twisting, cutting wind howling through me, turning the world upside down. I remembered after with Stacey and I standing under the street light. Remembered her eyes, turned storm-cloud gray, shining with fear as I asked her why... why hadn't she told me herself? *Because you'd have tried to talk me out of it,* she'd said. *And, I might have let you.*

Might have let you. That's what kept her hook in my heart. *Might have.* Later, over and over, I'd examined that statement of hers, searching for what she *hadn't said* to me. Searching for *I love you* somewhere between the spaces of what she *had* said, hunting for some clue. Had I been just grasping at straws? *Might have let you.*

I looked at Stacey standing in the middle of my room. Her green eyes were staring transfixed at something invisible to me. Smoke from her cigarette curled around her face like a frame. *Do you love me?* I silently asked her.

That night at the club under the street light, had she been waiting for me to say the words aloud first? Was she waiting for me to say *I love you* now? The words sat on my tongue and I opened my mouth.

I can't stop loving you, it's useless to say, Ray warned me.

I shut my mouth. Was Ray's voice a sign?

"Want a drink now?" Stacey asked.

"Yeah." I nodded.

I watched her fix it while I listened. Ray said he couldn't stop, but it was useless to keep loving, so he was giving up; he was settling for living on yesterday's dreams. *Giving up.* The thought of my doing that opened up a dark place in me. I couldn't stand the idea of Stacey belonging to somebody else forever. How could I give up and live with that? I went over and switched off the radio.

Stacey brought the drink to me, her expression solemn. "Frank, I think I know why you asked me to come tonight. It's about Ned and me, isn't it?"

"Yes," I whispered. My throat had closed up.

She gave a little nod and sat, wine and cigarette in hand, cross-legged on the floor, "Sit here, Frank," Stacey patted the floor.

I did, feeling off balance and struggling to find my way. Jumbled thoughts clouded my brain like worrisome gnats.

"Tell me."

I knew I needed to tell her how I felt. Needed to stop putting it off. And I gathered myself and took the plunge. "Stacey," I said, anxiety pushing my voice up a notch, "it's crazy, you being engaged to Ned."

"I don't think so." Her face closed up tight and her eyes—they'd turned a flinty gray, a sign that there was a storm brewing. Not good. But I pushed on.

"You don't love him, do you?"

She took a deep pull on her cigarette and examined the ring on her finger for some very long moments.

I found my cigarettes, lit one and waited. A ripple of fear wiggled down my throat. I hadn't meant to ask that. The question had slipped out. I hadn't wanted to ask because I was afraid of the answer.

Finally, she spoke: "That's not the point."

I was momentarily flustered by that answer. Then: "Well, how do you expect to be happy with him if you don't love him?"

"Happy is not my plan, Frankie."

"What? Then why—?"

Stacey interrupted me. "But it could turn out that I will be, Frank. Ned's a good man. He'll try to make me happy."

I wanted to tell her I'd make her happy... tell her I loved her, but I couldn't pull the words out because they were tangled on my tongue.

Before I could say anything, Stacey finished her point. "Besides, some things are more important than being happy."

I gawked at her in frustrated confusion. "Like what?"

"We're grown up now... and we—we have to do the right thing... do what people expect."

"What people expect!" Anxiety took my voice up to the roof.

"They say things will turn out all right if you do," she said in a tiny, high voice that seemed to plead.

"That's just bullshit, Stacey!" I was baffled at the way she sounded. Where was the woman I'd fallen in love with? Where was the Stacey that could chew up nails and spit them out? This Stacey sounded beaten. And afraid. I stubbed my cigarette out in the ashtray. "Just what do you think will happen if you don't do what people expect, Stacey?" I demanded.

She shrugged and went silent.

Unexpectedly, angry tears welled up, blurring my vision. For a moment, I thought I could see her receding into the distance. Out of my reach. I reached out and touched her hand. She was solid beneath my touch. Not fading away at all. Or was she?

"We've got choices, Stacey."

"Choices?" Stacey echoed. "What I have to remember is if I don't make the right one, I'll end up—" She stopped abruptly.

"End up what?"

She wouldn't say.

Why did she think she had to live her life doing what people expect? I knew it wouldn't be easy but why couldn't she just forget about them and live her life the way she wanted? Why did everybody else get to live free and be happy but us? It wasn't fair! I wanted to stomp my feet and throw a hissy fit. I wanted to scream at the top of my lungs. I wanted to fight like the fiercest of warriors! I didn't want to just give her up! I didn't know how.

At that moment, Vee, the teller of truths that I never wanted to hear, stepped up and shouted in my ear: *Tell her you love her! You've got to! Even though you're scared, you've got to!*

What the hell was wrong with me? I loved this woman so much that I couldn't see straight. Why couldn't I tell her? I looked into Stacey's face, trying to work up courage to go ahead with it.

"Stacey, are you happy when we're together?"

Her eyes changed to warm green waters. "You know I am, Frank." She reached out for my hand and squeezed it. "We're soul mates, aren't we?"

I nodded, squeezing her hand back. "If we're soul mates, then... how... how can you give us up for him?"

Long shadows flowed into the depths of her green eyes, reminding me of pictures I'd seen of desert wastelands—of bones seared and bleached under merciless sun. "We can't," she began in a voice low and full of unnamed fears, "can't always do what we want."

"Do you really believe that?"

"Yes," she whispered, touching my cheek with her left hand. The ring, winking in all its brilliance, seemed to suck all the air out of the room.

You better tell her! Vee shouted. *You better tell her or you're gonna lose her to Ned!*

Fear gripped my heart, snaked its way into my lungs and clamped onto my spine. Inside my head, the voices of my Flying Monkeys began screeching, warning me to *Stop!* Warning me that there was a drop-off cliff ahead. Warning me to turn back! Their voices brought me to the river. Made me see that it had never been the rule that had kept me silent all along.

Not really.

I was afraid. It had always been my fear that had kept me from taking the risk to tell her how I felt. Because if I'd told her, sooner or later, I would've had to ask her if she loved me. And what if she'd told me no? Told me, in no uncertain terms... said she'd never intended for love to come into the picture. Not at all. Not ever. And how could I live with that?

She got up, went to the window, and peeped out. "Can we see our ducks at night?" Watching the gray and white ducks at the nearby pond had been something special and private that we'd often done together.

"Don't think so. Too dark."

"You're right," Stacey said, turning the radio back on. "No ducks. But come look, Frank. I can see white clouds and there...the moon and a star."

Unspoken Words

Stacey held out her hand to me and I went. *Later,* I promised myself. *I'll tell her later.* Vee sneered at me for being the coward that I was.

Standing at the window, I put my hand in Stacey's and, together, we looked out. The sky was a dark blue backdrop against a smattering of clouds that cradled a crescent moon. At the top point of the crescent, a bright star twinkled.

"What's that star there by the tip?"

"I don't know. Maybe Venus."

"Isn't that the star for lovers?"

"Umm."

That sweet feeling of *rightness* came over me like it used to when we were together. She leaned in close and kissed my neck, just below my earlobe. Something as hot and bright as the sun flowed out from her to me. I could almost see it, rising, boiling up ... overloading my senses. Stacey kissed my fingertips and turned my hand over to let her tongue trace the lines in my palm. I caught my breath, remembering other times like this, breathing them in like perfume. Her heat pulled at me, traveled along the nerve lines of my palm, then raced down between my thighs to glow there, like a candle's steady flame. She held my hand while I led her away from the window toward the bed.

When we sat, I lifted her hand to my lips. As I kissed it, I looked into the ocean of her green eyes. The words. They were there hiding inside of my heart. Desperate for me to coax them out. I wanted to say them now. Finally. At this moment. I wanted to wade through the long, dark night of my fear and say *I love you, Stacey*.

I wanted to.

Meant to ...

Instead, I drowned in her eyes.

Masquerade

"Some conflicts in life are never resolved."
Ron Covington, Author

1. September 1966

I turned my navy-blue Rambler left onto Arbutus Avenue, a street in Indiana University's housing complex. "What's the address again, Cat?" I asked, glancing over at her.

She consulted the torn paper napkin I'd handed her. "1347," she said. "I bet it's over there." She pointed. "Where those guys are headed."

I slowed the car. "Can you see the numbers on the house?"

Across the street, a bunch of Black guys crossed the front lawn of an apartment heading to its door. Some had six packs under their arms; others carried bottles in brown bags.

"Yep. That's it. Party-time," Cat hollered, nodding in their direction. "Check out the guys with refreshments."

Despite the fading light of day, I recognized some of them. They were Alphas. Ned's frat brothers. I stopped the car and backed into a parking space. The thought of going into Stacey and Ned's love nest was about as appealing as barefootin it down a path of red hot coals. Since the semester had started, I'd made it my business to avoid every place on campus where Stacey might be. Now, here I was getting ready to go into her new home. For a house warming party, no less. This was crazy.

Then, why are you going to Stacey's? Asked Vee, sitting in the middle of my forehead, always asking about things she already knew the answer to.

Stacey called and asked me to come. You know that.

So what? Did you have to do this? When are you going to give up on her?

I was quivering with agitation. Suddenly, I wanted to run. Could I make an excuse to drive away from here? If I hadn't brought Cat to help me play out this masquerade, I could.

Cat had come round to my side of the car. "Hurry up, slow poke."

"Give me a second, Cat." I dug around in my purse. "I thought I had cigarettes somewhere here."

"Come on! I put some cigarettes in your purse before we left. Let's get going. I'm ready for this party," she said, looking at the apartment where the guys were headed. The door opened and a woman stepped out. Cat asked: "Is that Stacey at the door?"

Taking a deliberate breath to steady myself, I looked in the direction Cat was pointing. Stacey had stepped outside to welcome the guys.

"Yeah. That's her." My heartbeat had skipped into overtime. Heat charged up the length of my arms and pulsed into my chest. Stacey had cut her auburn hair short and swept bangs down to her eyebrows; the style emphasized her eyes. She was as stunning as ever. Maybe more so.

Cat pointed to my forehead. "You're sweating. Are you nervous about something?"

"Nervous? Course not," I shot back. "It's this sweater. Maybe I shouldn't have worn it. September's turning out to be warm this year." I tugged at the neck of my red pullover.

"No; you made the right choice. You look good in red. Besides, you'll need that sweater," Cat paused. "Nights are turning cold... good for snuggling. Right?" She winked and gave me a twinkling smile.

That smile. It flattered her cinnamon skin, dark eyes, and, of course, those killer dimples. When she'd first come after me, it was the dimples that had delivered me into her arms. Her dimples—and Stacey's eloping with Ned in last June.

2. Games

As I got out of the car, another knot of people came up and surged into Stacey's apartment. Before turning to follow them in, she took a last scan of the street. Which is when she spotted me. With Cat. Surprised, she stopped stock still. I knew she didn't know who Cat was. Or what she was to me. Stacey watched us, her expression in neutral, her eyes, green, calm waters. Hardly breathing, I masked the conflicting feelings zigzagging up and down my spine. *Why had she really called me?* Vee had implied that I was a fool to put stock in fairy tale happy endings. Maybe I was, but I wanted to believe love came out the winner—in the end.

When the three of us came face to face, I said: "Stacey, this is a friend of mine. She's a new transfer student." I tried to look at Cat during the introductions, but I couldn't quite take my eyes off of Stacey.

She molded her mouth into a smile—not particularly warm, but passable as polite. "Hello," She said, barely looking at Cat before she turned the full force of her eyes on me. "I'm glad you could come, Frank. It's been awhile."

I could feel Stacey's mojo reach out and pull me so that my insides trembled like Jell-O.

"Yeah," I said, "a while." Her eyes held me like a silk cord. The wings of her butterfly mole just above her left eyebrow were way up. That meant trouble was brewing.

"On the phone you said you weren't sure you could, Frank." Now, she gave me an easy smile. The effect was disarming. "But you were able to make it after all." She made a deliberate pause, then purred: "And you brought somebody with you. How nice."

I felt Cat bristle. "Not somebody. My name is Catherine. Cat, for short."

Stacey briefly cut her eyes at Cat and stared for a couple of beats before turning away in dismissal. "Come on in," she said and opened the door. "Welcome."

Inside, Cat stood on one side of me and Stacey on the other. Frat brothers, sorority sisters, party people from all over campus were talking, drinking, snacking, and dancing. On the hi-fi, Martha and the Vandellas belted out:

Nowhere to run... Nowhere to hide from you, baby.

Frankie Lennon

As I scanned Stacey's apartment, jealousy marched into my breast and pitched camp. This was a top of the line apartment. The large living room was decorated with warm-toned furniture—a couch, several chairs, granite-top tables—comfortable and pricey looking. Abstract sketches hung on all the crème walls. On a mantle over a cozy-looking fireplace, there were photos framed in heavy brass and silver. I couldn't tell if they were wedding pictures and I didn't want to find out. Sadness choked me as I imagined the days and nights she was spending with Ned now.

"How do you like it, Frank?"

Bitter tears swam in my chest. "It looks like you, Stacey."

She acknowledged my weak compliment with a smile and a small nod of the head. "Make yourself at home. Drinks and beer in the dining room. Snacks are everywhere." Stacey left us and crossed the room, stopping here and there to joke or laugh with her guests.

Cat looked appraisingly at me and said: "This is going to be an interesting party, I think."

Then she drifted toward the cooler of beer. Briefly, I wondered how much Cat had put together about me and Stacey—if anything. But, at the moment, I didn't care. I glared at Stacey as she made her way to Ned, the Collie dog. Still panting all over her, he put his arm around her waist; she leaned into him and wrapped her arms around him. I fumed, put my back to them and I lit up a cigarette, then carefully waved at this person and that one in the room.

Was she happy with him? I hoped not. I hoped she was as miserable as I was. I prayed she would always be miserable. Guilt and jealousy took turns jabbing me in the chest as my head raged with hurricane force winds. Home free. Safe because she'd done what was expected. Acceptable. The crowd wouldn't throw her to the wolves because she'd kept the rules: Girls must be with boys.

Who the hell had made the rule that girls had *to be with boys?* I asked Vee.

She didn't answer.

Masquerade

Lord, I hated rules. Who'd made them anyway, and by what right? Not long ago, people had gone down south to show they weren't going to follow White people's prejudiced rules anymore that kept Black people from voting. What would happen if I and Stacey decided not to follow the rules?

Some days I missed her so badly that I felt like I was bleeding to death inside. Why couldn't I be dead and done with it? I grabbed the nearest bottle of scotch and grimaced as the drink burned going down my throat.

Cat planted herself in front of me with a napkin full of Ritz crackers and cheese. "Girl, what are you frowned up about? Steam is coming out of your ears."

Embarrassed that my mask had slipped, I mumbled, "Nothing."

She x-rayed my face and gave a little nod. "Here, have some cheese and crackers to go with your scotch. Maybe that'll fix you." She dumped the whole thing in my hand. "I'm going to see if I can get into the card game."

At the dining room table, the Bid Whist players had lined up drinks and eats, cigarettes and ash trays at their elbows. One of them, Tommy, shouted: "Boston! Time for you ladies to rise and fly!" And he slammed his cards down on the table. The two women who'd lost got up.

Cat hunched me with her elbow. "Come on," she said, darting to one of the empty chairs. She gestured for me to sit in the other.

But I was too slow, Morgan slid into the chair. She was a striking woman with skin like ripe, dark plums and who, some said, suffered from an over-abundance of ego. "I'm going to be your partner, dear." She announced, without waiting for Cat to say yea or nay.

Cat looked at Morgan and shrugged. "Okay."

Morgan reached across the table and took the stacked cards. She said to Cat. "You came in with Frankie but I didn't get over to meet you. I haven't seen you around campus before." She looked directly at me first, then, Cat, taking her measure as she introduced herself. "I'm Morgan."

"Cat."

I moved to stand just behind Cat's shoulder. I could feel Stacey watching us. *Good. Let her watch. I want her to be jealous!* Though Stacey didn't know it, Cat couldn't hold a candle to her. But Stacey didn't know that. And I wasn't going to tell her.

Vee purred in my ear: *Quite the little manipulator, aren't we?*

Morgan shuffled the cards. "Anybody can tell you I'm a good player." She gave Leo and Tommy a smirk as she began a fast deal of the cards. "So don't sweat, Cat. We'll take them to the cleaners."

"Damn straight," Cat enthused. She was one of those ferocious card players.

Leo peeped at the cards she'd dealt him and put in his bluff. "Get serious. You can't touch this action here."

Morgan swept up the cards piled in front of her and put them in order. "Actions," she declared, "speak louder than words. We're gonna be rompin and stompin all over the place. Right, Cat?"

Cat deliberately caught Stacey's eye, smiled her cutest, sugar-dumpling smile, and winked. Then she said: "They won't know what hit 'em."

I looked at Stacey. Her deep frown said she wasn't buying Cat's cute act.

Stacey came over. "Come on into the kitchen with me. I'll fix you a fresh drink."

I looked in her face and a wave of charged heat made a bridge between us. That wasn't supposed to happen. Unless things weren't what they seemed. Ragged hope, snuggled in the bottom drawers of my heart, peeped out. *Could she want us to get back together?*

Foolish girl, said Vee. *Don't even think it.*

Could she? Excitement sped up my heart. *Why else had she called me to come today?*

You're going on a fool's errand, Vee warned me.

Stubborn hope surged up, nevertheless, as I followed Stacey out.

3. In the Kitchen

Stacey went straight to the refrigerator. I looked around at all shiny surfaces and gleaming appliances. On the table, a fifth of Johnnie Walker Red stood along with a silver and leather ice bucket. There was an ashtray, too. I sat, holding my breath, waiting for her to say something. But she kept silent, her back to me, doing something or other. It made me nervous that she wasn't talking. Her silence was draining my anticipation away.

The air in the room seemed heavy. Too full of feelings unnamed. Too full of choices made and… consequences. Once, we would've been cracking jokes and kidding each other. Happy to be in each other's company. Laughing. Chattering away. Sexual desire inching higher and higher. Once upon a time. Maybe we could get it back… all of it. If only… Hope kept wanting to push forward, but I kept hold of it, scared to let it have its head.

Frowning, I sat down at the table and stubbed my cigarette out. A thin trail of smoke spiraled up and away. Tears suddenly welled up in my eyes. I turned to brush them away before Stacey noticed. Was I setting myself up to be crushed again? Was what we'd had really gone? It was my own fault though. I never told her how I felt. Always waiting for her to say how she felt first. Why was I such a coward?

Stacey carried ice trays and two crystal tumblers to the table; her pensive expression said she was turning something over in her mind. Maybe it was stupid, to think that she was going to tell me she loved me and was leaving Ned … but could it be? I sucked smoke from the Pell Mell between my fingers, my hand trembling with anticipation. What was going on? It was frustrating just sitting here waiting for her to say something. Because I knew that she'd asked me in here for more than fixing me a drink.

"Tell me when," she said, holding the bottle to pour.

"I'll do it."

She shrugged and pushed the scotch bottle toward me. I poured my drink, staring at the ice bucket and the crystal tumblers, wondering, if they were wedding presents. I could feel resentment slithering in, taking the place of anticipation. Her wedding. The last time I'd talked to Stacey was when she'd called last summer to ask if I was coming to her wedding. I wondered then if she'd been trying to twist the knife deeper in my soul. *Are you crazy?* I'd asked her then. *Why would you think I'd come?* She'd never answered that.

"Why?" I repeated aloud.

She looked at me, bewildered. "Why what?"

"Why would you ask me to come to your wedding?" I could still feel my outrage, my jealousy, and the stinging rejection of not being chosen.

She didn't answer right away, but hesitated, her eyes going a soft green. "Because you're my best friend. And I... I wanted you there." Her voice broke a little on the last word.

"Bullshit," I paused, put my cigarette to my lips and inhaled. "Since you eloped, it doesn't matter anyway. Forget it." My sharp, angry tone hid the ache I felt.

"I guess it doesn't," she snapped back.

For a rare moment, her feelings lay naked on her face and I could see that I'd wounded her. What did that outright show of emotion mean anyway?

Well, welcome to the club, I thought. *You started it. You hurt me first.* Still, I regretted it... felt ashamed about it. But, Lord knows, seems like I had a right to be angry. Trying to ignore the pain peeking out of Stacey's eyes, I took a swallow of my drink.

She went to the counter and was fumbled with a huge bag of chips. I stared at the bottle of Johnnie Walker Red who'd become a very close friend of mine. Last spring and summer, I'd been in free fall... plunging down, grabbing for liquor and whatever else I could, trying to find some balance, some sense of being all right. Drinking was supposed to be a cure for a lot of things— only it really didn't cure love. Or grief. Oh, yes, it whisked you away for a while on its magic carpet. But then you had to come back. And the landing was never smooth.

I knew I was smoking too much, drinking too much. But, hell, you find your crutches where you can. No matter which of us was to blame for this mess, I still loved her and it was a dangerous game coming here today, I realized now. Like playing Russian roulette. I shouldn't have come. But I wanted to know what was on her mind.

Still standing, Stacey had turned, leaned against the counter, and was gazing solemnly at me. Finally, impatience reared up and I opened my mouth to ask her what was going on when, without warning, the kitchen door swung open.

It was Cat.

"Hey, you two," she said, showing off her dimples in an angelic smile. "What're you doing in here?"

Her entrance was a bucket of cold water thrown in our faces. I shook myself out of Stacey's aura. I don't know what we looked like, but Cat paused and gave us the once-over. "Having a deep conversation, are we?" She asked, moving further into the room.

I opened my mouth to speak but Stacey was on it. The full force of her green eyes took aim at Cat. "We're old friends, Cat. Just taking a minute to catch up." She leaned back on the counter, smiling. "You know how it is." Pause. "With *old* friends."

They stared at each other for a few naked beats. Neither was the street-fighter type and I didn't think they'd go to blows, but you could take a shower in the tension soaking the air. You might say that Cat was the scrapper type—tiny, wiry, ready to jump. Stacey, on the other hand, had height, self-assurance, and sleek grace. Some might put a bet on Cat, but Stacey was no pushover. She radiated danger in a way that was hard to put your finger on. Probably, it was her eyes that did that. They could be lethal. At the moment, they'd turned a scary gray. And she was using them to bore holes into Cat's skull. I kept my mouth shut and pulled hard on my cigarette, watching them. The tension was turning ugly though it did flatter my ego to think they had thrown down a gauntlet because of me. What would I do if they really did start fighting?

Cat stepped behind me and put her hands on my shoulders. "I snuck away from the game so I could get a cigarette from you, Frankie."

She was up to no good. I knew she had her own brand in her purse. Plus, she was a menthol smoker and she hated my brand. To reach my cigarettes on the table, she leaned over me from behind. It was a deliberate move. And a provocative one. If I had turned my face just a bit, my lips would have brushed against her breasts. So I kept still, tracking Stacey's eyes. They blazed as she watched how Cat had draped herself over me.

Cat gave my shoulder a little squeeze and lit the cigarette Moving to stand next to me, she said, "Come on back, Frankie. Me and Morgan have a winning streak going. The boys won't admit it but we're cleaning their clocks." Then, she turned to look dead into Stacey's face. "Sometimes," she said, "people need to admit when they've lost out, right Stace?"

A warning glowed in Stacey's eyes. "The game's not over til the fat lady sings though, Cat. I don't have to tell you that."

"Right," Cat laughed. "But if you notice, the fat lady's standing center stage and the orchestra's cueing her solo." She paused. "Obviously, some people don't see that yet." She moved toward the kitchen door. Over her shoulder, she half-sang, half-said: "There's none so blind as those who won't see." And walked out.

I sighed, relieved that Cat was gone. The interruption had put a damper on everything. I didn't know why Stacey had called me in here, but I did know that now she was royally pissed. I didn't have to look at her to know that. Her vibe was heating up the room like a furnace. Silently counting to ten, I freshened up my drink. Then I looked up at Stacey. I could see green fire in her eyes. It had gathered to take aim at me this time.

"So, tell me about Cat," she said, moving toward the table.

It sounded more like a command than a request. And I resented that. In my head, I answered: *She's my lover and what's it to you?*

Aloud, I said: "I told you about Cat, Stacey. She's a transfer student."

Stacey gave me a sharp look. "You know that's not what I mean, Frank."

Masquerade

Usually Stacey didn't have to work hard to get whatever information she wanted from people. With a little nudge, it would come spilling out. Especially with me.

She sat down across from me. Eye level. It was an old trick of hers. Since my answer didn't take the direction she wanted, she decided to change lanes. "When did you meet her?"

"Last summer, I think. But maybe it was spring."

"Uh, huh. And?" Her exasperation was showing.

"And what?" I asked.

"Well, where?"

"Here at school."

"So. What's the story with you two?"

I was getting exasperated myself with her questions. But I was secretly pleased that she cared enough to give me the third degree.

Ned might be your ace, Stacey, but Cat trumps him.

"Look, is this why you called me in here? To question me about Cat?"

"No, I didn't." Now, Stacey shifted gears. Came at me direct. Which was unlike her. "But I'm curious. I mean, that little scene she just played in here... she seems to want to keep you all for herself. Maybe she thinks I'm the big bad wolf... that I'm going to gobble you up."

"Was that a pun?" I asked with a twinkle.

Stacey gave me a look.

I decided to give her some of what she wanted. "This is the story. I needed a roommate. Cat's fun to be around. So it worked out for both of us."

"I saw you with her, Frankie." Something in Stacey's face and voice changed. "Last spring." Her tone of voice was faltering. Soft. And the wings of her butterfly mole had lifted. "You said you met her last summer, but it was last spring when I saw you together. The day I'd asked you to meet me in The Commons. I was late getting there because Ned had called me and I couldn't get him off the phone." She picked up her pack of cigarettes and fiddled with them.

I remembered. It was springtime. I hadn't seen Stacey in

months, not since January. And I was excited because she'd called. Excited because I was hoping she'd tell me the wedding was off.

Stacey said: "I was at the order window across the hall when I saw you two together. I'd stopped out there to buy something." She paused, as if she was searching hard for the right words. "You didn't see me, but I saw you two. Both of you were laughing."

When I'd gotten to The Commons, I'd looked around for Stacey. Cat had been there, sitting at a nearby table. As I'd passed, she'd spoken to me, reminding me that we'd met recently. I could see her in my mind's eye: Petite, dimply, and baby-cute. She'd struck up a conversation as I waited for Stacey. I remembered that Cat had gotten me laughing about something. Had turned all of her attention on me, as if I was the only person in the world that mattered to her. I remembered being flattered by that. Being filled up by that in a place where Stacey's absence had left a gaping, hungry void.

"I saw something—something special in your eyes, Frank. I used to see it when we were together. And... and you were looking at her—like—like that." Wavering, Stacey's voice had dropped so low that I had to strain to hear her.

A sudden shudder went through her and she folded her arms across her breasts as if to warm herself. Head bowed, she looked like a wounded bird all hunched into herself like that. I wanted to go over and put my arms around her. I wanted to say: *You were wrong. Cat was nothing to me.* Instead, I waited for her to go on.

"I was—surprised, "she whispered. "Shocked, I think... because I didn't know. Didn't think there'd be—be somebody. So soon." Stacey broke off, shaking her head, hugging herself tighter.

"So, you left without saying anything to me, Stacey?" Surprise lifted my voice higher.

She nodded.

All that time, I'd thought that she'd stood me up. Jerked me around, toying with me. And I'd been angry because of that. "You never said a word. Didn't call, didn't come by. Nothing.

Until you called about your wedding."

Again, she nodded. Her green eyes dark as a forest at evening.

Stacey was about to say something else when the phone rang. At first, I didn't think she was going to answer it, but it kept ringing and, finally, she got up. The change in the air was palpable. A moment had passed.

"Look, Frank, I know *your girl* wants you back out there, but hold on, don't leave."

Nodding, I let the sarcasm pass.

Last spring, Cat had come along just when I'd realized that Stacey wasn't going to change her mind and give Ned up. In fact, while Ned was up in Stacey's face night and day, Cat had been charming me, making me feel wanted, and making herself available to me 24-7 if I wanted. All the right moves and *Bam*! She'd hooked me. I'd let her, of course. Out of hurt. Out of revenge. Because the hole in my gut kept insisting that I'd been tossed overboard to drown. I was splashing around in deep water and I needed a life jacket. Cat volunteered for the job.

Stacey was saying something on the phone. I stared at her with unmasked longing.

What can I do to get her back? I asked Vee.

No answer.

I sighed. Well, maybe I wouldn't have to do anything. Maybe she was going to tell me she was coming back. If we could just get our little conversation off the ground without anymore interruptions.

Stacey hung up the phone. As she turned toward me, suddenly, without planning to, I asked her: "Are you happy, Stacey?"

She sat down facing me again.

"The only time I've ever been happy is with you, Frank. You're my soul mate. You know that."

For a moment, hope thrived. "Well, why—"

Stacey interrupted: "There's something I need to tell you."

"So tell me."

"Okay." She paused a long time.

I held my breath, looking in her ocean-green eyes for some sign of what was to come. They'd gone unreadable.

"I'm pregnant." She said in a flat voice devoid of emotion.

I couldn't stop holding my breath, or stop staring at her beautiful mouth. I was sure I'd heard wrong. Sure what I'd thought I'd heard wasn't true. I stared, waiting for I don't know what. Finally, something clicked in my brain. I pulled in a ragged breath. A doorway—no matter where it might have led—had closed between us.

"Why did you do it, Stacey?" I whispered, barely able to get it out.

Her eyes were haunted. The expression on her face was one that I'd seen before: a stark wasteland of shadows. "Because I needed ... somebody," she whispered, "somebody to love me."

I flinched. Everything in my soul wailed like a banshee: *But I love you, Stacey. Don't you know that?*

No, she doesn't, said Vee. *And it's your fault since you never told her.*

Swampy, black despair flooded my throat. I pulled my eyes away from her face and pushed away from the table to escape, glass in hand, to the kitchen window. Outside, in the back yard, falling leaves had stripped tree limbs bare. They stood out in dark relief against a somber evening sky. Everything was dying out there. Turning into cold ash.

Why had I set myself up like this? Why had I kept on hoping for something that wasn't going to happen? It was so stupid of me. So *damned* stupid! I took a healthy swallow of scotch. Tears threatened to drop, but I dammed up their bitter waters, wishing I could wave my hand and disappear... run far, far away. Or just stop breathing. Just stop.

Ned burst into the room carrying an armful of bowls. "Hey, baby, we need more snacks out there!" He shouted to Stacey, dropping bowls onto the kitchen counter. I watched while he grabbed Stacey playfully, circling his arms around her waist and planting little kisses on her neck and lips.

The moment Ned had come in, a mask had dropped over her face. And mine. Nothing showed. Ned's presence erased us out of being. I started for the kitchen door.

"Hold the door for me, Frankie; I'm going out." Ned said as Stacey was loading up bowls and putting them into Ned's arms.

"Okay," I said, gathering my drink, putting my cigarettes in my pocket. I used my shoulder to push the swinging door back and stood there holding it, waiting for Ned. "Ready when you are."

I looked over at the four card players at the dining room table. Tommy and Leo were taking a beating—and thoroughly pissed about it.

Everybody wants to win, I thought. *And so did I.*

I glanced back at Stacey just in time to see Ned kissing her full on the lips. A stinging sadness seeped in around my eyes. "Come on, Ned," I said with an edge in my voice.

He pulled away from Stacey and walked quickly past me. "Thanks, Frankie."

"Sure thing."

I was about to let go of the door and go over to Cat. She and Morgan were raking in cards as fast as they could slap them on the table.

"Hold on, Frank," Stacey said, coming toward me with a huge bowl of potato chips. "Take this out, please, and put it anywhere."

As she put it into my hand, her fingers purposely brushed my wrist. It was just a brief touch, but in that second, a current of heat crackled between us—a fierce blaze of fire-banked emotions: unremitting, unspoken.

I took a step back and away, deposited the bowl of chips on a nearby table, and poured myself another drink.

"Boston!" Cat shouted, beaming at me. She and Morgan had won the game.

Pulling my face into a smiling mask, I nodded at her while I felt myself doing something inside, making an effort to find a corner where I could leave my feelings in the dark. The drink in my hand beckoned me. As I brought it to my lips, it occurred to me that I'd always believed in stories that ended with the idea of "happily ever after." I looked in Stacey's direction.

Frankie Lennon

Vee said: *You always did believe that things got straightened out in the end.*

Yes, I answered.

You believed you could fix things if you tried hard enough and everything would turn out all right in the end.

Yes. That things would be resolved. I looked at Stacey once more. *But that's not true, is it, Vee?*

What do you think? Vee asked me.

Sleeper

"Nobody ever did, or will, escape the consequences of his choices."

Alfred A. Montapert

"Waking up is hard to do."

Frankie Lennon, author

Crossings

"There are no 'what ifs.' You have to jump in. You go all the way or back off completely."
Michele L. Rivera, author

1. The Wrecking Crew

"Hey," I said to Joyce. "Gorgeous day, huh?"

"Yep." She sat beside me on one of the beach chairs. Her carrot-red hair and pale skin always reminded me of Lucille Ball.

I was relaxed, stretched out in a beach chair by the big pool. Huge trees filtered noon sunlight on the fern-banked hills surrounding Teri's glass and stone house. It was May and the end of my second year of teaching at Evansville College. I was ready for summer. Ready to party.

Joyce held out her paper plate to me. "Have you tasted Teri's German potato salad?"

"*German* potato salad? I've never heard of it."

"Try it. It's good." She handed the plate over to me. "Who'd of thought Teri, the rich suburban housewife, could cook? I hate cooking. I was so bad at it that my ex hired a cook to do it for me." We giggled.

Joyce's sense of humor was one of the things that I liked about her. She'd introduced me, last fall, to The Wrecking Crew. The group of people I was currently running with. We were all at Evansville College, in our late twenties to thirties, three of us teachers, the others, students. Every one of them was White except me.

Sometimes I'd catch myself thinking: *What was I doing running with White people?* It *was 1969*, after all. Black Power was on center stage; Black people were organizing and preaching Black Pride, telling White people to kiss our collective asses.

And here I was, some would say, fraternizing with the enemy. I glanced at them lounging around the pool, eating, talking, and drinking.

Any misgivings I had about being the only Black person in the group had gotten kicked to the curb by my need to stop feeling all busted up inside. Those emotions had put me on the hunt for a way to get rid of the load. Whatever distractions I could find were welcome. The Wrecking Crew fit the bill.

I watched Danny dive into the pool and come up with his hair and handlebar moustache dripping water. A self-described rabble-rouser, Danny was an ex-Marine who put himself in the same radical political category as the Black Panthers or as Tom Hayden. Being a rebel myself, I liked that about Danny. When I looked at his hair, I thought of the Rumpelstiltskin story of spun gold. He brushed his hair out of his blue eyes and looked straight at me for several long seconds before giving me a lazy, Prince Charming smile. After which, he swam away.

"Somebody is seriously interested in you," Joyce said.

"Maybe."

"Don't be coy, Frankie." Joyce smiled broadly.

For an answer, I made a noncommittal face and winked at her. "This potato salad is delicious." I gave the plate back to her. "If I don't get my own plate, I'll eat all of yours."

Joyce nodded and gave me a knowing look. "Go ahead. We'll get back to this later."

I made straight for the feast Teri had laid out. In the past few weeks, it had gotten obvious that Danny had his eye on me. My ragged emotions led me to think about being with Danny. On the plus side, he was cute and his rebel attitude fascinated me; but this situation was a mixed bag of contradictions. Things that brought me up short. It wasn't that he was a man. My basic, natural attraction to women didn't mean that automatically men turned my stomach. In college, I'd had sex with a boy. Even though I liked him, nothing that happened in that bed had changed who I really was: a girl who liked girls. What I was tussling with had to do with his race. How could I get past that he was a White man? A southern White man. *A married, southern,*

Crossings

White man. I grimaced to myself. The whole image of me being with Danny fell right into classic stereotype of White Massa beds Black wench. Just like the movie, "Mandingo." Hell, forget movies, it was like real life history! I took a big swallow of my scotch. Given my Jim Crow childhood, I didn't know if I could get past that. Times were dangerous—for Black people, for radical young Whites. Cops were looking for an excuse to beat heads bloody like they did in Chicago at the Democratic Convention or in Selma. And with cops, you had to watch your step all the time. Like today when I was on my way here to Teri's house.

2. Goliath

Driving into Teri's neighborhood with its quietly elegant homes surrounded by manicured lawns, I felt out of my league and nervous about it. I thought I could hear the houses screaming: *No Negroes allowed! And positively, no poor people here! You're not welcome unless you're the maid or the gardener!* Which made me wish I'd had a drink before leaving the house; I'd decided not to because the cops might be lurking in Teri's neighborhood. In case they were, I kept adjusting my speed so I wasn't going too fast or too slow.

Where I'd grown up had left its mark—deep and tender around the edges. Back then, Blacks weren't supposed to be hobnobbing with White people. You were supposed to get out of their way and stay on your side of the street. That's the way you survived. Used to be, everybody stayed in their own backyards and in their own social groups. Each to his own. America was really no melting pot. I'd figured out that its true nature relied on divisions. Class divided. Race divided. Gender divided. Money and education divided. Who you were attracted to divided. It was all about categories and cubby holes.

While I was mulling that over, my eye caught a flashing of red lights in the rear view mirror; a black and white patrol car had crept in behind me. My heart jumped into my mouth and stayed there as I braked, pulled over, and sat waiting with my hands visible on the steering wheel. These days everybody was jumpy and you couldn't be too careful. Cops everywhere were on a mission: To put down the *nigras*—ungrateful bastards!—who'd risen up against "their masters."The sight of any cop made me very edgy. They were the enemy. And I had sense enough to stay put while a White cop in black uniform climbed out of the car to approach me. He was big enough to be Goliath. Before he got to my window, I had arranged my face in a way that I hoped made me look stupid and unappealing. If you're a colored girl, you never know what appearance to take, what mask to wear with a White cop. In their universe, only two kinds of Negro women exist—Aunt Jemima, the maid-cook-nurse, or Sapphire, the whore. Dressed in an ordinary cotton skirt and sleeveless blouse, I hoped I looked plain as pudding.

The cop walked up to my window and stopped. The thumb of his right hand was hooked loosely into his gun holster. He took a good, long look at me, ready to rescue his White folks from whatever terror I might represent.

Was I some kind of radical ready to burn the neighborhood down? While his eyes crawled over me, I lowered my eyes respectfully as I'd been taught so long ago. And waited. I knew better than to ask him why he'd stopped me.

"I need to see your license."

"Of course." I nodded. "It's in my wallet. I'll just pull out my wallet out of my purse."

I had to tell him what I was going to do because any sudden moves might be fatal. Slowly, I lifted my purse and held it so he could see that there was no gun or knife hiding in there. I pulled out my wallet and the license. Suspicion etched canyons of this cop's face as he checked it.

"Let me see your vehicle registration." He spoke in a monotone. Like a robot.

I pointed to the sun visor just above my head. "It's there. I'll get it for you."

He inspected it and said: "Stay in your vehicle until I return." At his car, I could see that he was calling in my registration and license.

My nerves sent a frenzy of signals to my brain. *Shitfire! Is he going to arrest me? If he takes me to jail, what can I do? Should I ask for a lawyer? A phone call?* My head ran on its squirrely way, scaring me so bad that I thought I was going to pee on myself.

After a few minutes, he came back, handed me the license and registration. "Where are you going?"

I gave him Teri's husband's name. He was a City Councilman and a prominent lawyer. He peered at me then nodded. "Go ahead and watch yourself."

That went without saying as far as I was concerned. As I started my car, I let go of my breath, although I hadn't been conscious of holding it. While I drove away, I watched him in my rear view mirror watching me. It's always been their job to watch us Colored folk for Massa. The sight of him released the sour stink of a childhood memory.

3. A Georgia Road in 1953

Afternoon. Smoky, white clouds smudge blue-white sky. Daddy is driving his big, black Buick with shiny chrome. Mama is in the front seat with him. As our car rolls along a Georgia road, from the back seat, I am looking out at the play of sun and cloud shadows chasing each other on the green countryside. Crickets sing in the heat. It is hot and my eyes are getting heavy. Lulled by the heat, the crickets' song, the car's movement, I doze off.

When I rouse, Daddy has stopped the car. He and Mama are sitting very still in the front seats. Neither is speaking. Curious, I scrabble up on my knees, ready to ask them why we are stopped when I see a White giant glide out of half shadows. He stops at Daddy's window. Still on my knees, I inch closer to that side of the car where the cop stands. Beneath the big cowboy hat, the whiteness of his skin shines like a pearl. On his chest a silver badge glimmers. At his waist, he wears a heavy black belt. From it hang a thick black baton and handcuffs and a holstered gun. Looking at him gives me the creeps. His hand rests on the flap of the holster while he stares at our car, lips so pressed tightly together that they seem to disappear into his angular face. His empty blue eyes move, like a spotlight, from Daddy to Mama, then me. His eyes linger on Mama's face, trying to figure out if she's White or not.

"Say, boy. Where you goin in this car?"

"Just passin through, sir," Daddy says, his gravel-rough voice soft; his head dipped low. "Goin down to Atlanta to see some of our folks."

"Uh, huh. Where you from?" The cop's eyes stay on Daddy's face. His hand is gripping the handle of the holstered gun.

"Tennessee. Knoxville, Tennessee."

"Don't the culluds say 'sir' to a White man up there? Lemme see ya driver's license."

"Yes sir. I'm sorry, sir."

Daddy takes his license out of a holder over his head and hands it to the cop. I notice Daddy's hands are trembling and that he keeps his eyes down, never looks at the cop. Mama is still and, silent. As if she's trying to make herself invisible. Copying her instinctively, I get quiet as a mouse in the back seat. But I sneak to watch the giant White man.

The cop looks over Daddy's license. Looks at Daddy. Looks at the car again. "Might' nice car for a cullud boy. Sure you ain't stole it?"

"No sir." Daddy's voice trembles a little.

The cop moves closer to the car, leans down, hooks his hands on the car door, and looks in once more. Standing there, he seems to blot out the sky. Under the cowboy hat, his white face is streaked with sweat. The badge he wears gleams in the sun. As he looks at each of us, at me, I lower my eyes and pull all of my breath in. Crickets sing loudly in the trees and field. The air is damp hot and heavy. I keep holding my breath and never move. Not even when my nose starts to itch.

"All right, boy, you git along, now," says the cop finally. "You want to mind y'manners. And don't come back to these parts no more in a White man's car, you heah?"

"Yes sir," says Daddy, starting the car.

Crossings

My nose is keeps itching as we drive slowly away, but I still don't move. In Daddy's rear view mirror, I can see the big cop, like Goliath in *The Bible*, standing there watching us. I let a little of my breath go, watching him watching us. He never moves... only stands, a soldier on watch. I still hold my breath as our car moves further and further away. He shrinks smaller and smaller in the mirror, but he keeps standing, keeps watching. I still hold my breath. When I can't see him anymore, I let all of my breath go.

4. Boiling Pots and Boxes

"Hey, let's turn on the news," Gavin yelled. Three months ago, he'd gotten a job as a television reporter and, now, he was forever checking out the competition. Huntley and Brinkley were the brightest stars in his firmament.

Teri switched on her pool side television set. The NBC five o'clock news drew everybody's attention. We all came closer, circling around. Watching the news everyday was like sitting center stage for a three ring circus. You never knew what kind of crisis would be presented this time. It could be more pictures of American G.I.s gunning down unarmed Vietnamese or Cambodian villagers—another massacre like My Lai, live and in living color. Or, it could be film of Stokely Carmichael scaring the bejesus out of Whitey by exhorting crowds of Black people to take up the idea of Black Power. Or maybe, perhaps it might be the suddenly sexy, all powerful, globe-hopping Secretary of State, Henry Kissinger, who looked like the Hunchback of Notre Dame to me. Today, the film clip was about the Black Panthers— Black men and women dressed in Black pants, turtleneck sweaters, and leather coats, their bushy Afros like halos around their heads. They were serving eggs and hot cereal to impoverished, Chicago, school children, feeding them breakfast before school so they could concentrate when they got there. Hungry kids don't learn anything, The Panthers told the world. The film clip focused on Mayor Richard Daley's cops had rousting the Panthers while they served breakfast. My anger simmered and bubbled as they swung their clubs, barely missing the children, and handcuffed every Panther in the room.

"Fuckin Daley and his cops," muttered Danny.

"There're just running dogs for Hoover's F.B.I.! They can't stand that the Panthers stand up for their own; it scares them." The ex-Navy man, Malcolm, put in.

The next news story was about the latest antiwar protest at Columbia University. Some kept watching the screen; Danny, Tony and some others drifted away, talking.

"Think I'll have another, "Malcolm said to me, holding up his empty glass. "Give me your glass and I'll refresh you." He took it and wandered away to the bar. Malcolm had a kind of square face, heavily shadowed with a beard that seemed impossible to shave away. He reminded me of good-ole-boy, southern cops. And yet, Malcolm was my drinking buddy. Here was yet another irony in my present life, I noted.

These days, all kinds of unexpected stuff was happening. Like a pot of water left too long on the heat, things were rising up fast and boiling over. People were furious, vocal, hot and bothered about the cards they were dealt. Everybody was demanding a different mix of cards from the dealer... looking for a different hand to play than the one traditionally assigned to them.

And me? Here I was, mixing it up with a bunch of radical-thinking White people. Who'd of thought that? How and why had we been drawn to each other? Probably something about the times. The heady, swirling waters of the last year or so had, maybe, drawn us together, each of us struggling to free ourselves from the boxes America expected us to fit ourselves into. Joyce had broken with her family's Catholicism when she'd filed for divorce and come to college. Teri was itching to crash out of her upper middle class, married life, and break into the New York Theater. Ava and Edgar, both college professors, regularly spouted anti-war-anti draft ideas in their classrooms despite the fact that their tenure track positions had been threatened by the college. Scared but determined, we pushed for the right to shape our own lives.

Malcolm handed me a fresh drink and then slugged back his own. Malcolm stayed drunk most of the time. In fact, more than half of us lived our lives fueled by alcohol, always in a state of high drama, personal crisis dogging us almost constantly. Usually, we ended up making a mess—mostly because of the way we went about solving our problems, and making decisions.

I really couldn't be pointing any fingers though. Maybe I was getting ready to make a mess, too. I looked at Danny. The whole idea of taking him as a lover made me feel crazy. Like I was in the funhouse of mirrors where I could only see a distorted reflection of me and my surroundings. Was this what I really wanted? A man? For no reason, I, suddenly, remembered being a kid at Alease's birthday party.

5. Spin the Bottle

In my head I can see a boy, a little older than the rest of us, wearing a white shirt, kneeling on the wooden floor, spinning a coke bottle in the middle of the floor. Us girls are standing around him in a circle and I'm squinting because the sun's brightness floods through the windows and throws the rest of the room into shadow. In memory, I can only see the outline of their bodies... a group of children dressed in their birthday celebration best.

"Whoever the bottle points to when it stops spinning, I get to kiss," The boy says, looking like a big-ole, brown turtle to me.

"Ooh, no! That's nasty!" All the girls screech, although their mouths are smiling. They giggle with delicious anticipation.

Beams of sunlight float through the window while I watch the boy, Tommy, who is still on one knee, bending over the Coke bottle that sparkles like a found treasure. Feelings of doom gather over my head like a rain cloud as I wait, trapped in a circle by the hands of the girls on either side of me.

Boy-kisses! Nuh Uhn! I think. But if Kathy, who is standing next to me wanted to give *me* a kiss, I'd let *her*. A warm feeling skitters through my chest at the thought of her kissing me. That would be nice because I like Kathy. A lot.

Holding my right hand, she leans toward me: "Tommy's so cute, don'cha think so, Frankie?"

I look at Tommy again without answering. He still looks like a big-ole, brown turtle to me. *Why does she think he's cute?* I wonder. *She's the one that's cute... not him.*

Tommy flips the bottle into a whipping spin. "Round and round she goes," Tommy hollers out in a sing-song voice, "where she stops, nobody knows!"

Everybody watches, laughing, tittering. Everybody, that is, but me. As I watch my stomach—full of chocolate ice cream and birthday cake—churns and spins, too, like Mama's old washing machine, and panic shoots through my veins at the idea of the boy putting his lips on me. I start inching backwards, trying to slip away, but then I remember that I can't because I'm in a circle holding hands with girls on either side of me.

The spinning bottle slows, slows, and slows. Finally, it stops and points, like a finger. I choke back a strangled sound as Tommy jumps up, facing in my direction.

One of the girls in the circle screeches, "It's you! You, Kathy!" And they all dissolve into laughter as Tommy, suddenly shy, shuffles over to her.

When he plants a big, wet kiss on her lips, she beams. He sticks out his chest. And I grimace while my head races to figure out how I can get out of here before they start the game of Spin the Bottle again.

6. Crossings

Danny had gone back into the pool while I'd been remembering secret thoughts about girls. I'd dreamed of them all the time when I was a kid. My woman dreams of Hollywood's screen goddesses. My woman dreams of Black women who wore high heels and black silk stockings with rhinestone butterflies fluttering at the seam. My woman dreams of girls whose breasts budded and bloomed like mine.

Nobody wants a girl like you! Nobody! Whispered Auntie's voice.

Crossings

It had to be true because, so far, my luck with women was zero. After grad school, Cat had left me before I got the job teaching here at Evansville College. As for Stacey, she'd gotten a divorce after she'd had her child. Then she'd moved east.

Carrying a torch might look beautifully romantic in a movie script, but in reality, there wasn't a damn thing beautiful about it. I kept shoving Stacey into the shadowy corners of my mind. Leaving her there, however, was another matter altogether. That job was going to take distractions.

I looked at Danny. A crazy kind of thrumming rushed through me. Scary and exciting, like I was about to dive off a high, rocky cliff into the sea miles below. If I dived, I might bust myself up on the rocks. Then again, I might not. Who knew? It couldn't be any worse than what had happened with Stacey. Or Cat, for that matter, could it?

Vee gave me her two-cents worth: *You're jumping out of the skillet into fire and it's gonna burn your ass to a crisp.*

She always had something to say. As usual, I didn't want to hear it. *So what the hell do you suggest that I do? Stand around and wait for Stacey to come back. Or Cat? That would be stupid!*

She didn't have an answer. But her warning had shaken me.

Cross, Whispered a voice I didn't recognize. *Be like the rest of the girls. Take up with men and never, ever look back. Cross.*

Danny swam to the edge of the pool and climbed out. Was I ready to do that? To cross? If I did, Danny would be the bridge. And I wouldn't look back.

Without another thought, I stood up and smiled at Danny. He was standing by the edge of the pool, toweling himself dry. My nerves were buzzing like hornets ready to sting as I crossed the patio toward him.

Legacies

Legacy: anything handed down from an ancestor.
Webster's Dictionary

1. Mourners

Rain pelted me as I ran from my car and ducked into the entrance hall of the Morrow Funeral Home. It smelled of dampness and old wooden furniture. For a moment, I stopped, feeling tension radiating from my neck into my shoulders. I would've given real money to be able to turn around and walk out. Instead, I gave myself a push to see this through. Mama would have wanted me to be here. It had been a hard six hour drive from Evansville this time, with rain all the way, but the tightness in my neck came more from my feelings. From not wanting to be here. From my old habit of trying to avoid Auntie as much as possible. I dropped my umbrella into a stand by the door and shrugged out of my raincoat.

The funeral was going to be in the small, plain room, just off the hallway. When I stepped quietly in, I stopped for a moment at Auntie's casket. *Finally gone,* I thought, staring at the casket's flower spray, a blanket of white carnations. Their sweet, cloying smell never failed to remind me of death and funerals. My stomach clenched sharply. Growing up, I'd always liked carnations, but now I hated their smell. Before I could head them off, bad, sad memories flashed across my memory screen— Mama holding me up over Grandma's open casket and me screaming my head off when I saw her in it; Mama's closed casket in this very room a few years ago; Uncle Frank's funeral shortly after. Depressing. It was depressing to realize that my family was thinning out.

Sylvia, my stepmother, looked up and nodded at me. Her mahogany face always reminded me of a beautiful African mask. If I didn't dread the sight of her, I might have thought her striking with her full nose and lips, and her high cheekbones. I nodded back at her as I quietly walked over to where she and Daddy were sitting. I took a chair beside him, and Daddy gave me one of his lopsided smiles. I smiled back and squeezed my fingers around his chubby hand. Sylvia cut her eyes at the affectionate gesture.

Stepmothers, I thought. *Were they all a pain in the ass?*

Although I'd tried to genuinely like her, I felt like she was the interloper at 1919 Dandridge; after all, it was my home before she came, so I felt I had first territorial rights. Very soon, it had become plain that she didn't agree. She'd been in my life since a few months after Mama's death. You might say she unceremoniously burst into it. The way it happened was just tacky, I remembered. She'd let me discover her with Daddy in his bedroom. Too neat to be an accident, I decided. I think that she had a plan and was so sure of herself with Daddy that she didn't have to be discreet. An accident? Not hardly. First, why would she come to our house, knowing I was in town? Everybody knew college students were home for Christmas vacation. Surely, Daddy had mentioned it. Second, although I was out at a wedding when she and Daddy had arrived at the house, she'd had plenty of warning when I returned because you could hear cars when they pulled into our driveway and parked. Three, when I came in the front door, I'd called out to Daddy. Four, I'd knocked at his bedroom door before entering. She'd had time to pull herself together for the sake of discretion.

My brain replayed the scene I'd walked in on in exquisite detail. I'd opened the bedroom door and there she'd been, in a pink lace robe, lounging in the bed beside my sleeping father. "Oops, ex*cuse* me!" I'd said. She just gazed at me without opening her mouth. Didn't seem to have any shame about the situation although I did. Red-faced, I backed out of the room, shut the door, and retreated to the living room to pour myself a long, strong drink. I was young and over twenty-one, but I wasn't stupid. I knew Daddy, recently widowed, had physical needs.

Legacies

Still, the scene gave me a helluva shock. That bedroom, after all, had been where I was used to seeing Mama.

In about five minutes, she came out, smoothing down her lace robe, to offer an apology. "Oh," she laughed sheepishly, checking me out. "I'm sorry. I didn't realize you were here. Coach, umm, he, uh, fell asleep."

"Um, hmm." I nodded.

"I'm Sylvia."

I nodded again. She stood there expectantly, but, frankly, I didn't know what to say: *Nice to meet cha and thanks for screwing my father in my house?* We eyed each other. She was at least ten years younger than Daddy. In her late thirties or early forties. The bloom was still there but her colors were fading. After some seconds, she turned on her heel and went back into the bedroom.

After that day, I'd assumed that'd never see her again. Wrong. Apparently, she was in the market for a good catch and her chance was at hand. Once she and Daddy were married, she'd thrown the gauntlet down and shown her true colors. She'd gone through my drawers and closet, and thrown out all of my precious high school and college mementoes and pictures. To make matters worse, she'd thrown out all Mama's pictures—which I'd intended to keep since they were my only keepsakes of her life. (Well, not quite. There *was* the letter.) How would it have hurt her to ask me, during one of my visits home, if I wanted any of those things? I still hadn't forgiven Sylvia for it, but I hadn't said anything to Daddy about it. What could he do? By the time I'd discovered it, everything was already gone. Besides, I didn't want to put Daddy in the middle of us two. She was his wife, after all, and he might not have taken my side. That, of course, would've been a big win-win for her.

Anger and resentment rose up and sloshed around in my gut, thinking about all of that. Death always brought out panicked, unruly feelings in me. To take the edge off of them, I glanced around. Behind me, six rows of straight-backed chairs had been set up to seat mourners. They were decidedly empty. You noticed how many people showed up to pay respects or mourn when somebody died. Aunt Bessie, one of Mama's longtime friends, had come. I turned and smiled a greeting to her. She nodded back without a smile. It had always fascinated me that she looked like a tall, big-boned White woman. Her milky, translucent skin and light brown, graying hair—so straight that it couldn't hold a proper curl—told a story about her ancestors. She could've passed if she'd wanted to—a lot of Knoxville Black women could have, including Mama.

There were two other women seated together near Aunt Bessie that I didn't know. Both were elderly. One was freckled, light-skinned, and slender. The other, darker, heavy-set. I wondered if they'd been Auntie's church members. Or Bible Study friends of long ago are a memory, tinged with acid shame, drifted up, like smoke. The living room of her Alcoa house materialized in my head with Auntie moving about among members of her Bible study. They were all old ladies, dressed in their Sunday best, properly hatted and gloved, seated primly in a circle, each holding a Bible in her lap. It was the only memory I had of other people being in Auntie's house. She had asked me to play a hymn for them to sing. Since Mama had insisted on my taking piano lessons, Auntie thought I ought to be able to perfectly play any hymn by sight. Of course, I couldn't, but she had urged me to do it with eyes full of thunder. So I sat at her piano with a tight chest and trembling hands. From the opening chords to the end, I stumbled, unsure of which notes I should be playing. But the ladies sang right along, not seeming to notice. At the end, I'd slid off the piano stool and glanced up at Auntie, hoping that she hadn't noticed either. But her face—a black, threatening cloud—told me she had.

Again, I peeped at the two women. Had they gone to see Auntie in the nursing home? Except for Aunt Bessie and me, I never knew of anyone else who visited Auntie.

2. Nursing Home

Legacies

When I was a sophomore in high school, Auntie came to live with us. I don't think she liked the idea of moving to Knoxville. I didn't and Daddy's closed-down face told me that he didn't. But Mama said, "Sister is getting up there in age." So Mama and Daddy tore down the garage and had a studio apartment built for Auntie, located at one end of the house. Before she moved in, I thought she'd come out of the apartment and talk a bit with us from time to time. She didn't. If I was in the kitchen and she had her door open, I'd see her. But that was only now and then. Mostly, she was a hermit back there.

A few years after living with us, she'd fallen in her room. Hearing a strange noise behind Auntie's shut door, Mama knocked and went in. Auntie was crumbled on the floor.

"Sister!" Mama cried, rushing over to her.

Mama checked for broken bones and sprains; there didn't seem to be any. Bruises and a little head bump seemed to be the worst of it. Because Auntie had always been skinny as a bag of bones, Mama had bent down, put her arms under Auntie's body and tried to pick her up. Bad idea. Mama went down herself with Auntie half in and half out of her arms. Both ended up sprawled out on the floor.

After that, Mama was faced with the reality that Auntie had gotten very feeble and needed constant watching and care. Which Mama, who was still teaching, couldn't give. So reluctantly, she'd put Auntie in the nursing home.

After Mama died I knew she'd expect me, after she was gone, to visit Auntie in the nursing home. I didn't want to. In fact, I'd hated doing it. When I'd come home from Evansville, it was my first stop. I'd drive up and park in front of the red brick building, wishing I didn't have to go in, and knowing if I didn't, I'd have to carry a mountain-load of guilt. To avoid that, I'd take a deep breath and in I'd go.

In the hall, the smell of dust and stale sheets gave me greeting. That alone was enough to prod me to hurry up and get the visit over with. As I'd step inside Auntie's room, she'd indifferently look my way, her eyes yellow with age. Each time I saw her, she looked thinner, darker… more and more unrecognizable, except for her white, cotton ball hair. Even the little golden earrings that I'd seen her wear all her life no longer dangled from her ears. The skin, covering her dusty bones, reminded me of delicate, old parchment paper. Often, I wondered about her age. Was she in her eighties? Her nineties?

"Hi Auntie," I'd say, hating my false, cheery tone. "How are you today?" It was a sad attempt at conversation and I suppose she knew that my asking was a sham. Empty words. Without sincerity or feeling.

Likely as not, she'd say nothing. The sterile room in which she now lay seemed to pulse with silence. That always unnerved me, made me even more desperate to have done with the visit, but since I was duty-bound to be there, I'd try to break through her barrier.

"Auntie? It's me. Frankie. I'm home for the weekend. Just came by to see how you're doin."

She'd turn her head away. Nothing. My words would sit like stones in the usual strained silence between us. Which would make me feel that I'd done something horribly wrong for which I must dearly pay. Nervously, I'd circle the room, smoothing the blanket or bed sheet, straightening up her religious things that lay on an old table under the window—the *Bible*, a dozen pamphlets depicting a seated, blonde-haired Jesus surrounded by a gaggle of little White children.

Finally, unnerved and desperate to have done with this visit, I'd try again. "Auntie? You feelin okay today?"

Her habit was to never answer me... to just keep her eyes closed tightly, and I was reminded of how I'd felt invisible all those years when she'd babysat me in her neat, bare-bones Alcoa house. I gritted my teeth. Leaving the nursing home too soon would invite the guilts to come and smother me alive, so I'd worked out a strategy ahead of time. I'd stay until I counted to fifty. Just time enough for a respectable visit. Countdown to fifty. That, I'd decided, was the magic number giving me permission to break out of there. Once I reached fifty, I'd ask the last question: "Is there something I can get for you, Auntie?"

"Lemon drop candy," she'd usually mumble.

Legacies

"Okay. I'll bring it back by in a day or two." That said, it was all I could do to keep from sprinting out of the door and down the hall. I felt bad about not staying longer and not trying harder to connect with her.

Feeling bad about it never changed anything, I reflected, hearing a piped-in melody from another room. I recognized it as "The Old Rugged Cross," one of Auntie's favorite hymns.

Once or twice, I'd thought I'd seen her wipe away a tear as she sang, but I couldn't be sure. It surprised me because it had never occurred to me that she *could* cry. I don't know why I thought that. Maybe I thought she'd been born without tear ducts. Or more to the point, without feelings. On the roof of the funeral home, rain beat slowly at first, then changed into a rapid downpour. It sounded like the world was drowning. And it brought back another Auntie memory.

3. Storm

One evening, when Mama and Daddy left me at home with Auntie to babysit, the storm came.

In my mind's eye, I can see myself outside in our back yard on Mee Street playing alone when I hear thunder coming. It sounds like huge wooden balls rolling heavily along the floor of the sky.

A mild wind—warm, not hot, not cold—ripples through the air, ruffling the hairs on my arms. Just then, I hear Auntie calling me.

"Fran-*keee*!" She hollers in that peculiar way, dividing my name into two parts.

The thunder answers for me, coming closer, sounding louder. I look to the west where the sun has dropped almost below the horizon. The sky is dark purple smudged with orange. *Creepy,* I think.

"Fran-*keee*!"

"I'm comin, Auntie!" Up the steps I run. She sounds like she's getting ready to be mad like she always is if I'm slow coming after she calls. She's leaning out, holding the screen door open for me. As I scoot inside the kitchen, I notice that her dark forehead is wrinkled with worry. Her snow white hair is plaited and the tiny braids are pinned down neatly.

"Storm's comin," she says. "Git on in the liv'n room."

"Yes, mam." While I go, I wonder why I have to go into the living room.

I hear her shuffling footsteps following me. "Wait," she commands and we both stop in the dining room. "Pull down that shade there," she points. Her arm and fingers remind me of an old, leafless tree branch sticking up toward the sky.

Why do we have to pull the shades? But I don't ask. I always have questions to ask about all kinds of things. Although Mama and Daddy don't mind, and my first grade teacher, Mrs. Bryant, doesn't mind, Auntie doesn't like it. She thinks I shouldn't ask questions, just keep my mouth shut and do what she says. Standing on tiptoes at the window, I can see our next door neighbor lady in her kitchen. She waves, smiling, and I raise my arm to wave back at her just as thunder hits the air.

"Hurry up 'n do what I said, little girl!" Auntie barks.

I pull the shade down and look over at her, waiting for her to tell me what to do next. The shade at the other window is still up. As Auntie reaches for it, lightning streaks so bright that the gold of her little hoop earrings flash like sunbeams. Auntie jerks back from the window with a funny look on her face.

"Come over here 'n get this un, too," she demands.

I do it quickly.

"Go over theah and pull them shades 'hind the davenport. I'll do the others."

In the living room, I hop up on the couch and pull the shades. Pulling them all the way down will make it darker in here—too dark—and I don't like dark. So I deliberately leave the shades a few inches up from the window sill; that way, a little light can come in.

"Little girl, you better mind me!"Auntie threatens. "Ya think I cain't see you ain't pulled 'em all the way down? I'm old, but the good Lord ain't tookm'eyesight. Do what I say."

Legacies

"But it's gonna be too dark to see," I whine. She stares at me with those milky gray eyes of hers until I pull the shades all the way down.

"Ya don't need to see nuthin out there anyway. Sit on that davenport and don't talk." She sits in the chair, wrapping a sweater around her thin arms, and closes her eyes.

It's not exactly pitch black in the living room now, but it's dark all the same. The rain is doing a fast tap on the roof. The sound of it drowns out everything else. The creepy quiet makes me want to move around. Do something. I hate sittin in the dark. I hate bein bored; so, I slide over to the big brown radio and turn it on, hopin for the sound of one of my cowboy or detective shows. Instead, noisy-noise leaps out of the radio—Daddy calls it "static" or something—and Auntie almost jumps out of her chair.

"Turn that thing off!" She hollers. "Din't I tell ya to sit!"

I slink over to the couch. "Yes ma'm."

"Don't be movin around neither."

"But I don't have nuthin to do!" I protest. The storm gets louder… like all the rain and thunder in the world is crashing down right outside the front door.

Her eyes get wide as the storm gets louder. "You be still. Don't need to do nuthin. Oughter have respeck for the Lord doin His work out theah." She settles back and closes her eyes again.

The rain is coming even harder now, and I hear the wind, soundin like a million bees buzzin in the air. I look up at the roof and over at Auntie. Her thin lips are pressed together and her arms are wrapped around herself real tight. I shiver and ask: "What about the lights? Can we turn one on?"

She doesn't answer. I hate it when grownups do that… when they don't answer you… when they act like you're a big, fat zero. The thunder crashes again. That scares me. It's so dark… so dark. If I could just have some light. I stare at the lamp closest to me and wait another few seconds before I put out a dare. "Auntie, it's too dark. I'm gonna turn on a light." I stand up.

"No!" She hollers.

"Well, why not?!" The question has slipped out before I can catch it. Auntie opens her eyes and turns her head to glare at me.

I'm scared of her, but more scared of sittin in the middle of a storm in the dark.

"You a sassy little hussy! I don't know how yo mama stands yo sass. Nobody likes sass! If ya mama die, you gon end up by y'self. I done tole ya before, nobody wants a sassy girl!"

Hurt wrapped itself around my heart and squeezed. "Yes, mam," I mumbled.

"You jes do what I say from now on an' shut up!"

Thunder crashes like it's comin through the roof. "But I'm scared!"

Auntie jumps in her chair. "Oh, Lord, have mercy! We got to be still. Thass what Jesus said: Peace and be still. We got to be still, I tell ya. So stay still."

I look at her real good. Her lower lip is goin up and down like she's chewin somethin. "Ain't you scared, Auntie?"

"Jesus 'buked the storm. Said: 'Peace and be still.'" I see her hand digging into the bottom of the chair and squeezing it hard.

Thunder crashes and cracks, like the sky's getting ripped apart. I push myself back into the couch, trying to hide from the awful sounds of the storm. Auntie's mouth is going, like when she prays to herself, but no sounds are coming out. Wind roars and thunder screams at us. I'm glued to my seat and Auntie doesn't have to tell me again to stay still. We sit in the dark like that until the storm passes.

4. Pictures

The preacher entered and laid his Bible on the small podium at the front of the room. He intoned: "We have gathered here today to remember Annie E. Reynolds."

I wondered what the other people in the room remembered about her. To me, she was a fierce woman. Unyielding. As if she had put a diamond-hard shield around herself. Funny though that she was scared of storms. That didn't fit with my other picture of her at all. She'd believed you could protect yourself by sitting quietly in the dark until the storm passed. Had she lived her life like that, by staying quiet in the dark until danger passed? I'd already found out that there's plenty in life to scare a person shitless, and take you down a peg or three. When the tiger is about to eat you, you grab for whatever protects you—a crucifix, Mother scotch, a big stick, or a quiet corner. Protection comes in all shapes and sizes. But I'd never figured out what could protect me from Auntie's mean mouth... always putting a curse on me.

You a sassy little hussy! Ain't nobody gonna want ya!! Nobody.

It was a dark legacy to leave behind you. When I stopped to think about it, I was sure there was malice behind it. What had I done to her? Why didn't she like me? Was it because Mama had married and had me, instead of staying with her? Or was it something she had seen in me that had invited her hostility? Why had Mama even left me with her? Surely Mama had noticed how Auntie felt about me.

The preacher said:"Until she came to Alcoa, Tennessee with her sister, Annie E. Reynolds lived in Fort Smith, a rural town in Arkansas...."

My head painted a sepia-toned main street in Fort Smith with a dusty road lined by one or two-story buildings, with men in stove pipe hats, with horses pulling wagons past a railroad depot. I tried to picture a young Auntie in a long dress with ribbons in her hair. Mama had once said Auntie was a party girl. Said that when she was young, Auntie had liked to dance and have a good time. Laughing? Dancing? Auntie? That picture of her didn't fit. Mama had once said that Auntie had had two husbands. (*Two? I couldn't picture her with one, much less two.*)That Auntie had given up the second one because she had to choose between him and keeping her promise to raise Mama. When Auntie's mother lay dying, she'd made Sister promise, Mama had.

An old, black and white photograph of Auntie and Mama came to mind. Date stamped, August, 1956, it was taken at the Alcoa house. It was the only picture I've ever seen of Auntie, and the only one taken of the two of them together. They stand in a dreary, dead-looking backyard with a waist-high, wire fence separating Auntie's yard and the weed-choked, empty field next door. Neither is facing the camera straight-on. Mama is wearing a light-colored, casual, summer dress, and she is squinting at the camera... not squinting, frowning, looking irritated. Standing slightly behind and to the side of Auntie, Mama has her arms locked around Auntie's chest. Auntie's hands are folded placidly on her stomach. She has an uncharacteristic smile on her face, a secret smile, and she is looking down. Auntie, who usually doesn't wear glasses, is wearing them here. Her white hair is pinned up away from her face and she has on her gold earrings. Her dress is trimmed with large white collar. I have gazed more times than I can remember at the details of the photo, willing it to speak across the gulf of years to me ... willing it to reveal the secrets of the two of them, dead and gone. I don't know what this photo is saying, but it tells me something... something in mysterious hieroglyphs.

5. Identity

When had I first noticed that Mama and Auntie didn't have any similar features? That Auntie's skin was ebony and Mama's almost lily white? And if I had noticed years ago, why hadn't I asked Mama about it?

You take certain things for granted when you're growing up. Like who your mother is, who your father is. Before I read the letter she left for me to read after she died, I thought I knew who I was. Before, I'd thought: "I'm a Lennon, on Daddy's side. A Smith on Mama's." But her letter wiped out the past I thought I had a place in.

Vee whispered: *You should've asked Auntie about what Mama said in the letter.*

Dear Frankie, Mama's letter read, *I think I should tell you of my side of your family background. I was an unwanted child and my family gave me away after administering severe beatings to me for being born. The Nathan Tolbert Smiths, of Fort Smith, Arkansas where I was born (Sister's father and stepmother) adopted me when I was less than a year old. When I was five years old, Mrs. Sarah Smith, my adopted mother, died, pledging Sister to rear me. I know nothing of my blood parents.*

Legacies

Half of my identity—wiped out. Just erased. Why had she waited to tell me? I had so many questions—and they'd never be answered.

I kept staring at Auntie's closed casket, picturing her in it, still as night. *Vee, would she have told me anything?*

No way to know, answered Vee.

I'd been too much of a coward to ask Auntie for anything she could refuse me. Her refusal would've been a savage twist of the knife she'd stabbed me with more times than I cared to remember. (*Don't nobody wantcha, yasassy little hussy!*)If she could've shed some light, I figured she wouldn't, given her hostility toward me. Now, I regretted not having tried.

Some men in dark suits came in to carry Auntie's casket out. I took stock of my feelings and knew I didn't feel sad that she was gone. I thought about how her voice had followed me down through the years. Stalked me and haunted the corridors of my mind. Why would you tell a little girl that if her mother died, her Daddy would walk away from her and nobody else would want her? The room rustled with life as we gathered our things and rose to our feet in respect for the dead. I watched Daddy reach out to help Sylvia with her raincoat. In my little girl's heart, I felt like Auntie's prediction had come true, that Daddy *had* left me after Mama died. Although in my grown-up heart, I knew he hadn't. I understood that Mama's death had left him alone. And lonely. I understood that he needed Sylvia. Still, Auntie's voice had left a wound. Maybe one day the wound would disappear.

Outside, Daddy turned to me: "I'll see you at the cemetery unless you want to ride with us."

"I'll follow you in my car."

Daddy and Sylvia headed for their car. The rain had let up for a moment although the sky was still a patchwork of fuzzy, gray clouds. I puffed my cheeks out, sighing deeply. As I watched the dark-suited men put Auntie's casket into the hearse, the sigh turned into a breath of genuine relief. Finally. I was done with her.

Are you? Whispered Vee.

Emerald City

"I am Oz, the Great and Terrible. Who are you and why do you seek me?" From The Wonderful Wizard of Oz

1. Over the Rainbow: June, 1970

It was summertime, warm, and we had been walking, Jay and I, through the streets of Manhattan. He was smoking furiously, puffing and puffing, walking too fast for me, his long legs striding forward as if he might break out in a run any minute. I had on heels, so walking fast was difficult. To keep up, I had to do a little skip now and then. He didn't seem to notice. Nor did he notice the restaurant ahead although we were supposed to be looking for some place nice to eat dinner. *Bernardo's*, said the red sign. I slowed, thinking we'd go in. Instead, Jay kept up his brisk pace. Already, we'd passed half dozen restaurants this evening, but he was too preoccupied to notice.

Enfolding and surrounding us, skyscrapers—a timberland of them—rose to the clouds, drawing my gaze upward. For the last five days that we'd been in New York, I'd wanted to see a whole field of blue up there without tall buildings intruding on it. *There are too many of them* I'd thought. Uninhabited sky, breathing room was what I was used to. As we moved along the street, a river of people flowed by, eyes ahead, back straight, wearing scowling or tired or perplexed faces. They seemed unaware of each other, unaware, too, of the different noises colliding around us—honking cars, street singers, people ranting through loudspeakers, music blasting out of bars. It was all so overwhelming. The noise, the people, the skyscrapers—they made me uneasy, set up a cascade of misgivings about whether I could make it living here. I'd been fighting off the misgivings each day because I'd left Evansville, Indiana to come to New

York, the city of cities—my Emerald City—where I could write... where I could fly.

I peeked at Jay's pecan-brown face set in tense lines. What was going on with him? I was afraid to ask. Since the second day we'd been here, there'd been a strange gulf between us. He wasn't talking much. And in bed, which was our root connection, he wouldn't touch me. That set off deep alarms, but I was afraid to pay attention to them. Ignoring the clanging in my head as best as I could, I'd told myself he was just getting used to living in a new place.

Abruptly, Jay stopped and plucked the stub of a cigarette out of the corner of his mouth. "Let's go over there," he said, nodding in the direction of a pocket-sized sandwich stand with a couple of lawn chairs and tables in front of it.

Without waiting for me, he went over and sat down. I followed and sat across from him. Tension crackled in the air like a live wire too close to water.

"I'm going back," he said, flipping the cigarette butt out into the street. "You stay." His voice was as thin as the evening light.

What he was saying didn't register with me at first. "Stay?" Confusion swarmed in my brain. "What're you talking about?"

"Look," he turned to face me. "I'm leaving, but you should stay. This place," he gestured at the stream of cars, the smooth, swift flow of people, "it ain't for me."

"Why? What's wrong, Jay?" This was a question I really didn't want to ask because I sensed I was facing a hunk of reality that I didn't think I could fix. I held my breath, waiting for him to tell me what was wrong, but there was nothing else. He shrugged my question away without trying to explain any more. And why should he? The whole idea of coming here to live had been my idea.

"I called the airline and got a reservation," he said. His voice had dropped so low I could hardly hear above the hum of tires, voices, and footsteps in the street.

His face, shadowed with unhappiness, told me that begging him not to leave would do no good. Though I wanted to. Very badly. Instead, a shaky voice came out of me: "When... when will you go?"

"Tomorrow afternoon."

I looked around. The streets changed, instantly, into a narrow, foggy path winding away into the dark and I heard the wings of fear—my Flying Monkeys—beating. They were coming for me. There—beyond Jay's left shoulder. If I let them slip inside my head, they'd swoop and dive and bite at me, yammering in my ears that the path ahead, was rocky, treacherous, and steep. That I wouldn't be safe on it. That if I followed it, I might lose my footing and fall. And fall and fall. To keep The Monkeys at bay, I silently screamed at myself: *You're a grown, twenty-six year old woman! Get some backbone! You can do this without Jay!*

Nonetheless, I could see them. Coming closer.

2. Tornado

I watched Jay push his toothbrush and a comb into the side of his open suitcase. He'd been avoiding my eyes since we'd gotten up late this morning. Breakfast had been dry cereal, milk, and some orange juice. Our room at The Colonial, a residential hotel just this side of seedy, was as big as a postage stamp. The breakfast was the best I could do, given the room's makeshift kitchen, hidden behind an accordion screen.

Silence churned the air between us. I wanted to scream, *Don't leave!* But I had to hold my feelings in check. Embarrassed and at a loss as to what to do with myself, I cleaned up the breakfast leavings, just to give myself something to do while Jay finished gathering his things.

After that, I stood at the window looking out. Blocks and blocks of tall and taller buildings—vaults of smooth stone and glass—kept the city's secrets. In my head, long ago, I'd named New York after Dorothy's Emerald City: The sparkling place where dreams, where wishes came true. Where you got your heart's desires.

And who wouldn't want that? But I couldn't quite ignore the reality that since we'd been here, Jay and I had been floundering, searching around for our niche—our pond, like the one we'd left in Evansville. Surely, I'd told myself, we'd find it soon. And we'd adapt. I'd brushed doubts and warning bells aside. Pretty soon, I'd told myself, Jay would find a job that would give him heart; I'd get my dream job at an advertising agency or publishing house and, soon enough, I'd be writing. If just ignored the warning bells, they'd stop. Soon.

That was getting to be a habit of mine, I'd noticed—ignoring painful, scary stuff. At times, ignoring worked; other times, it backfired. I didn't keep score of which was winning. It was best to ignore that, too.

Right now though, I couldn't ignore the feelings roaring inside me like a dangerous mob. Shame and unbridled panic battled in me. Shame screamed that it was my fault that Jay didn't like New York. Taunted me like a schoolyard bully, telling me I'd been rejected. Again. That someone I cared about was leaving me. Again. Then panic galloped through and stirred up its choking dust. *Jay would be gone soon. I'd be alone. Then what?* I trembled.

The question triggered a sharp warning sensation from The Corners—a dark place below my conscious mind where I'd stashed painful Stacey-feelings, stifled desires, and subtle, swampy fears. With Jay around, The Corners were silent, unmoving because I'd put Jay dead center on my radar. With him around I could put on blinders, black out my feelings for the woman whose candle forever glowed in my soul. When he left, how would I keep those buried thoughts of Stacey from rising out of The Corners and eating me alive?

Jay snapped his suitcase shut. "I'm ready to go."

I turned around. Wearing the navy suit I'd bought him, he looked like a model straight out of *Ebony* magazine. I'd told him before we'd come here that modeling was something he ought to pursue in New York. He'd blushed at the suggestion without commenting.

"You look good," I told him.

Smiling self-consciously, he fiddled with his suit jacket. "I borrowed $300 from your stash. I'll send it back to you."

"No, it's okay." I waved away the suggestion, and immediately wondered why I'd said that. I'd need every penny of the $2000 I'd brought here. If I was going to stay, that is.

"I've called the cab already."

What was going on in his head at this moment? Did I want to know? Probably not. "What time will you get back to Evansville?"

"Six or seven tonight."

The crowd in my head roared and I dropped my head so he couldn't see my eyes. Was he going to miss me? I was going to miss him. A big lump sat in my throat. Was I going to cry? I couldn't let myself cry in front of him. I had to scrounge up some kind of pride.

Jay came over and put his hand on my shoulder. "I belong in Evansville, Frankie."

"I thought—"

He didn't let me finish. "Like I said, this place ain't for me. But you— you'll be all right."

I mumbled: "Maybe." Although a bitter stab of betrayal wanted me to say: *I thought you'd see me through the unknown.* Hadn't he promised—outright or by implication? I thought he had, but I couldn't remember for sure.

A tentative smile hovered around his lips. "You'll make it here, Frankie. I'm not worried about you."

I was. I'd hoped he was going to change his mind at the last minute. The realization that he wasn't had me in a cold sweat.

"Give yourself a chance at it."

I kept my mouth shut. It was all I could do to fight the roar of the crowd in my head and the terrifying picture of me living alone in New York. How would I make it without him to hold onto? You needed somebody to hold onto because even though you were walking along nice as you please, *Wham!* you always got hit with something you never saw coming. Life had the habit of picking you up, and like a tornado whipping you around every which-away, then dropping you in some turf where you had to figure out how not to get eaten by the local wild life.

He picked up his suitcase. "I'm going down now. The cab should be here soon."

"I'll come with you."

We took the elevator downstairs in silence. Would I ever see Jay again? *Not likely*, Sadness told me. It was an unbearable thought. I couldn't let him go. Couldn't. But what choice did I have? My mind ran like a mouse in a maze looking for an answer. *Say something to stop him!* I screamed at myself. But what? The elevator lumbered on down.

Outside, a yellow cab was waiting. The pale-faced driver was listening to a baseball game. His expression registered boredom. He got out and took Jay's suitcase without a word to us. My tongue had frozen. The man I cared about most in the world was leaving me and I couldn't speak a word. I wanted to hug him. Touch him, let him know how much I was hurting. Instead, I clinched my shaking hands together with tears standing in my eyes.

Jay opened the cab door and turned back to me. "I wrote you a letter to try to explain more," he said, pulling a small white envelope out of his suit pocket and handing it to me. Printed on the envelope's upper left-hand corner was the name of the hotel. "Take care of yourself, Frankie. Call Allen's and let me know how you doin. Okay?"

I held the letter, looking into his face. His eyes were unreadable. "Okay," I said, heart-stricken.

He kissed me on the cheek, and climbed in. The cab pulled out into traffic. I waved, watching as it disappeared into the swift stream of cars and busses. My eyes rose to the skyscrapers—a labyrinth of concrete, steel, and glass. They glistened, tall, and silent under the golden glare of the afternoon sun. While Emerald City went on about its business, I turned, heading back upstairs.

3. Yellow Brick Road

I stepped into my room, having already read and cried over Jay's letter in the downstairs hall and elevator. Other than what he'd already said, the letter didn't add much. He hadn't said he loved me or would miss me, but I wished he had—to take the bitter edge off his leaving. Did it really matter though? Truthfully, had I fallen in love with him?

Truthfully? I wasn't exactly sure. In bed, he had sung me a siren's song that filled my heart... that worked magic and inspired forgetfulness. Because of it, I'd been able to drop Stacey into a trunk hidden in The Corners. His lovemaking, potent and more skillful than I'd ever experienced, almost convinced me to forget her... although I knew in my heart that I really hadn't.

I dug cigarettes and matches out of my purse. His being gone was going to upset the careful balance of The Corners... how I'd stacked, arranged, and covered things up. That wasn't good because they didn't like being messed with. To remind me of that, they zinged me with a peek at my past—a peek at some wounds that seared my soul. Instantly, I pulled down the shades of memory, hard, and pushed a cigarette between my lips.

As I struck the match, I sank down on the lumpy bed and scooted around, in vain, to find a soft place. I sighed, thinking back to six days ago on the plane. That's when I'd picked this hotel... by doing an "Eeny-meeny-miney-mo from the three references Malynda had given me. I glanced around the room. There wasn't much to look at. A bedside table where a black telephone crouched, a rickety floor lamp, a beat-up table with two hard-backed chairs squeezed under it. I blew out smoke, knowing I was going to have to find someplace else. Fast. It was bleak enough to remind me of *No Exit,* a play about being sentenced to your own personal version of hell. Maybe this room was mine, my punishment for talking Jay into leaving his family to come with me to New York.

I missed him already and he'd only been gone—I checked my watch—fifteen minutes. It felt like more. Much more. *Gone... he's run out on you.* On the heels of that angry thought, I pictured myself throwing all my things helter-skelter in my bag and hailing a taxi to go after him.

"You can't go back. You just got here," I whispered to myself, gritting my teeth against the urge.

Jay's note had said he hoped that I'd find what I wanted. And what was that? I thought I knew, but when I asked myself, fog swirled about in my mind. I shook my head to clear it and thought of Tori, my college soror, who knew that I'd wanted to start a writing career in New York after I graduated. A month ago, she'd driven down from Bloomington to say goodbye.

When we'd settled on my couch, piled high with stuff I was packing, she'd said: "I admire you for what you're doing—going to New York."

She hadn't known that for the last three years, I had wanted, dreamed of going, but The Flying Monkeys kept whispering fearful things in my ears. Kept telling me that Black girls didn't throw away good teaching jobs to go to New York for some crazy pipe dream. Kept exclaiming that it was madness to think I could write and support myself by doing it! Why, they taunted, you haven't even finished that pitiful little novel for your Master's thesis!

After I'd graduated, I'd tried. I would sit at the kitchen table in my apartment, expecting some rush of words to magically leap from my fingertips. I would grit my teeth and will the words to come. But they didn't, and I'd always end up frustrated, staring at a blank sheet of paper, afraid that I didn't have the talent to write. Because if I did, why couldn't I? Maybe because I needed to be in New York. If I lived in New York, I'd be writing all the time. With that thought, I'd take out Mother scotch and pour myself a hefty one while I'd imagine life as a writer in New York. If I could just get there my dream would come true. I daydreamed about it and watched the calendar changing. Nineteen sixty-seven became 1968 and that year melted into 1969. Before I knew it, 1970 was here. Time was running off with my life. When I heard from my high school and college friends telling me about how they were living their lives, how they were following their dreams and goals, I'd break out in a sweat, thinking about what wasn't happening in my life. What was I doing still living in Evansville? It was supposed to have been a stopover. A temporary resting place. If I was going to go to New York, I needed to make a move soon. My blood had heated up with the urgency of it. Still, fear—The Monkeys—strangled me and kept me stymied. Until I tricked them. Pulled a surprise maneuver and I talked Jay, my lover of eight months, into coming with me. He'd be my companion in facing the unknown. Jay and I were going to set out on the yellow brick road, go to Emerald City, like Dorothy, the Tin Man, the Scarecrow, and the Lion. That reassurance had thrown a net over The Monkeys. And I'd been on my way, at last.

So. Here I was. In Emerald City. My eyes crawled around the room and I thought that without another human being's comforting presence, this could very well be my hell. Like the Alcoa house. Which I hadn't thought of in years. The sound of crickets at evening and cars whooshing by came back in full sensory recall. Once more, I was there, marooned in Auntie's cold, silent house, waiting in vain for my parents to come for me. Shivering, I wiped away the memory and mashed out my cigarette. I wasn't in Alcoa, Tennessee with Auntie babysitting me. I was in Emerald City. And wasn't this the dream I'd said I wanted all along? I got up and hurried out, headed for Malynda's apartment.

4. Courage

I smoked and sipped a ginger ale while Malynda was reading Jay's letter, wishing I could get rid of this ache that had set up shop in my gut. I wanted a drink, but Malynda didn't believe in taking a drink until after five p.m. The turned-down edges of her full-lipped mouth made me nervous about what she was thinking. She was a pint-sized dynamo, who, as a rule, didn't disguise or soft-pedal her opinions. I hoped she wasn't going to tell me I was a fool about Jay. Although I suspected I was, I didn't want to hear it.

Everything aggravated my nerves. Her small apartment did, for sure. As you came in here, there was a narrow, galley-like kitchen which opened to the one room apartment. The couch I was sitting on was a let-out bed. The plain, dark furniture belonged to the apartment. With family photos of her parents, aunts, cousins scattered around, a colorful floor rug, knick-knacks here and there, and some fancy place mats for the dining table, she'd made the place hers. Even so, it was almost claustrophobic and the walls seemed to be closing in on me. It was almost as depressing as my hotel room. How much was she paying for it, I wondered. Would I be stuck renting a place like this? It was likely that I would. Space in Manhattan was at a premium, they said. That prospect pushed my spirits down even further.

"He put the standard married man stuff in here," Malynda said, then read aloud: "You're special in my heart but I have to go back. My wife and kids need me." She grimaced. You could almost see her brain cells making connections. She knew Jay because she was from Evansville, too, and the place was small enough for everybody to know everybody. "I remember his wife, so I'm sure they do. Hmmph! Didn't stop him from leaving though." She folded the letter and slipped it back into the envelope before handing it back to me. "It's almost like he didn't plan to stay."

I'd thought of that myself. But I didn't like the feel of that idea. It smacked of double-dealings and trickery. Which made me feel more the fool. I hurried to knock down her speculation. "But if he was just planning to stay awhile, like a kind of vacation, why didn't he stay longer? Have some fun?"

"Hmm." She considered that a moment and said: "Look, let's not waste any more time on him. He's gone. It's shitty that he let you down. But, honey, that's men for you. You gotta count on yourself."

Uncomfortably aware that I didn't want him to look bad, I opened my mouth to defend Jay's honor—say something to excuse his leaving. The acid expression on Malynda's face told me not to bother. I shut my mouth. He'd left me. Why did I care how he looked anyway?

She dismissed him with a wave of hand. "Like they say: One monkey don't stop no show. Time to move on, if you ask me. That is, if you want to move on." She lifted her sculpted brows, giving me a speculative look. "Do you, Frankie?"

Emerald City

Did I want to move on? Jay had been the sole focus of my affections for almost a year. "I guess I have to try." An evasive answer if there ever was one.

She let that go and went to her kitchen. I could hear her opening her tiny refrigerator. "So what's your next move?"

My next move? How did I know? I was still trying to take in the awful fact that Jay had left. Right now, my brain, like the proverbial deer caught in headlights, was deep in the grip of paralysis. I mumbled, just above a whisper: "I don't know."

"What did you say?" She asked, coming back out carrying a coke. Then she switched tracks: "Oh, I forgot. What about McGraw-Hill Publishers? You said you'd be taking your transcript to apply for something there. Did you go yet?"

The paralysis lifted long enough for discouragement to seep in again. "I went yesterday morning. No openings now." The hard-faced woman interviewer had made it obvious that my transcript didn't impress. The company wanted experience. And a White face, I suspected. Remembering left a sour taste of failure. Why had I thought getting a job writing in New York would be easy as counting one, two, three? +

Malynda sat in a chair positioned near the couch, cigarette and coke in hand. "Did you make any letter inquiries before you got here? To give you some leads?" She struck a match and lit her cigarette.

I shook my head. "No. I didn't know where to find any company names and addresses." I felt stupid saying that. Like I should have known better or somehow found a way.

She seemed to understand. "Any ideas about where to look next?"

"No." Reality was catching up with me. How was I going to start? What would I do? Somehow, I'd convinced myself that, once I was here, everything would—well, just fall into place. Again, I felt stupid and, now, embarrassed for not having thought things out. Trying to sidestep the fear that was working hard to keep me in Evansville hadn't allowed for it. When the monsters were chasing you, you didn't stop to make a plan.

"I know you want to do something that has to do with writing. I mean, that's why you came. But have you considered teaching? Until you can get something else, I mean."

I could feel my hackles rising. I shook my head, my mouth set. "No teaching. I want out of that trap."

At Indiana University, I'd done it to help pay for graduate school, and because I'd needed a job when I was about to graduate, I'd applied to teach at Evansville College and gotten it. But I had never, ever wanted to teach. That was what my parents did—teach. That's what everybody in Knoxville had expected me to do. I didn't want to do what everybody expected me to do. I wanted to be my own person. Whoever that was.

She peered at me. "Yeah. I can dig it. Between teaching those snot-nosed kids everyday and living in Evansville, I was going nuts." She paused and blew out smoke. "My parents thought I'd lost it two years ago when I told them I was coming to live here. Giving up a good, stable, respectable teaching job? But my God, the thought of living in Evansville and doing that for the rest of my life—I thought: Why don't you shoot me and get it over with?"

She chuckled. I tried to join her but my laughter died on the vine. I was too close to tears.

"I can see that right now you're shook up about Jay and it's got you turned around." She paused for a moment to gather her thoughts. "Let me give you a tip. It's been hard establishing myself here. But I've learned that you can't let a bump in the road throw you off. If you want something bad enough, you've gotta stick it through and keep going. Pull up some courage inside so you can stay on course, Frankie."

I nodded, feeling tender as a newborn kitten left on somebody's doorstep. How would I stay on course? Where would I get courage from? How did you *do* that? I wished she had a magic wand to hit me on the head and give me the strength she had gotten from somewhere. This business with Jay had sideswiped me good and hard.

"Okay," she went on, "here's a lead on a job I accidently found out about yesterday." She reached for a piece of lined notebook paper on the coffee table and handed it to me. "You'd be selling copy machines for a new company, Xerox Corporation. Wanna check it out?"

A sales job? Lord! I couldn't think of anything I'd hate more. Except maybe teaching. I looked down at her neat handwriting and then up at her. "Malynda, what in the world is a copy machine?"

She smiled. "I'm not surprised you don't know. I didn't know myself, coming from the teaching field. It's not in widespread use yet, but I think it will be. A copy machine duplicates. You want a copy of something... you slap it on the machine, and it makes it for you."

"You mean, no more typing with carbons or mimeographing?"

"That's right. I think it's going to catch on big soon. For this job, you'd be going around to businesses to demonstrate how the machine works. Should be easy to sell it after you show them the advantages of getting one for their business."

And if I got the job, how would I get around these businesses? I wondered. Take the bus? The subway? The prospect seemed overwhelming. But I gave her a bit of a smile because I appreciated what she was trying to do.

Malynda could see my response was less than enthusiastic and she tried another tact. "This Xerox thing is open right now. So you'd be working. You gotta live while you're waiting for a bite from any publishing or advertising companies you apply to. And you could find an apartment. Move out of that hotel."

I nodded. "Yeah, I definitely want to get out of there."

"That bad, huh?"

"Early tacky tends to be depressing." I tried to work up some excitement about her lead.

"I don't mind telling you that I've been thinking of going for this job myself if you don't want to. I think it has possibilities and I'm on the lookout for something better. Anyway, you let me know. Look, I'm sorry we can't have dinner tonight. I've got to get dressed for a date. Let's try for tomorrow. Okay?"

"Okay," I said, getting up to leave. I hid my glum feelings behind a smile. "And thanks. I'll go Monday to apply. Like you say, I've got to make a living."

Pleased, Malynda smiled back at me. "Good."

I slipped out the door, thanking her again. Once in the hallway, I sighed. Things were not going the way I thought they would. I wished I could step out of time. Step back to when Malynda and I were in the dorm at I.U. Back somewhere in time where things were predictable—classes and homework, weekends and partying. You knew how things would go. You knew what was coming—the next test, the next dance, the next semester. Now, you didn't know. The image of Jay getting into the yellow cab scrolled across my mind. I hadn't seen what was coming with him. Why hadn't I paid more attention? Maybe I could have stopped it. Behind Jay's image, I saw a shadowy glimpse of Stacey's smile. I'd been blindsided by her, too. So badly that I couldn't let myself remember her face without pain and anger wrapping their fingers around my throat. Near tears, I sighed again. Would I ever know how things in life would go?

5. The Wizard

From where I was sitting at the bar, I could see a slice of the streaked, orange and purple evening sky through the front windows. In front of me sat the remains of a hamburger. It was waiting for the drink I'd ordered. After I'd left Malynda's and gone back to the hotel, panic had me pacing the floor for almost an hour. To keep the walls of that wretched room from closing in, I finally grabbed my purse and ran out for a walk.

A couple of blocks away from the hotel, I'd seen this place, *Marty's*, and looked through the window. Seemed to be clean and decent. So I'd come in. It wasn't fancy. A medium-sized place, tables and booths covered with red-checked tablecloths, a huge, gilded mirror hung behind the bar. At booths and tables sat a smattering of couples and quartets talking, laughing. Instead of hearing music, I listened to low-pitched conversations floating in the air. No juke box in sight. Whoever heard of a bar with no music? In Allen's, people were forever pumping the juke box full of quarters to hear their favorite tunes. But this wasn't Evansville where you stayed in your neighborhood bars and drank with people who looked like you. I'd have to get used to this. Feeling a twinge of loneliness, I wondered what other things I'd have to get used to.

The waitress brought over my drink. "Anything else?" She asked, smiling vaguely. Her translucent skin needed some sun in the worst kind of way and she looked dead-on-her-feet.

"Not now. Thanks."

She nodded and went away. Watching her go reminded me of the waitresses, Sally and Katie, who'd be moving through the crowd at Allen's right now. I could see my drinking buddies, Syl and Clyde, at the bar, laughing it up with Les, the bartender. The music would be loud. People would be dancing. I looked around again for a juke box. None in sight. It was just a little thing, yet its absence revealed differences that added up to something important. Overhead, The Flying Monkeys circled, reminding me that here, I had no group of friends to trade laughs and drinks with at the end of the day. Nobody would be recognizing me. Nobody would be calling out a hello. Those realities didn't sit well. I wanted to feel the familiar, not something alien. A pang of homesickness hit me like a stomach cramp.

To shake it off, I took a swallow of my scotch, thinking about Evansville. A place, like my home town, where you grew up knowing your neighbors, your church members, the local schoolteachers, the parents of your buddies and classmates. It was a place you could easily fold yourself into. There were drawbacks, sure, like people getting into your business, and like no places to go for entertainment unless a hotel or a bar was bringing in a big-name singer, or unless the Drama Department of Evansville College had mounted a play. Still, in a place like Evansville you didn't feel adrift. You had a niche. You could figure out, more or less, what was coming next.

In a booth, the laughter of a couple—lovers, I could tell, drew my attention. They put their heads closer together, whispering, then got up to leave. Looking at them prompted my mind to take me places that I didn't want to go. It flew, before I knew it, to a hidden memory in The Corners: To Stacey and me whispering together, sharing a moment that belonged only to us. The memory opened a raw misery in my chest. Deliberately, I pushed away from it hard and in Jay's direction. I watched the lovers going out the door and wondered if they'd make love as soon as they got home. Did he satisfy her?

Satisfaction. Until Jay, every time I got up out of a man's bed, I'd be singing," I Can't Get No Satisfaction." Danny, I remembered, had circled me a long time like a bull in heat. When he'd made his big move, it had been particularly disappointing. And frustrating.

The waitress came back over with another drink and set it beside the dregs of the first. "The guy over there," she nodded in the man's direction, "sent you a drink."

Surprised, I glanced over at him. He raised his drink in salute. I nodded my thanks, deciding not to make any moves that might be interpreted as an invitation. He looked decent enough, a young Black man dressed in a suit and tie. But I wasn't interested. I had enough on my plate right now.

I lit a cigarette and sipped the fresh drink as my mind threaded its way back to meeting Jay. Danny had been gone a month when I'd met Jay at Allen's Sycamore Tavern. It had been raining cats and dogs that day, and Jay had come in wearing a soaked-through suede brown jacket. He'd plopped down beside me at the bar, his jacket smelling like a wet dog, introduced himself, and I'd found out that he'd dated my ex-roommate when they were in high school. That tidbit gave us common ground to chat—and to begin dancing around each other. We danced awhile as he pursued. Soon enough, I let myself be caught. Taking up with Jay pleased The Corners—the Stacey memories piled in there stayed quiet, thank God. They didn't pop out at random times during the day to hound me or seep into the fabric of my dreams at night. As long as Jay was on my radar, they kept still. But what would happen now? I took another sip, shuddering at the thought of their awakening.

Emerald City

I had to make the effort to put all that aside, to focus instead on where I was... where I'd got myself to. And why. In my mind, this was Emerald City. Land of Oz. The home of the Wizard who'd make your dearest desires come true. In the story, Dorothy and her friends had slipped into his throne room, ready to ask for what they wanted. *Who are you and why do you seek me?* He'd demanded of them in a threatening voice. *What is it that your heart desires?* When they'd told him, he'd given them an impossible task to complete to prove that they'd go to any lengths to get their hearts' desires.

From somewhere in the night boomed the voice of the Wizard: *Who are you and why do you seek me?*

Though doubt was setting into my bones like hardening cement, I answered: *I'm Frankie and I want to be a writer.*

Outside the bar's window, darkness had dropped. Time to get back to the room, I realized and signaled for my bill. I frowned at myself. Did I really want that? When you got right down to it, what would I write about? And how? I thought about the unfinished novel. At school, I hadn't finished it because, number one, I didn't have enough money to get it printed up for proper presentation to my Thesis Committee. But that was only part of the truth. The other part was that I didn't know how to finish it. I'd waded out into waters that I didn't know how to swim in.

In my Writing classes, I'd waited in vain for the teachers to teach me how to do those mysterious things that writers do. I'd listened to the lofty discussions about other people's work, searching the face of my instructors for some clue. For the key. For answers about how to swim in these waters. I wanted to ask: *What is the secret of putting a story together? How do you begin? How do you find your characters? How do you find the end of your story?* Instead of asking those questions, I'd looked at the oh-so-confident White faces of the students surrounding me, feeling unsure of whether I had anything meaningful to say. Or any talent to say it. I'd never asked my questions. I'd simply gone on feeling ashamed that I didn't know. And hiding it.

Who are you and why do you seek me? Boomed the Wizard's voice.

The waitress came with the bill and I counted out my money. As I gathered my purse and rose to leave, I realized that I'd never thought consciously before about writing. About the how of it. About what I knew and didn't. I'd never turned those experiences at I.U. over in my mind and examined them. But now—a cold sweat crawled over me.

As I was going out, the man who'd sent the drink smiled warmly at me. Vaguely, I nodded in his direction. My mind was spinning with something new to consider.

6. The Flying Monkeys

Outside, the night was very warm and without a breeze. My hotel was nearby and I hurried along, all the while, groping inside myself to find a sense of being all right... of being at ease in the city. A brisk procession of cabs and cars rolled by, and, on the other side of the street, there were a few lone walkers. My side was empty except for a Black couple strolling toward me. They looked to be about my age. I nodded a hello to them, acting on the old southern custom that Black folks should always speak to each other. They didn't look my way or return the acknowledgment. *Not like folks back home*, I thought. A strange sense of things being off-key dropped over me stronger than before. It made me uncomfortable.

What is it that your heart desires? Asked the Wizard.

I didn't know anymore. And if I didn't, what was I doing in New York? I didn't have a job. No decent place to live. No group of friends to circle the wagons around me. Fingers of sadness pressed down and squeezed my skull. Where could I fit in Emerald City?

My brown, brick hotel was now just a few steps away. I trudged in. The lobby looked respectable enough. But it had a forlorn feel to it. The furniture was a bit worn out. The décor, a bit out of date. And there was an unpleasant whiff of something old, like mildew. I rolled my eyes at my surroundings in disgust. Such as it was, it was tolerable. Down here. Upstairs was another story. At the elevator, I pushed the third floor button. Instead of taking the usual four or five minutes, the elevator came down right away. Just my bad luck. Every second I could spend away from that room up there, I counted as a blessing. By the time I stepped into the hallway of my floor, dread was settling into my stomach. I fought to push away the feeling while I unlocked my door. I hated going in. Hated the smothering loneliness in there. But I had no place else to go.

Inside, I sank down at the table. Under my nose, *The New York Times* was spread out on the table, the job classifieds pages open and waiting to be scanned. I'd bought it yesterday morning. So long ago. Ages. Silence hummed in my ears. A job helped you feel not out of place. A job gave you kind of anchor. Malynda's lead was something, at least although I didn't like the idea of trying to talk somebody into buying something. Even in elementary school, I remembered, I'd hated selling Girl Scout cookies. It felt wrong to me, strong-arming somebody into doing something they might not want to do. But it was a lead and I ought to be feeling grateful about it; instead, I was felt guilty that I didn't feel grateful.

I looked down at the classifieds. Something had to be in there that I had the right background for. My background might get my foot in the door to do proofreading, maybe even editing for a newspaper, or a magazine. As for advertising, wouldn't they need writers? The Flying Monkeys brushed me with their wings, sending me a tremor of fear. It wiggled around in my head like a caterpillar. Truth be known, after I'd gone to McGraw-Hill, the interview had all but scared me out of even looking for jobs where I thought I'd fit. I lit a cigarette and paced the room. Would all of them ask for experience, like the woman at McGraw-Hill? Jesus, how were you supposed to have experience before you actually got a job that would give you experience?

I paced over to the window and looked out. Street lights winked at me, sparkled like diamonds on a woman's dark breast. Would anybody give me a chance to learn? I'd wanted to learn back at I.U. but the secret things that the other students seemed to know about writing had slipped by me somehow. I'd felt like a stupid, country clod then. At McGraw-Hill, I'd felt the same way.

A boiling wave of resentment surged up inside me. Shame peppered the mix and made me hate lumbering around, begging all these sophisticated, smart White people to let me into their world.

That was a lethal brew of emotions. And I didn't want to feel any of them. I ground out my cigarette, wishing I had another drink. Why hadn't I bought a bottle at the bar? Coping with all these feelings stirring around… it was too much. I backed away from the window and flopped down on the bed.

What is it that your heart desires? Asked the voice.

To be a writer… that's what. But how was I going to do that? How could I be a writer if I didn't know any of the secret writing things that writers do to make stories? I went back to the window and looked out into the shadowy outlines of the city's skyline. In the dark, beyond the window pane, buildings crouched together guarding Emerald City's mysteries. I'd promised myself that I'd come to New York so I could be writing all the time. I was aware of the silence around me. I'd never really been alone and on my own before. There'd always been somebody. Always somebody to travel the road with, so to speak. But now—staying in New York would mean I'd have to sort things out by myself. Be willing to walk on an uncertain path alone. If I was going to stay here, I was going to have to step up and plunge, head first, into my own life. Into writing. Whether I knew how or not. That was something that I hadn't faced squarely before. Something I hadn't wanted to face.

The Flying Monkeys, waiting like roosting vampire bats, smelled blood then, and dropped down from the ceiling. They zoomed straight at me, crowded round, cutting off my breath with an iron-tight band of stark, white terror. I dropped into a chair, trying to breathe, and gazed out the window, once more, at the high columns of stone crowded together, scraping the sky—sentinels standing guard in dark shadow. In that moment, I saw how things stood. Saw that I'd been fooling myself all along. This was not Emerald City. This was New York City, not a fantasy, or a storybook place. The McGraw-Hill woman's hard face materialized in front of my eyes. This was a *real city* in a *real place* where *real people lived.*

My mind went to Jay and tears stung at the corners of my eyes. He'd be landing about in Evansville about now. He'd take a taxi, go to the bar, have a drink, and then go home to his wife and kids. Loneliness burned into my gut like alcohol in an open wound. How did I ever think I could live in New York?

I had to go back.

The Sandman's Bag

"Come sweet slumber; enshroud me in thy purple cloak." Max Headroom, character

1. No Backbone

Sitting in Club Paradise next to a bank of windows, I had a perfect view of Lincoln Avenue, the main drag for Black businesses in Evansville, and I reminded myself to keep close tabs on the time because I was on my lunch. The waitress, Edna, was smoking and drinking a beer at the bar. She didn't come to take your order until she was good and ready. Which might be five minutes or sixty-five minutes after you sat down. You had to play by her rules and you best try to look patient if you wanted to be waited on at all.

Edna put her cigarette out and trudged in my direction. The perpetual scowl on her ugly face was like some kind of sign. *Stay the fuck away,* it blinked. *Don't mess with me if you value your life,* it threatened. I shrank back in my chair, wishing for my friend, Willa, so I could ask her to do the ordering. That way I wouldn't have to even meet Edna's stony eyes.

When she reached my table, she put one hand on her hip and challenged me to open my mouth. "Yeah?"

How many people had she turned to stone with that Medusa face, I wondered. "Scotch on the rocks and water back," I said.

She turned away without a word.

"And some lemon slices, please." I added in a tiny, begging voice.

"Hump!" She grunted over her shoulder without missing a step.

Ordinarily, I preferred the friendly waitresses at Allen's Tavern, but the Paradise was air-conditioned. That came in handy on a roasting day like this one. I hated August in Evansville. Between the humidity and the sweat rolling down my body, I felt like I was living underwater. Or in a steam bath. But what could you do?

You could leave this city, answered Vee. *You don't have to live here.*

Vee was stirring up shit as usual. To ignore her annoying remark, I pulled out my cigarettes and lit a Pall Mall. The stuff she'd been nagging me about lately took backbone to face and I just couldn't muster any. Easier to have a drink, easier to let Mother scotch soothe me and ignore all that stuff I didn't want to deal with it. Like running back to Evansville from New York City.

Because you were too scared, whispered Vee.

True. New York wasn't easy. It had dared me to climb its hard, stone heights. It offered no soft place to dream. Or hide in.

Now look at you and the job you're stuck in, Vee taunted.

I grimaced, thinking about what my job was like. Ace had helped me to get in at the Neighborhood Youth Corps. It was a non-profit program, courtesy of the Nixon administration; it was supposed to help put Black drop-outs on the high road to productive employment, instead of leaving them at poverty's dead-end.

Well, what kind of job did you expect to get coming back here from New York? Asked Vee, with a nasty edge in her tone. *After all it* is *Evansville.*

I blew smoke out and tapped the end of my cigarette in the ash tray. She wasn't going to give me a break I could see. Wouldn't be satisfied until my mind replayed what had happened once I'd gotten back from New York City.

2. A Job Is a Job

It wasn't a pretty story. Reality had jumped up and slapped me hard in the face: Where was I going to get a job? Since I had kissed the English department goodbye at Evansville College before I'd left town, there would be no going back. But I'd

The Sandman's Bag

figured I had a good chance of getting work in the Evansville school system. There were only a few Black teachers and, after all, I had two college degrees. I was sure I'd qualify. But I didn't. They said I didn't because I hadn't taken any Education courses in college. On top of that, the three biggest manufacturing corporations in town had slammed the door in my face, saying that I was overqualified. Over qualified? Who'd have thought that being a Black woman with two college degrees would hold me back? Degrees were supposed to get you equal time on the playing field. Not shut out. What was going on? By the time I'd gone to see Ace, I was in full panic mode. That's when he'd given me a short, but eye-opening lesson.

Ace looked like a Black Mr. Clean—shaved head, muscled chest, the whole nine. He worked in the relatively new local Black organization struggling to get Black men into union apprenticeships for skilled trades. Since he knew a lot of people, I'd gone to his office for some help. He asked me where I'd been looking and I told him with frustrated anger dripping from every word.

"Cool down, Frankie, and think. In Evansville, where do you see most Black women working?"

The faces of my friend, Willa and of my ex-roommate immediately came to mind. Both of them worked in a garment-sewing sweat shop. Although my roommate finally had moved to Gary for a better job, Willa was still bent over a sewing machine every day. Other faces came to mind... Dorothy, Sally, Nannie. They worked as maids, or cooks for hotels. An overwhelming number of Black women did. Others had husbands that supported them. A few women taught in the school system. One or two drove school buses. None taught, or even worked at, either of the two colleges.

Ace said: "If you look closely, you see that, generally, Black faces aren't hired for jobs that require interacting with the public. Most Black men here work as unskilled laborers. Vance, the postman, is the only exception I know of." Ace shook his head. "It's about competition for jobs. And the fact is, the system won't be changing until it's forced to."

Hope plunged as panic surged up three or four notches. "Ace, this is 1970. Looks like things would be getting better."

"Looks like' is the key phrase," he said. "The power structure plays those political, smoke-and-mirrors games with our heads. They offer us a carrot on a stick and we follow it, thinking that if we do what they tell us, they'll play fair, open the gates, and let us in to compete. That's the game. The catch is that they always switch up the rules on us and keep the gates closed."

"Damn! That's not fair." My expression must have shown my growing alarm. If Ace couldn't give me some hope, I didn't know what I was going to do.

He studied my face. "Don't worry. What I'll do is speak to Clark Johnson about hiring you. They're doing some expansion of the Neighborhood Youth Corps Program. Have your resume ready."

Thanks to him, I'd been hired as a G.E.D. exam tutor to help drop-outs study for their high school diploma. During the eleven months I'd been there, nobody had ever shown up for tutoring—except once. That was when our teen recruiter, Clarence, a fast-talking nineteen-year-old from the streets, had managed to drag in a sixteen-year-old boy—God knows how, either under duress or bribery. That boy stayed just under an hour before he managed to make his escape, telling Clarence he'd "be right back" then disappearing into thin air.

To keep myself looking like I deserved to stay on the payroll, I'd moved quietly into the role of receptionist. For one thing, we didn't have one and, besides, there was nothing else for me to do. Every morning, I'd sit at the big desk, arranging and rearranging the message pad, pen, and phone, trying to look busy in an office where hardly anyone phoned or came in. It was depressing. To occupy my mind, I read books and told myself it was a job. And a job is a job. It paid.

Edna appeared at my elbow, interrupting my trip down memory lane. "Scotch," she mumble-barked and set my scotch, water, and lemons on the table.

My money was already waiting for her. "Thanks." I pushed it in her direction. With a tip. She rolled her eyes at the tip and scooped it up, showing me her broad backside as she went away.

I gazed into the golden depths of Mother scotch and sighed.

What's happening to me? I asked Vee.

Bored. You're drop-dead, screaming, crazy bored, said Vee.

She was right. My bladder signaled me to go to the bathroom. I put out my cigarette and headed for the back of the club.

3. Bathroom Confessions

The Paradise was a huge place… easily the biggest Black club in Evansville. Besides me, the only others here were an older couple sipping beer. We exchanged nods of greeting as I passed. Chairs and tables took up floor space all the way back to the shadowed dance area and stage.

As I went into the bathroom, the door squeaked loudly in deserted, spooky silence. While I answered the call of my bladder, my nose wrinkled at the stale beer smell layered over the acrid odor of cleaning disinfectant. Last Saturday night when George had booked in The Ohio Players, you could smell mingling scents of perfume and whiskey in here. Shrieks of laughter had burst overhead like fireworks as lines formed outside bathroom stalls, and voices had urged those inside the stalls to hurry up. Women had taken turns in front of the body-length, wall mirror checking their lipstick, adjusting miniskirts, and fish net stockings.

In the club, the crowd had roared and finger-popped all night to the music. I'd had fun dancing with Bob, my favorite dance partner, but fun couldn't erase the sharp edges of my disappointment that Jay wasn't around. Of course, he was at Allen's bartending; he'd come to my place afterwards and we'd have a few hours—the usual arrangement—but I was getting so I didn't like our catch-as-catch-can routine. I didn't like it that we couldn't go out as a couple… that he only came over when he could get away from his wife or when he didn't have to work nights at Allen's. Truth be told, Allen's was where I saw him mostly—when I was sitting at the bar and he was behind it. I didn't like it, but had I really expected things to be different between us when I'd come back to Evansville? I sighed, realizing that I probably had.

Which, I saw in a flash, was really, really stupid of me. Before I could catch them, my Stacey-thoughts—locked in a corner vault of my brain—burst free and showed me what I was doing and why. It came back to me trying, over and over, to smother the memory of Stacey into lifelessness. It came back to what I needed to do: Live my life without her. And Jay was the way I'd devised to do that. I stepped in front of the mirror and touched my face. The black, Cleopatra-style eye shadow I wore seemed to emphasize my desperation. I didn't have the right to complain about the routine with Jay. Or anything else. Because, I nodded at my reflection, I'd made this bed and put Jay in it. Suddenly, a lonely wind blew its empty night into my soul. I shivered and wanted to cry.

4. The Sandman

By the time I got back to my seat, that wind was roaring inside me. I had to stop it. I couldn't afford to be lingering in this misery of feelings. I tried to shake them off by reassuring myself that everything was going to be okay. That one day I'd be with Jay all the time. That he'd get a divorce, and we'd get married, and I'd be safe and sound. No loneliness. No Stacey-Jones. I'd be living in the "happily ever after." Wasn't that what my heart had desired? Why I'd come back? I lit another cigarette. Of course, it was.

Vee jumped in with both feet. *If that's the case, why does everything feel so chokingly tight and tangled up inside you?*

I took another swallow of scotch, wishing I could get high right now. I wanted to get high enough so my life would stop looking like shades of gray. High enough to leap over the rainbow to a place where my life would show up in living color. Where boredom and loneliness didn't exist. Over the rainbow was where everybody lived "happily ever after."

The Sandman's Bag

What fanciful thoughts, said Vee.

I tapped my cigarette ash and looked out of the window. The streets and sidewalks were deserted except for a lone figure in the distance. It was coming closer... striding with long, even steps that spoke of purpose. I stared at the figure... then blinked. He was dressed in a monk-like gray, shapeless gown and he carried a sack slung over his shoulder.

Where had he come from? I glanced up and down Lincoln Avenue. Nothing moved except him. *What a bizarre sight.*

Except it wasn't, really. Almost a year ago, after I'd come back here from New York, I'd been catching sight of him at the edge of my vision. From time to time, I'd see a glimpse of him standing, knapsack across his shoulder, just there at the very edge of sight. If I turned around to look at him full-on, he'd disappear—like he was playing hide-and-seek with me.

Who is that, Vee? I asked, mesmerized by the sight.

It's The Sandman.

Yeah? I peered at him, even more fascinated. *I didn't think he was real.*

He's as real as you need him to be, Vee said.

I glanced back at my drink and picked it up. There were about two swallows left in the glass. I took one. Mother scotch felt good going down. Very good. I wanted more because I wanted to keep feeling good. But, there was my boring job. Though I wished I didn't, I had to go back to it this afternoon. My eyes went to the window again. The Sandman was across the street now. Closer. That scared me. Just a little.

What's in his bag, Vee?

You know as well as I do.

The stories say it's sleep dust. Is it sleep dust?

Yes. And when he gets close enough to you, he'll douse you with it... if you want him to.

I thought about it: *If I wanted him to.* I kept looking out the window. The Sandman stepped off the curb and crossed the street, all the while, clutching his bag.

Vee, what would happen if I let him?

Frankie Lennon

You know. Things would be the way you want. You'd be numb... shut down. Asleep all the time.

Would I care? Vee let me answer that one myself. I wouldn't. It would be a relief, to tell the truth, not to have to think about stuff anymore. I didn't want to. It was too hard to think about stuff. I just wanted things to be easy—to float along without my having to make any effort.

The Sandman opened the door of the club. As he and came toward me, he dipped into his bag. I lifted my head a bit and he threw a handful of dust in my face. It drifted down like falling stars.

Feels so peaceful, I mumbled and took a drink.

The Sandman dipped into his bag again, and pulled out another fistful of dust. *It's time to sleep,* he said, and slowly sprinkled, covering me from head to toe in a silver-dust fog.

My eyelids drooped. "Time to sleep," I mumbled, as my mind folded up... and clicked off.

Scotch on the Rocks

1. Night Flyer

I was late for the play at Evansville College, my dashboard clock told me. I muttered a curse. If I hadn't had that last drink at Allen's tonight, I wouldn't be crunching the accelerator to gain some extra minutes driving down Lincoln Avenue. The rain-spattered windshield had me squinting to keep inside the road's yellow line. I blinked to clear my vision, easing up on the accelerator pedal a bit. It was annoying that the damn line kept wiggling. How was I supposed to drive on the right side if it didn't stay straight? The frantic swish-swish of the wipers dancing across the windshield was getting on my nerves. If only I could switch on some music. That would drown them out. But the radio was on the blink. To calm myself down, I stuck a Pell Mell between my lips, pushed in the cigarette lighter, and waited. In a few seconds, it popped out and I lowered my eyes to grope for it. My fingers found the lighter and as I looked up at the road again, out of the darkness, a parked Volkswagen materialized inches away on my right. Startled, I jerked hard on the steering wheel just in time to keep from side-swiping the car. A shaky breath escaped my lips as I gripped the wheel firmly with both hands.

"That was a narrow escape," I whispered to myself.

The light turned red ahead at Kentucky Avenue and Lincoln; I braked and tossed the cigarette in the ashtray. The urge to smoke had evaporated. A peep at the clock, while I waited for the light to change, needled me, once more, to keep hurrying. It was in my favor that the streets folded up this time of night in Evansville. No cars out and about meant I could go faster for the rest of the way down Lincoln. I gazed at the red light. *Come on, come on. How long are you gonna stay red?* Ahead, streetlights threw out yellow shafts of light. A couple of cars sped across the intersection in front of me, their tires whistling on black pavement that glistened with raindrops. My eyes shifted to the painted line ahead down the middle of the street. It still shimmied like a snake, so I closed one eye and looked again. The line seemed to straighten.

"No more shimmy, shimmy like my sister Kate," I bragged to the empty car.

The light turned yellow. Then green. My toes pushed down on the accelerator and the car jumped forward to cross Kentucky Avenue, the line of demarcation between Black folks' home ground and White folks' territory. Outside my windshield, I noticed the outlined shapes of trees streaking by, then melting into pools of black shadows. Further back, big, brightly lit houses sat comfortably on broad expanses of lawn. It was getting hard for me to make out what was shadow and what was substance. I scooted forward, squinting. Because the rain was now no more than a few drops, my car's wipers began to screech and scrape. I twisted the control dial to intermittent and glanced at the clock. It was five minutes after eight and the play would be starting now. The speedometer needle pointed at thirty-nine miles per hour. There'd be no more stoplights for a few blocks, so I could get away with just a little bit more speed. *Must go faster*, I told myself and pressed down on the accelerator.

Then, out of the corner of my eye, I thought I saw a puppy dart out into the street. I slammed my foot on the brake, hard. And as soon as I did, the car skidded to the right. For a moment, my mind froze. Was I supposed to turn the car into the skid or away from it? I couldn't remember. Following instinct, I steered left instead of right. The Pinto spun like a whirligig, weaving across the street's middle line. Everything was out of control. Not far ahead, I saw the lights of an oncoming car. Desperate to get out of harm's way, I hit the accelerator, at the same time, tugging at the wheel. A corner appeared out of the darkness and I jerked right sharply, swerving in. *Too fast!* My mind screamed as the car barreled toward parked cars on my right. To compensate, I pulled the wheel to the left, but too far. The car surged into a driveway and up the incline of a yard. Wind rushed past my cheeks from the half-opened windows. Suddenly, a huge Magnolia tree loomed up out of the yard, directly in my car's path. I tried pulling the steering wheel to the right to avoid the tree, but it wasn't quite enough. Bark flew and I closed my eyes, hearing the sound of screaming metal as the Pinto plowed in and sideswiped the Magnolia. I could feel the driver's door buckling while shattered glass popped like firecrackers; shards flew into my hair, fell on my coat, and into my lap. The car came to rest with the driver's door jammed shut, and its nose bulldozed into the Magnolia. I groaned when I realized the car and I were sitting in the front yard of a Georgian style, two-story mansion. *Shit-a-mile!* No way could I play this off; these folks would be calling the cops for sure. Maybe they wouldn't smell the liquor though. I fumbled for some breath mints as a young, blonde woman came running out of the front door to find out if I needed an ambulance. I told her I didn't, then threw a couple of mints in my mouth as I climbed out on the passenger side. It was gonna be a long night.

2. Q. and A.

A young man with sallow skin sat before me, staring down at a pamphlet. I inspected him warily. Sunbeams streaming through the window bounced off his straight, jet-black hair. The November afternoon sun backlit the man the way a Hollywood cameraman might, sculpting his face in granite planes and hollows. Although he wore the uniform of an older, corporation man—a gray suit with narrow lapels, a crisp, white shirt and a tightly-knotted, navy tie—he looked to be about my age, in his late twenties, but a bit frayed around the edges. I looked around me. The office was a cubbyhole: A desk, a couple of chairs, a tall, gray file cabinet in the corner, and an overflowing wastebasket. The office was tiny enough for my I-hate-cramped-places phobia to kick into gear, but it was checked by the huge window behind his desk. Without shade or blinds for cover, it opened wide on the levee and the Ohio River beyond to give you the illusion of space.

The air hummed with silence. It felt surreal, like I'd been plopped down in the middle of a movie set where the director had called for quiet. Pinpricks of painful humiliation stabbed me every time I thought about the driving under the influence ticket that had got me here. I drummed my fingers on the big, red purse in my lap, wishing I could comfort myself with a cigarette. But, a few minutes ago, when I'd pulled out my Pell Mells, the man had said right off that I couldn't: "It's against the rules. This is a smoke-free office," he'd said, his eyes looking like a bottomless, black pool.

What a bitch! Sentenced to a session with an alcohol counselor in a smoke-free office! Who thought up this kind of torture anyway? My toes twitched anxiously. I glared at him. What was he reading anyhow? Did it have something to do with the questions he'd said he'd be asking me? I crossed my legs because I didn't know what to do with myself. God, I wanted this over quick, so I could head out for Allen's. Today was Friday and the eagle was flying; people would be swooping in on its wings, ready to trade those dollar bills for a good time. Besides that, a scotch on the rocks would soothe my jumpy nerves just fine about now.

Without preamble, the counselor spoke into the silence. "When you drink, how many would you say you ordinarily might have?"

I swallowed and laced my fingers together to hide my shaking hands. "Two. Maybe, three." The lie rolled off my tongue as easy as pie.

For a few beats, the black light in his eyes searched my face. That steady gaze set my toes to itching. I rubbed the front of my right foot up and down the back of my left leg, hoping for relief. At the window, blue-bellied clouds had drifted into view. While I watched them, he wrote something down.

Looking down at an open file folder on the desk, he began again. "You crashed into a tree the night of the accident." The

Scotch on the Rocks

man paused, looked up at me, and asked: "How many drinks did you have that night?"

The question embarrassed me. I mumbled an answer, then began to inspect the new red boots I had on for scuff marks.

He didn't let me get away with it. "How many?"

I lifted my head. "Four, I believe." Actually, I knew I'd had more like six or seven drinks that night. Desperate to escape his bottomless, black eyes, I shifted mine back to the window. The large, single pane was almost invisible, as if you could dive right out of it and into the river's rippling, dove-gray waves.

After flipping to another page in the file folder, he said, "This is your second D.U.I. Are you sure about that?"

Hot anger bubbled up under my skin. I played it off by shrugging and smoothing my skirt. What the hell was this jive turkey tryin to say? I didn't want to hit the puppy that's why I had the accident!

The counselor studied the pamphlet on his desk again. When he looked at me this time, his expression was questioning. "Why did you have four that night when ordinarily you drink less? Was something bothering you?"

"Nothing was wrong," I said, hoping I wouldn't get caught in the lies I was weaving. Sweat popped out under my armpits as my eyes slid away from his to the window. I pictured myself leaping out of it into the Ohio River, then swimming away with easy, deliberate strokes.

He shifted in his seat and smoothed his tie a bit. In an off-handed tone, he threw out another question, "How long have you been drinking?"

Twelve years of my past flared up and a tide of liquor swept by: Chugalugging rum with Steve before a dance, sipping Seagram's Seven undercover in Carol's dorm room, guzzling vodka with Shari at a house party. Half-pints, fifths, and quarts of whiskey, rum, gin, scotch. Cans of Schlitz, Colt 45, Budweiser, Champale. Sipping martinis, gimlets, daiquiris, champagne. Drinking at the bar after work, in the kitchen playing Bid Whist, outside at the softball games on Sundays, in the living room on Saturday afternoons. Cocktails, nightcaps, toddies, and hair of the dog that bit you all washed by in waves. An ocean of memories. A smile almost touched my lips at the thought of them, but other, more recent things flowed in around the edges, spoiling memories of the good times: Hangovers, memory lapses, car accidents, the shakes, guilt driving me to say I'd only have one drink and then waking the next day to realize that one had somehow turned into ten or twelve. I wrinkled my nose at the rotten smell of my own shame. *What happened?* I asked myself silently. *It used to be so much fun.*

The man leaned forward, pressing me for an answer: "How long? Months? Years?"

I wished he would stop being nosey, stop poking around into my business. "A few years," I said, avoiding his question with vagueness. How long was I gonna have to sit through these stupid-ass questions?

He consulted the pamphlet and came at me again. "When did you take your first drink?"

I stared at him, realizing that I wasn't going to be able to think fast enough to get him off me. The questions, the probing jabbed my insides like a knife. I could feel a sharp ache in my side, draining away my resolve to sidestep him.

"Do you remember?"

It didn't matter if I told him the truth this time. "Twelve years ago. At college." Hearing it was eerie somehow. *Was it that long ago?*

"First drink at college." He repeated, making a note.

"When I was a freshman. Before a fraternity dance," I added. And reminded myself: *In the cab with Steve.* He'd asked me if I knew how to drink and I'd said yes. Then he'd poured a paper cup full of Bacardi's rum, splashed some coke in it, and smiled, nodding for me to try it. The rum had burned my tongue.

"What kind of experience was it for you, good or bad?" The counselor asked.

"Good," I said, but it really wasn't. The moment Steve had said, "Drink up," I'd felt scared. Like I'd signed up for a big contest that I didn't know how to win. Scared because I was an imposter, posing as a sophisticated lady all dressed up in a rose,

Scotch on the Rocks

satin cocktail dress with long, black gloves. Scared shitless, looking down at the dark liquid in the cup because I was a liar. I'd never had a drink before. But I drank it all up like he told me to, and ended up with my head hanging over the toilet stool, my stomach heaving, trying to vomit the stuff up.

Remembering brought back smothering feelings of shame. To push them away, I let my eyes wander to my escape hatch—the office window. More clouds had linked up with the blue-bellies. The new gray-colored ones had fat, dark bottoms. I wondered if it was going to rain and if I had an umbrella in the car.

"Do you mostly drink alone, or with others—say at dinner, at a bar, something like that?"

His question pulled me back into the room. I uncrossed and re-crossed my legs to give myself time to consider whether to lie or not. "Sometimes alone, other times at bars or at dinner with other people."

Without pause, he launched into the next one. "How often do you drink? Every day? A couple of times a week?"

I blinked at his attack. It took a moment before I could put together an answer. "Once or twice a week." The lie came out of me in a squeaky, uneven voice.

He gave me a doubtful look. "Once or twice? You don't drink more than that typically in a week?"

"No," I said sealing the lie with defiance and a good deal of resentment.

A distant sadness glistened in his eyes. Then, his face became even more grave and still. "Do you think you have a drinking problem?"

White heat exploded in my chest. To keep my hands from going for his neck, I choked my purse for dear life and bit my tongue. Mr. Langley, my boss and the Director of the Library, thought I had a drinking problem. He'd told me so as big as you please. Called me into his office two weeks ago after the accident to let me know his secretary, Miss Hardy, had seen my name in the paper under the court records. I could still picture the two of them tsk-tsk-tsking about my name in the paper. *Shit-a-mile! What kind of secretary combs the local rag for gossip to report it back to her boss anyway?* I was still seething with resentment. I had to concede he had a right to call me on the carpet. It did look bad to have your Community Relations Coordinator going to court for drunk driving. All the same, when that little Napoleon had fixed me with a severe look that made me feel lower than dirt, I'd felt like slapping his ass into next week.

The counselor repeated his question: "Do you think you have a drinking problem?"

I didn't know what to say. Anger and shame fought it out in my head while a red-hot poker burned in my chest.

"Please answer the—"

"No, I don't," I almost shouted. Then, I took a breath and stammered out the rest. "At least, I, I don't think so." *Where had that come from?*

He closed the folder and lifted his eyes to mine. "Would you like to quit?"

Quit? My mind nudged the idea like it was an alien thing, and white-hot fear gushed up, like lava, surging into every cell of my body. *Quit?* Scotch was my Linus blanket. My protector. My mind zoomed away, imagining a life, a future without scotch. A future that looked like a long, dark, winding tunnel. One that was unknowable and unpredictable. Who knew what might be waiting? Most likely, scary things you couldn't see coming. *Quit scotch?* My mind scrambled away from the idea as if it was a fully-hooded, swaying cobra poised in my path. I just couldn't feature it. How the hell did anybody just up and quit?

Aloud, I said, "Uh, uh. I don't think so. Why should I give up partying? Everybody wants to have a good time. Right?"

He stared at me as if he were contemplating something; then he licked his lips and said, "Sure, people want to have a good time, but alcoholism is a serious disease. Deadly, in fact. I think you ought to take a hard look at your drinking."

I wanted to cuss his raggedy-white-ass out, calling me an alcoholic right to my face. But I didn't want a bad report to go to the judge, so I said, in my meekest voice, "You're right, sir."

He shuffled some papers on his desk and put them into a neat stack, then, looked at me once more, as if he were taking my measure. "Okay, Miss Lennon. You can go." He swiveled his chair around to the file cabinet in a gesture of dismissal.

Glancing at my watch, I rose quickly from the chair. It was a relief to see that I'd be able to catch the five o'clock crowd at Allen's. Before I turned to go, my eyes were drawn to the window once more. The late afternoon sun had stained the sky with oranges and reds.

3. What's Goin On?

The five o'clock crew at Allen's Lounge was off and running. The place buzzed like a busy hive. Compared to the worn and threadbare Sycamore Tavern, this new bar of Allen's was almost classy-looking. It was larger and brighter, a far cry from the old tavern hunched on the corner like a dark, ancient crone. Despite the "Lounge" that Allen had adopted to signal a higher status for his bar, those who considered themselves high-class snubbed Allen's in favor of Club Paradise on Lincoln. Basically, the crowd at Allen's remained the same: Blue collar with a smattering of white collar here and there.

What's goin on? I heard Marvin Gaye ask over the chattering hum of the crowd. *Home free! That's what's goin on,* I answered in my head while situating myself on a barstool. *No alcohol counselor and his stupid questions around here!* I nodded hello to the regulars lining the bar like pigeons waiting for bread crusts. Behind the bar, Allen, tall as an ostrich and dark as bitter chocolate, counted bills and change to balance the cash register. Jay iced down the beer while Les, looking like a sad-eyed, basset hound, poured up half-dozen drink orders as Katie, the waitress, reeled them off.

I lit a cigarette and glanced up at the huge, lighted mirror in front of me; the crowd's doings immediately snagged my attention. Scattered at tables, men in blue or gray work uniforms, just getting off from work at Whirlpool or Alcoa, drank quarts of Budweiser or shots of whiskey, smoked cigarettes, traded lies, hawked the women, and speculated on which one might want a just-for-tonight lover. The women, in bright colors, sat in groups of two's and three's, cutting their eyes at each other, whispering behind their hands, or throwing their heads back in noisy laughter. Most of them sipped pretty drinks—the kind I never had much use for—like Tom Collins or Tequila Sunrise, although some toyed with a glass of beer.

I caught Jay's eye and winked. He was a beauty. An x-rated honey-dripper. Cinnamon skin, thick eyelashes, naturally arched eyebrows, sculpted, full lips. And so good in bed that I could pretend my woman-jones didn't exist. Sometimes, all his sexiness and beauty triggered my inferiority complexes. At other times, my ego swelled with the idea that a sugah-lump like him had picked me to be his woman.

"What's up?" I asked as he came toward me

He shrugged, slapping a napkin on the counter. "Gonna be jumpin in here tonight. Allen's got me working the night shift, so I won't get by your place until 2:30. You want your usual? It's on me."

"Yeah, scotch on the—"

He finished it. "Rocks, lemon slice, water back."

"What else?" I smiled.

He grinned at me and started to pour. As he did, a voice hollered out.

"Give her another!" It was Sylvester sitting at the other end of the bar; he slammed two quarters down for Jay. I waved at Syl and nodded my thanks. He, in turn, lifted his shot glass ceremoniously in salute.

Jay put another glass down beside the first. Watching him pour a drink was mesmerizing. He made it high art. With a magician's flourish, he tossed the scotch bottle from one hand to the other, lifted it high in the air, and flicked his wrist to let the liquor flow in an even stream, first into one glass, then, without missing a beat, into the other. I'd seen him do it a thousand times and he'd never spilled a drop.

Jay put two drinks in front of me, went down the bar to collect for it, rang up the order, and trotted off to the john. I gestured for Syl to come over and take the empty seat beside me.

Scotch on the Rocks

He stood and hitched up his pants the way he always did, then, strolled over.

When he reached me, he said: "Gotta go. Got business to take care of."

"What? On a Friday night?" I was disappointed that he was leaving. Syl was one of my favorite drinking buddies

He shrugged. "Catch you later, sis."

On his way out, he stopped at a table to slap the backs of some men. I shifted my sight from Syl's retreat to the mirror behind the bar. It ran the length of the wall. The bottles, in front of it, artfully arranged in stair-step fashion, caught my eye. Like ladies of the night displaying their wares to the highest bidder, the shimmering liquor winked and promised good times: Scotch in emerald green bottles, whiskey in topaz brown bottles, vodka and gin in diamond-clear bottles. I picked up my glass and sipped. *Nothing like the first scotch of the day*, I told myself while savoring the bitter, slightly oily taste of J & B.

A good feeling began to settle over me. But before the good feeling could make itself at home, out of nowhere, I heard the counselor ask: *Do you want to quit?*

Spooked, I glanced over my shoulder, frowning as I scanned the crowd. Was that ass hole of an alcohol counselor in here? Did he follow me to Allen's? But, no. There were only Black folks here, getting down to some serious partying. I stared into the golden liquid in my glass. *Do you want to quit?* He'd asked me. An icy tremor passed through me. How could I give it up? My palms felt clammy and I wiped them together.

There'd been times when I'd thought about it. Especially when I'd come into Allen's, and somebody at the bar would ask me if I remembered what I'd done the night before. I hated that question. It shamed me. They knew what I'd done, but I didn't. It was unnerving because a big, black hood had dropped down over my brain. What I'd done the night before was gone. Wiped clean. When someone asked me, I'd drop my eyes, afraid that I'd made a fool of myself. Afraid that somebody was going to rib me for it and I wouldn't be able to, couldn't play it off. How could I when last night was a bunch of empty pages scrolling in my head?

I pulled on my cigarette. Why couldn't I remember? What was happening? Maybe I should seriously consider quitting. But when that line of thought came to mind, I had to have a drink since thinking about quitting was unnerving. By the time I'd finished drinking and thinking, mother scotch had moved the whole idea to the back burner.

What's goin on? Marvin asked me, his voice fading on the last notes of the song. I took a long swallow of scotch, almost draining the glass as The Isley's kicked "Love the One You With" into high gear. It was then that the door swung open so hard that the hinges squeaked and sang. I turned my head to see who was coming in. There at the entrance stood Jay's wife—a harmless-looking, brown terrier with the soul of a war dog. For a millisecond, she was motionless; then, she swooped in.

Thank God, Jay was in the john. If she had come in a few minutes earlier, she'd have caught me sitting here carrying on with him. But she didn't need to catch me to know I was guilty. When Jay was here, nine times out of ten, I was, too. Marsha knew, like everybody else in Evansville, that I was Jay's sideline woman. It was a common practice. Husbands took lovers; wives looked the other way. Marsha didn't frequent the bars, so ordinarily Allen's Lounge was safe territory for me and Jay. But not, it seemed, today. In the mirror, I watched her double-timing it straight to me, her jaws tighter than Dick's hatband. She stomped up beside me and stopped, hand on her hip, glaring. Without looking at her, I lifted my glass to drink, weighing the threat of danger her presence signaled while cold sweat inched down my stomach.

"What the hell," she addressed me in ringing tones, loud enough for everyone to take notice, "do you think you're doin in here with Jay?"

At the sound of her voice, the bar's noisy crowd suddenly came to attention, slipping into the I-was-a-witness mode, drinks forgotten as eyes turned to watch local drama.

Marsha moved a step closer. "Ain't I tole you bout this shit before?"

Scotch on the Rocks

Survival instinct screamed for me to get the hell out of the bar, but my feet had turned to concrete. Careful not to look her in the face, I took a drag on my Pell Mell and tapped some ashes off the tip.

She took the drama up a notch, playing to every person in the room. "I hope," she proclaimed, "you don't think I'ma jus sit back in some corner while you fuck around with my husband."

I could feel her breath on my neck. Was she going to jump me? My heart was thumping in time with the record's beat. Since I'd never been a fighter, I had zero confidence about myself when it came to fisty-cuffs, but if she made a move to beat my ass, would I just sit here and let her?

The crowd hung with bated breath on every word. She huffed and puffed for them. "I'ma tell you one more time to leave Jay alone."

I kept silent, gambling that she'd interpret my silence as browbeaten humiliation and leave me be.

She pronounced her final threat with a flourish. "Don't let me have to tell you bout this shit no more!" A dramatic pause, and then: "You hear me?"

The challenge hung in the air. Despite the fact that I was shivering in my boots, the smart-ass in me finally reared its head, ready to deliver me to the hangman's noose. I opened my mouth with the intention of sarcastically assuring Marsha that I had, indeed, heard her. But Jay glided up before I could say a word, and quickly steered her out of the bar.

The door slammed behind them, and the crowd came back to life, jabbering excitedly. Although I felt frazzled, the mirror showed me looking cool as a cucumber: Permed hair pulled back into a long pony tail, Cleopatra eye makeup unsmeared, gold earrings dangling. Underneath it all, fright churned my guts like a washing machine. To steady my galloping heartbeat, I finished off the rest of the scotch in glass number one, pushed it away, and pulled glass number two into drinking position.

Katie, on her way to put in order, stopped beside me. "Don't let Marsha bother you. She be all bark and no bite."

"You think so?" I asked, glad she was rallying round me. It softened the hard edge of guilt that poked my ribs when I thought about Jay's wife and family.

"Hell, yeah," she said, looking for all the world like somebody's teddy bear as she waddled toward the waitress station. "Don't sweat the small stuff, baby girl!"

On the jukebox, The Isley's played out and Gladys Knight swung in on the grapevine with the Pips backing her up. I took a big sip out of scotch number two, feeling a nice buzz as I watched the boogying on the dance floor. Before long, Jay rushed in and trotted behind the bar, giving Allen an apologetic look. Allen shook his head in disgust while Jay began to busy himself with glasses that needed washing, and beer that needed icing.

I blew out a long stream of cigarette smoke. Wisps glided together. A pale face with deep, black, mocking eyes materialized and floated just above my drink. It looked like the alcohol counselor. I stared, fearfully, at the apparition.

Do you think drinking will make The Corners go away? It asked.

Why was I seeing things? And how did it know about The Corners? Nobody knew about The Corners. *Go away!* I shouted wordlessly, shutting my eyes. I didn't like to think about The Corners. Although Marsha had rattled my cage, she wasn't the scariest thing in my life. The Corners were. I was twenty-nine years old, and scared to death of the lightless places where I'd shoved things in my life that I couldn't deal with; scared of The Corners—shadowy, murky places, where I'd hidden the truth about me. The memory of Stacey languished there. Dreams and desires lay abandoned there. Unclaimed and suffocating, my life lay buried there, gasping and clawing to break free. Pitch-black, dark and deep, The Corners haunted me. I was afraid of them and the things dying there. When I opened my eyes, and looked at the apparition, it grimaced at me with disapproval.

Why are you living your life in a bar? It asked.

I'm not! I screamed at it silently, and the face broke apart, leaving tendrils of smoke drifting in the air. Thoroughly shaken, I gulped down most of my drink.

Scotch on the Rocks

Charlie, standing nearby, stumbled over. He studied my face. "You look like you could use another," he said to me, swaying on unsteady legs.

"Yeah, guess I could," I agreed. I needed it to calm the dread trickling, like acid, into my stomach. Besides, I never refused a freebie.

"Les," Charlie said, "set her up. I'm buyin. And bring me another rum and coke."

As Les filled the order, the head of the alcohol counselor suddenly popped out of thin air. The disembodied head reminded me of the Cheshire cat in Alice in Wonderland. I blinked at the hallucination.

How much do you drink? It demanded to know, black eyes fixed on the almost-empty scotch glass in front of me.

Charlie yammered away, apparently noticing nothing out of the ordinary. I took a deep breath, grabbed the drink in front of me, and chugalugged it, hoping the head of the counselor would vanish.

It didn't. Instead, it continued interrogating me. *How much do you drink?* It pressed, dark eyes flashing, daring me to lie.

Not as much as Charlie. He's a stone drunk! I shot back in my defense. I always marveled that it took so little for Charlie to get high; after two or so, he'd be three sheets in the wind, where it would usually take half-dozen or more for me to get there. The head scowled at the thread of my argument. I ignored the scowl and taunted: *Well, Mr. Alcohol Counselor, what'll you say to Charlie? Tell him he has a serious disease? Ask him if he wants to give it up?*

Les put fresh drinks in front of Charlie and me.

How many drinks does that make for you? The head asked quietly while its eyes probed my insides like a scalpel.

Just leave me alone, I snarled, my stomach trembling like jello.

The thing stared at me, its face fixed in a grim, schoolmarm expression. I felt like it was dumping a load of squirming guilt into my stomach. God! I wished I'd stop seeing things. It was ruining everything.

Charlie pushed a dollar bill to Les and picked up his rum and coke. "Be seein ya," he said to me. "I'm playin pool over there with Marcellus."

"Okay. Thanks, Charlie," I said.

Allen's door opened, and I turned away from the floating head to see Billy strolling in. I waved at him, then looked back at the spot where the counselor's head had been hovering. But it had disappeared. I sighed, deeply relieved.

Billy sat on one of the empty barstools nearest the door and ordered a coke. I checked out his appearance. You'd never guess by the way he was dressed that he operated and owned an automobile repair shop. If your car had a dent, or a bent fender, he was your man. Accidents seemed to hover around me—the Magnolia tree accident being a case in point, so Billie had made a good piece of change off me. Everybody knew that there were side benefits in taking your car to his place. For one, he made the best barbecue in town, bar none. Not only did you get his barbeque when you took your car to him, you'd also get to share his bottle or, if you preferred, the beer in the fridge. I passed on his beer, but never on his bottle. Now, Billy was definitely somebody who drank more than I did. Though it didn't seem to get in the way of his work because when he did my cars, you couldn't tell that I'd misjudged here and there, and sideswiped a car, a tree, or run into a house.

Lately, though, there was a change in Billy's drinking habits. Used to be, he'd order a double Four Roses and coke. Not now though. He'd told me he'd stopped. And his appearance showed it. The old Billy always came to the bar in his wrinkled coveralls, stained with engine oil and paint dust; the new Billy showed up, pressed and righteously put together, in a suit and shined shoes. Like today.

Something tugged at me to get up and go over to him. Without consciously thinking about it, I moved to his side just as Les shoved a glass of coke at him.

"What's up, Billy?" I greeted him. It was always good to see Billy. Something about him reminded me of Uncle Matt. Maybe it was his maple-colored skin.

Scotch on the Rocks

Smiling hugely, he said, "Nothing much. I'm lookin for one of my customers. Ain't you off early? Thought they didn't let you outta that library until six."

Since he'd fixed my car himself, Billy knew I had to go to court. "The judge sent me to some alcohol counselor, so I had to take off."

I watched him drain some of the coke Les had put in front of him. Billy puzzled me; he didn't act like he missed the ole Roses at all. An icy finger touched the back of my neck and I shivered, wondering: *Was it that easy for him just to stop cold?*

A couple of guys near the pool table suddenly laughed loudly. I jumped at the sound, and I thought I saw Billy give me, for a second, a strange glance.

"There's my customer, Marcellus," he said. "We got business." He glanced at my empty hands. I'd left my drinks at my seat. "Want a drink?"

"Sure. I never turn down a drink," I said automatically.

Billy caught Les's eye and nodded at me. Les set a whiskey glass on the bar, shoveled in some ice and poured my J & B in it. After Les put the drink in front of me, Billy pulled out change, dropped it on the bar, and heaved himself up.

As he started walking away, the alcohol counselor's face floated up into my vision. I saw his pale, stern mouth. *I think*, the mouth said, *that you ought to take a look at your drinking.*

The words made me quiver inside, like an arrow striking true to its mark. Before I knew what I was doing, I was on my feet, and at Billy's heels. "Billy," I said, gesturing for him to move a discreet distance away from any listening ears.

"Yeah?"

"I wanna ask you something."

He waited.

I lowered my voice. "Was it hard?"

He looked confused. "What?"

I felt a knot growing in my chest. "Quitting," I whispered, my throat constricting. "Quitting the drinking."

He gave me a sharp look. "Why you wanna know?"

I shrugged, icicles in my stomach. I couldn't have told him why; I didn't even know I was going to ask, but I needed an answer.

"Was it?" I pressed him.

Instead of answering me, Billy stood, as if he were rooted to the spot, hands in his pockets, staring at the floor. Some indefinable thing, dark as batwings blotting out the moon, flew across his face and twisted it, for a moment, into a mask of pain. At the sight of his reaction, I winced, dread touching my heart. *Maybe it would be better*, I thought, *if I didn't know. Maybe I should tell Billy never mind.* But looking at Billy I didn't think I could call the question back now. Katie passed close by, threw us both a strange look, and kept walking.

"Yeah," Billy finally said, on a breath that was hoarse and strangling. "It was hard."

My chest rippled in fear at his words. At what was behind them. At the things he wasn't saying. Once more, Billy turned to leave. But there was more I needed to ask though I didn't know exactly what. So I couldn't let him leave. If he went, the knot of terror swelling in my chest would burst.

"Billy," I put my hand on his arm to stop him, and the words tumbled out, "the counselor told me some things. A lot of things, really. Stuff I didn't want to hear. " I was babbling, but Billy let me. "He said, well, he said that I ought to take a look at my drinking." I paused.

Billy watched me carefully, saying nothing.

My throat felt like I'd swallowed a wad of cotton. I licked my lips and pushed on with it. "He didn't say I was an alcoholic, but he came damn close to it." The knot in my chest wouldn't let me take a deep breath. I sort of gasped, and the rest of it spilled out. "Billy, do you think I'm an alcoholic?"

I was afraid to breathe. Why had I asked Billy that stupid, stupid question? As soon as it was out of my mouth, he'd looked away from me. And who could blame him? Only a crazy person would ask somebody a question like that. The knot in my chest opened and spread its cold fingers. Everything inside me was as still and icy as the grave. I shivered as seconds seemed to stretch

Scotch on the Rocks

on the delicate silk of silence between us. Was he ever, I began to wonder, going to answer me? At last, he did. His voice was quiet . "Do you think you're an alcoholic?"

Disappointment fell on me. Why had Billy answered me with another question? He was supposed to be my witness for the defense. I'd banked on him to give a counter testimony that would wipe out the counselor's worrisome questions. But my witness had turned the tables. Now, I'd have to answer instead.

"Well, there are days when I don't drink at all." Yes, that was true. But there was more that I wasn't saying. Those were hangover days when my stomach twisted away from thoughts of liquor, and I suffered a tortuous thirst for water that gave me a churning nausea when I drank it. Even smoking cigarettes made me sick.

"I mean," I continued, deliberately not looking at Billy, "don't alcoholics have to drink every day? So, then, I wouldn't qualify. Would I?"

Billy gave me a penetrating look. "I can't answer that for you, Frankie. You're the one that would know."

For a ridiculously long moment, I felt like crying. Instead, I choked it back and said, "Well, thanks for listening to me." Now, it was me turning away.

"Frankie," Billy said.

"Yeah?" I half-turned, hoping that he didn't notice the tears standing in my eyes.

"If you wanna talk about this again. I, uh. Well, I always got time to listen. Right?"

"Right, Billy. Thanks a lot."

I picked up the drink he'd bought me and took it back to my seat. On the jukebox, Smokey Robinson crooned, *You really got a hold on me*, while I lifted the glass of scotch. I'd never particularly like that song. It was depressing. As I drank, I realized I really didn't like the taste of scotch. I put the glass down and stared into my drink. Random images flashed in memory: College. A movie date. Something about wine and roses. Jack Lemmon and Lee Remick drinking their way through marriage. Jack Lemon finally stopping after he goes to

Alcoholics Anonymous meetings. And Lee Remick unable to. In the end, I remembered, he leaves her.

I frowned at the two drinks in front of me. That movie wasn't like the ones I saw when I was growing up. In those, bars were romantic, exciting places where sleek, magnolia-skinned women—all done up in drop-dead black satin gowns, sporting layers of diamond bracelets—perched on stools drinking martinis out of stemmed, frosted glasses. Where were they, these sophisticated creatures who never drank too much? Did they turn into Lee Remick? Had I? Mentally, I shook myself. Why was I thinking about stupid movies? I pushed them out of my mind by lighting a cigarette and listening to Smokey again.

You really got a hold on me, he testified. Suddenly, I wanted to cry a bucket of tears. Maybe I'd take that counselor up on his offer. Just quit the stuff. I could do it. Couldn't I? I looked down at the glasses in front of me again. One was empty and ice was melting in the other. *Stop now!* Something said inside my brain. *Walk away from the stuff.* But could I? A thick, black cloud of fear swept into my heart.

Charlie stumbled up to the bar again. "Say, Frankie, you ready for another scotch, yet?"

I looked up at him and knew, deep down inside, that I was in bad trouble. As bad as can be. Because I couldn't keep myself from telling Charlie: "Sure, you know I never turn down a drink."

Trailblazer

Trailblazer: a person who blazes a trail; a pioneer, one of the first who goes before, preparing the way for others; settler of a new territory. Webster's Dictionary

"Our destination is to go where we have never been before." Peter J. Gomes, Minister

1. Lunch at the Country Club

Discreetly, I scanned the dining room of The Evansville Country Club. There were five of us seated as guests of Keller Crescent Advertising's top Account Executive, Randy Dillard. Randy was hosting lunch for our Magic Chef client, Brent, and the advertising copy team. There was Steve, our group supervisor, and Judy, the group's senior copywriter. I was the junior writer. And the only Black writer in our group—in the whole agency for that matter.

The club was full of White businessmen in dark suits wearing granite faces, and there were just as many lunching ladies of leisure who were married to men able to afford the expensive dues. When the ladies caught sight of the five of us, their bright, blue eyes lingered a few beats too long. Which caused me to wonder if I was "the first" to be invited into their private sanctuary. Maybe. Probably. Even though it was 1974 and things in America had changed a little, I had sense enough to know that time was a frozen dimension in White sanctuaries like country clubs.

A couple of the granite-faced men looked my way. Their glances set off a childhood memory of a Georgia back-road and a stone-faced White cop leaning in Daddy's car window. The flashback gave me the willies and I choked back panic by looking down at the brilliantly white linen tablecloth covering our table. A feather tickle brushed the back of my throat, signaling me that the coughing fit I'd had earlier in Randy's car might be coming back to embarrass me once more. *Please, God,* I prayed, *don't let me start again.*

Earlier, when Randy had ushered us into his car, saying we'd be lunching at The Evansville Country Club, that piece of information set off a tickle in my throat. Excited, Judy, had begun to babble while Brent and Steve laughed, delighted about the whole thing, but survival instincts had put my brain into high alert. The idea of going there had brought panic boiling up into my chest while sweat found a home in my armpits. Suddenly, hacking coughs had exploded from my throat. Although I'd tried swallowing repeatedly to wet my bone dry throat, they wouldn't stop.

Seated next to me in the back, Judy dug into her purse to give me a Kleenex. In the front seat, Brent turned around and trained his pale, sky-blue eyes on me. "Catching a cold, Frankie?"

"Something in my throat," I'd managed to stutter, grabbing the Kleenex Judy had offered, painfully conscious of looking like I might be spreading some Black folks' contagion. After several very long and very embarrassing minutes, the coughing had, finally—thank God—gone away.

Now, at the table, I sat rigid as a board, ready to dash for the ladies room if the tickle exploded into hacking coughs again.

"Brent, did you have a good flight in this morning?" Asked Randy, dark-haired and stylishly groomed.

"The best. Everything went smooth and by the numbers." Bent smiled hugely.

Inside, I grimaced; he reminded me of a very unappealing Ichabod Crane. When the waiter had seated us a few minutes ago, Brent had made a playful show of scooting his chair closer to mine. I didn't like him pushing the boundaries of his power as an important client and his privilege as a White man, but I'd swallowed my resentment. This was my dream job and I wanted to keep it.

"Hotel room to your liking?" Randy inquired, ever the solicitous salesman.

Brent nodded and, as he opened his mouth to add something, Randy leaned forward to give Brent his full attention. While they chatted, my instincts reminded me to keep checking out the territory since I was smack dab inside the lion's den; I turned the volume down on them and continued to look around. The perfectly coifed lunching ladies were still peeking our way. Not surprising. I knew I stood out like a sore thumb, even though it was possible that they might really be checking Judy out. Her outfit, a glorious mismatch of yellow and red stripes, plaids, and dots, screamed: *I'm an airhead hippie and I don't care who knows it!* Her long black hair, some of it piled this way and that, some of it hanging in her face without any particular rhyme or reason, begged for the services of a stylist who could make sense of the whole thing. Still, the ladies probably weren't just goggling at Judy. My afro, more than likely, was drawing their stares, as well. Afros said something frightening to White people... that we were stepping out of *their* shadow and into *our* sun, so to speak. Before I'd gone in to apply for a job at Keller eight months ago, I'd been tempted to straighten my hair. That I didn't could've hurt my chances because a lot of companies—like the very conservative Evansville Public Library where I had worked for a while—didn't like Black folks wearing afros. Luckily, in my job interview, Keller's Personnel Director hadn't blinked an eye.

"Steve," Randy suggested, "why don't you tell Brent about the general theme of the campaign we've put together for Magic Chef."

"Yeah, Steve, bring it on," Brent said and leaned forward.

Steve began to talk, stroking his black beard and pulling at his moustache the way he always did. I looked at him, but my attention was drawn away a bit when I noticed white-coated Black bus boys quietly crisscrossing the thickly carpeted room.

One of the white-coated men I recognized from Allen's Tavern. His name was Sonny Boy, a skinny, balding man who always radiated nervous energy. He moved quickly to our table and began to fill our water glasses. As he came closer to my seat,

I was plunged into confusion about how I should act when he got to me. On one hand, I was hugely embarrassed to be sitting here with him serving me. Not because I knew him—I didn't want him or any of the Black men to serve me in this setting—because I didn't want it to look like I was superior. I wasn't better than them, but in this setting—being here with White people in their private haven—it might look like I was expected to act superior to the Black guys—treat them like underlings. Sonny Boy was closer, now, and the thing was, I didn't want to ignore him, didn't want to act like he was invisible, the way Whites always treated us whether we were their servants or not. Should I try to catch Sonny Boy's eye and nod hello? I didn't know. I felt like I was cast in a movie without a script... cast in a role so unfamiliar and uncustomary that I couldn't fake my way through. In the end, he solved my problem for me because he deliberately never met my eye as he poured water in my stemmed glass. And as he moved away, I felt relief and sadness that we couldn't, didn't acknowledge each other.

The granite faced men and lunching women were used to seeing Black people as servants in these surroundings, not seated as guests at one of their tables. And that thought reminded me of my Jim Crow past. Its shadows reached out for me, and I was back in Knoxville in the summer of 1962.

2. Jim Crow's Shadow

I was back in the roasting, hot kitchen of a White woman who lived in the enclaves of the rich on Kingston Pike. Although she'd hired me for the summer as a nanny for her seven year old grandson, she'd made it clear that I was also to always help with lunch. Cook, a middle-aged, taffy-colored woman with gray-green eyes, was in charge of setting the white, lace-covered table for luncheon. That first day I was on the job, we'd put starched napkins, forks, knives, spoons, stemmed water glasses, and miniature bowls of water at each place setting.

"What's this little bowl for?" I'd pointed to the little bowl of water.

Cook placed each one just so beside the stemmed water glass. She didn't spill a drop. "To dip the fingertips 'n wash off stickiness after each course." She smiled, shaking her head. "Finger bowls they call em. Ain't that a pip?"

"What's wrong with using a napkin?" I asked.

"You tell me. I guess napkins ain't good nuff for these peoples."

I tucked that information away with all the other millions of things I didn't know about. Would I ever need to know about finger bowls? Maybe. I was straddling two worlds, so who knew? One of my feet was still firmly rooted in my southern Negro world, while my other foot was feeling around for a solid place in my White college world at Indiana University.

We finished setting up the fancy lunch table and, soon enough, served the food to the White folks. Now, in the kitchen, Cook was setting up our lunch table—a very small counter tucked into the corner of the kitchen. I frowned, wondering why we were eating at a counter barely big enough for one, let alone two, when there was a roomy table that Cook used to prepare food. As she carried our plates and forks, Cook saw me staring at the big table, frowning. "Miz Hoover," she'd said, "don't like me to eat at the big table. Tole me when I started here twenny years ago t'always eat ovah here. Thass where I'ma put you, too." She cut her eyes to the firmly closed swinging door that led into the dining room and lowered her voice even more. "You know how White wimmens be. You good 'nough to fix they food an' serve it, but ya cain't sit nowhere decent to eat, even in the kitchen." She chuckled. It was a dry, raspy sound. "They always gots to make sure you don't forget *yo place.* Now, honey, you come on an' eat 'fore they finish up and shove that li'l terror grandson back in yo hands."

That memory dissolved with the buzz of Country Club voices. I stared at Sonny Boy's retreating back. *Your place.* Those words chimed like a warning bell in my mind as I picked up the water glass and sipped to quiet my tickly throat.

A Black man that I didn't know wearing a gray vest and black bow tie put menus at each of our places, ending with Randy.

While we looked over the menu choices, he quietly turned to Randy."Would you like drinks while you're deciding on your orders, Mr. Dillard, sir?" His brown face was an unreadable mask.

"That'll be fine, Chester. I'll have a Tom Collins." Randy turned to Brent. "What'll you have, Brent?"

"Chester, bring me a tall scotch and water," he said in a hearty, glib tone.

As Chester turned to Judy, she said, "I think I'll have a glass of house wine."

Although I longed to order a scotch on the rocks because it would have hit the spot and soothed my nerves, I couldn't chance it. Sometimes, Mother scotch got away from me. Just took off and skedaddled down the road with me tucked helplessly under her arm. I didn't want that to happen today. Besides, I had to go back to work and I didn't need to be high when I got there.

"I'll have the same as Judy," I said.

"Make mine a beer... Budweiser," Steve told Chester.

"Give us some time to look at the menu, Chester," Randy said.

"Of course, sir." Chester nodded and went away to put in the drink orders.

"What's good on the menu, Randy?" Steve asked.

"The steak sandwich is always good here. And the Marco Polo sandwich. The Chicken Tetrazzini is the lunch specialty."

I wondered what a Marco Polo was. Sounded intriguing. So did that chicken dish. Should I order something familiar? I glanced down confidently at the spoons, knives, and forks fanned out on either side of my place setting. Whatever the dish, I knew which silverware to use for what course.

When I was growing up, on holidays, or for special meals, like the March birthday party for my uncles and Daddy, out would come Grandmama's good silverware that Mama had inherited. Mama had patiently taught me how to set a formal table, making sure I memorized where the soup spoon went, and the salad fork, and so on. I was glad my parents had prepared me for some things. But other things they didn't. Couldn't. Because how could they know what I'd be facing… what any of us would be facing when we stepped out of Knoxville's boundaries—out of Jim Crow's shadow?

We were the generation that Alabama's Governor George Wallace had dared to step into the White schools, the first ones to cross the boundaries. Trailblazers, going forward without a map. Mama and Daddy didn't know the lay of this land. Only White people knew it. Knew things about it—big and little—that helped you get on solid footing. A few of them had helped me. But there were others, one boss in particular who'd made me ashamed for not knowing things about social manners. And that had been a fiasco.

3.Hostess with the Mostest

Though it had happened a couple of years ago, I could still see myself in my boss' big office that afternoon. He'd called me in to assign me the responsibility for the Evansville Public Library employee's dinner. A short, dishwater blond man, Mr. Langley was always immaculately dressed—usually in brown suits. I had noticed he liked to change up his glasses, from gold rims to silver, to rimless, to complement his suits. Today, he wore the gold rims.

There was no offer to have a seat although two empty, tan leather chairs faced his desk waiting to make visitors comfortable. Library employees whispered that no one sat in the Director's office unless he offered you a chair. So, I stood, steno pad in hand ready to take notes as I listened.

"As the library's Public Relations Coordinator," he said, "you'll be in charge of making all the arrangements for the annual Christmas dinner for our employees. At the dinner, you'll be the hostess, working directly with the restaurant staff.

I shifted my weight to my right, keeping my face expressionless.

Using his thumb and index finger, he adjusted his gold-rimmed glasses and placed his manicured finger tips on the desk in front of him."Miss Adams always made our annual dinner a memorable occasion. I'm counting on you to do the same."

Miss Adams again. The middle-aged White woman who'd held the position before me. He intoned her name as if he'd crowned her with sainthood. He seemed to always expect me to be like Miss Adams. So irritating. Now, he'd thrown down the gauntlet one more time with this dinner thing. *What the hell,* I'd thought and sighed inwardly. Aloud, I said: "Is there a restaurant that the library likes to use?"

"Miss Adams always made arrangements with The Ranch House. Why not see if it's available for our affair? I'm sure it is. Just a matter of calling, you know." There was something of a challenge in his tone. He gave me a very frosty smile.

"Certainly." I nodded, wondering what Miss Adams had done to make herself so unforgettable. I'd never seen any evidence of what she'd done to promote library services, other than doing the weekly newspaper column called "New Books at the Library."She'd left no record of her publicity projects at all.

I'd never had Public Relations training or experience. when I'd started this job, so I'd had to figure out fast how to get things done, ways to talk and act like a professional, even when I didn't know what the hell I was doing. Within a short while, despite the fact that nobody gave me any direction or fed me any publicity ideas, I'd spotted some services the library offered that were unknown to the public, and I'd succeeded in getting months of coverage about the services by both city newspapers. I was no Miss Adams and so what? I'd done pretty well for the library although Mr. Langley never seemed genuinely pleased with me.

He slid a sheet of paper on his desk toward me. "Call the restaurant today. The phone number is here along with several dates that will do nicely."

I stepped forward to pick up the paper, glanced at the information and before I had a chance to ask questions, he shooed me out of his office. As I closed his door, smiling stiffly at his old battle-axe of a secretary, I realized he expected me to know how to handle the ins and outs of making dinner arrangements as if it was second nature. Little did he know, I'd never done anything like this before. To make matters more even more interesting, I'd gotten the feeling that I was on a short leash with this dinner and that I'd better not mess it up.

A few days after my meeting in Mr. Langley's office, the Assistant Director, Mr. Ross, called me into his. For some reason, Mr. Ross always reminded me of Tony Curtis in drag. Perched behind a desk too big for his small office, he'd asked, "How are you doing with the dinner arrangements?"

I mumbled something vague and he smiled. "Frankie, let me help you."

"Please do," I said and he gave me some key tips for which I was truly grateful.

The night of the dinner, I could see that everyone was enjoying themselves. The food was good and the restaurant, elegant. I thought I'd done everything right, thanks to Mr. Ross' help. When I was handed the bill by the maître d', I'd gone up to the dais where the big-wigs were sitting and given the bill to Mr. Langley to look over and sign at his leisure. Back at my table, I'd let out a sigh of relief, thinking that it had all gone smoothly. As I lifted a forkful of cheesecake to my lips, I glanced up at the dais and saw Mr. Langley getting up, bill in hand. At the same time, Mr. Ross was frantically signaling me that something was amiss. He needn't have bothered; I could tell I was in trouble by looking at Mr. Langley's face.

Frowning deeply, he glided over to my table like a pale ghost. He might have been short, but the power of his white skin seemed larger than life to me. His rimless glasses caught the room's light and turned them into sightless shades that blocked my seeing his eyes. Which reminded me of those southern sheriffs who wore dark sunglasses that made their faces unreadable and, in my eyes, dangerous.

When Mr. Langley was three steps from my table, I took a deep breath and put my fork down, willing my screaming nerves to calm down.

"Miss Lennon," he said, enunciating my name carefully, "Have you made other arrangements for the tip?" He put the bill under my nose.

Frankie Lennon

I flushed, sensing disaster galloping over the horizon and heading straight for me. "Tip?" I asked, feeling like a dummy.

"Yes, Miss Lennon. The tip. It isn't added into the bill I noticed."

"Uh, I, uh, didn't realize I was supposed to add it in. Uh, I thought maybe you..." My words drifted off. He wasn't going to help me through this embarrassment even though it was obvious I was on unfamiliar ground.

Truthfully, I hadn't added it in because I didn't know about tips, so I really hadn't thought about it. Leaving a tip was not a part of my life experiences. Why would it be? In Knoxville, Jim Crow wouldn't allow Black folks to eat out, and in Bloomington, on my college allowance, I didn't have the money for real restaurants. Neither did my dates. The pizza parlor had been the top of the line for us and nobody had ever mentioned leaving a tip.

Mr. Langley was just about breathing fire. "Miss Lennon, you are the person in charge of logistics and social amenities for this dinner. Making sure the bill is in order, including the tip, is a part of that responsibility."

I took the bill out of his hand. "Sorry, Mr. Langley." Not only did I not know how much of a tip to include, the plain awful thing was that I was going to have to bite the bullet and ask Mr. Langley about it. Playing for time, I dug into my purse for a pen. "How much would you say I should add on?"

As Mr. Langley stood there, glaring down at me, a memory flashed by. Mama had taken me out for a tuna sandwich at Walgreen's lunch counter when we visited New York City one summer. It was my first time ever eating out at the same place as White people. I'd been in sixth grade, thrilled at New York and at the freedom of being able to eat out at Walgreen's. We couldn't eat at any of the lunch counters back home. I'd felt all grown up sitting at the counter with Mama.

Mr. Langley's frown deepened. "I should think you would know how much of a tip is appropriate."

I could see me and Mama clearly in my mind. Mama had looked at the bill and was taking a dollar out of her purse. She laid it down next to the bill. Then, she'd leaned over me and said: *We have to leave a tip.* And she'd pushed a dime over to sit beside the dollar.

Why hadn't I asked her how she figured the amount? I gritted my teeth. Was I going to have to tell Mr. Langley that I didn't know how to figure out tips? *Lord have mercy!*

He kept standing there, waiting. I kept sitting there, humiliated, wanting to vanish into thin air.

Finally, he said: "Well. All right. I'll add it in myself." He picked up the bill and turned on his heel. Before he walked away, he threw a parting shot over his shoulder."Miss Adams always took care of things like this without a problem."

I wanted to throw my glass of water at his head while snarling a string of choice words at his pale face. I didn't though. Instead, I thought about Miss Adams, a middle-aged, white woman, my picture-perfect predecessor, the hostess with the mostest. In Mr. Langley's eyes, I'd never, ever measure up to her in this job.

The cold part was, at that moment, I'd felt ashamed that I couldn't.

4. Trying to Pass for Perfect

Mr. Langley had enjoyed nailing me to the cross for not knowing. For not being the perfect imitation of Miss Adams. Eventually, the library board had cut budget items which included cutting my position out. Though I didn't think so at the time, it had been a blessing in disguise. I was out of his shadow now. And thank God for that.

I shook off lingering shreds of shame as Judy asked the waiter about an item on the menu. He was setting drinks in front of each of us. Brent took a long, deep swallow of his. Randy and Steve ignored theirs. Judy sipped politely. I looked at my wine, wishing for scotch, and lifted the wine glass.

"You've got two really good writers working for you," Steve told Brent. "Judy came up with some great ideas for your sales team meetings. Frankie's working on copy for your new microwave product."

Brent looked at me and then at Judy. "What's the pitch for the microwave?"

Judy nodded at me to jump in. I put down my wine glass and said: "Well, we've got to convince women to use your new product. Since they don't know what it is or how it works, we'll do a little cookbook for them called "Tempt Her with an Apple."I pointed at Judy and she took it from there.

It felt good that Steve had given me credit. A few weeks ago, he'd really boosted my confidence. After looking over the Magic Chef copy I'd written, he'd said, *You've got good instincts, Frankie. Don't be afraid to use them. Trust them.*

I was still learning to. When I'd been hired, Gerry, another copy supervisor, had been put in charge of training me; my first assignment from him was to write a sales letter. In my office, I'd anguished over it, unsure of every word I typed, wanting to go and ask questions but scared to do that because I thought it would make me look dumb. When I'd finished, copy in hand, I'd gone to his office, trembling. At his door, I'd stood silently, waiting. Gerry, a gangling, loose-limbed old man, was typing rapidly with two fingers on an old typewriter. Except for a stack of white paper, a dictionary, and thesaurus, his big, oak desk was clean as a whistle. After he beckoned me in, I sat, as he read my copy, feeling way, way out of my league. My churning stomach had me wondering if I had made a mistake in applying for this job. What if he told me I should give up all notions of writing because couldn't write worth a damn? I bit my fingernails while The Monkeys in my head made up some other miserable thoughts that left me boiling in oil and wishing for a quick death.

Finally, Gerry held up the letter. "You're doing a lot of throat-clearing here."

"Throat-clearing?" I frowned, clutching my pen and yellow legal pad for taking notes.

"What I mean is you do a lot of getting ready to say what you want to say, instead of simply saying it. People have a habit of clearing their throats when they're unsure of what they're going to say."

I nodded.

"Look at this." He pointed to the first three sentences in the first paragraph. "These three sentences you can throw out. You're just circling the barn instead of going straight in." He thumped the paper. "It's the sentence after the first three that gets down to business."

I could see that he was right. I sighed, frustrated and disgusted with myself. Wasn't I supposed to known how to write advertising copy since I'd graduated from Indiana University with a Master's in Creative Writing? I'd thought I was. For a moment, I dropped my gaze, feeling some parts embarrassed and some parts dumb creeping up at the back of my eyes. *Stupid*, I called myself silently.

Which took me back to third grade where I sat facing Miss Netherland, feeling dumb, as I struggled in vain to learn what she was trying to teach me: the logic of counting change. *Why can't you understand this like everybody else?* She'd asked me in front of the class. After going over the same ground with me for the fourth time, she'd finally said, in disgust: *I'm disappointed in you, Frankie. From now on, you'll have to stay right here and practice during recess until you get this right*. Resenting the punishment, I'd been racked with shame as she'd sent me back to my desk. My classmates had stared at me wide-eyed. After some weeks, I gave up on truly understanding the lesson. To get out of the punishment, I imitated what she said in counting change without a clue as to what I was doing. It wasn't until a few years later when I was at the grocery buying something for Mama that it all somehow magically clicked into place for me. Still, why hadn't I caught on sooner? When it came to math, I was the world's biggest dummy.

Gerry snapped me back into the present by saying:"Listen, you aren't supposed to automatically know this stuff, Frankie. Make it your business to learn, instead of crucifying yourself for not knowing." He paused and gave me a penetrating look. "I know how it feels being part of the first wave. I've been there, you know, since I'm Jewish." He took a breath and went on: "Take some advice from me. Relax. Be willing to learn from your experiences. And stop trying to pass for perfect." He waved his hand and shook his head. "Perfect ain't what it's cracked up to be."

Back at my desk, I'd thought about what he'd said. He'd read me to a tee, and I'd been embarrassed that he had, but kind of relieved at the same time. Some lessons, I'd realized, were easier to learn than others.

5. A Good Thing

Brent was slouched back in his chair, enjoying the attention he was getting from everybody. Judy was finishing the run down. "And with the cookbook, your sales team will be able to demonstrate right in the store how the microwave works, so the consumer can see for herself that it's easy to use." Judy smiled.

"Easy and *fast*," I added. "The salesman will show her how easy it is to cook a whole apple in the blink of an eye, and if that's not a tempting temptation for a busy woman, I don't know what is."

"Sounds good." Brent was smiling hugely again.

"Brilliant," Randy nodded to Steve, Judy and me.

Pleased at Brent's response, all of us were grinning to beat the band. I looked around the country club, relaxed for the first time. Everything was the same, but it wasn't. The granite-face men and the leisure-time women were still in their places. It was the same, but...what?

I probed around inside of me. And found something different in there. Found that I was feeling, for some reason, steadier on this new ground.... surer of foot. And that change was a good thing.

"Who's ready to order?"Randy asked.

Predators

"Homosexuality is not a deviation; it is a variation. And people need to know that."
Peter J. Gomes, Minister

    Allen's black and white television sat on a beer cooler in a corner behind the bar, and you couldn't really see it unless you were sitting almost on top of it. From where I usually sat at the bar, I could see it fine if it was on. Today it was, and I was watching Les build my drink when the *CBS Evening News* came on. The anchor, Walter Cronkite, always distinguished, always credible, opened with the story of the "Save Our Children" campaign. It had started a short while ago, Cronkite said, pausing to glance down at the sheaf of papers in his hand, with Anita Bryant and her organization pushing for Miami to repeal the city ordinance prohibiting discrimination against homosexuals.

    As soon as the word homosexual rolled out of Cronkite's mouth in basso tones, everybody seemed to come to instant attention. I shifted my eyes away from Les to the television broadcast, feeling everything inside me go stock still, just like a rabbit that's caught the scent of danger in high grass.

    Out of the corner of my eye, I could see Katie, the waitress, headed for the jukebox, but Cecil, sitting at a table behind me, stopped her.

    "Wait up, " he said. "I wanna hear the news." Katie shrugged and backed off.

    That was unusual. Watching the news got very low priority even when there were only a handful of us at Allen's, so my nerve endings went on alert. Plus, I'd heard about Bryant's campaign. Which in itself was enough to get anxiety skipping through my veins. The campaign was getting a lot of national play and in Evansville, people were paying attention. At the very least, conversations gave it a passing nod if not full blown commentary. Not long ago, a man that I'd thought was open-minded and liberal had stunned me.

"Anita Bryant is right," he'd raged after I'd asked him what he thought about her campaign. "That scum should be hunted down and put in a concentration camp somewhere away from normal people." I particularly remembered his eyes while he'd said it. They'd gone hard and black and lightless. It was his eyes that had frightened me the most. He'd shown me his Mr. Hyde face, a part of him that I didn't know. And that part had drawn a line of separation in the sand with me standing one side and him on the other although he didn't know it. Didn't know about Stacey, about my woman dreams, about the real me I kept chained in secret corners. Nobody here did.

Glancing around, I realized that only a couple of familiar faces, the regulars that made Allen's so comfortable for me, were here today. Clyde, on the barstool in the corner and John, next to him. The rest—Cecil, Sonny, Nance, Gloria, and Betty—came in less often. As always Les was behind the bar and Katie was waiting tables, but there were a few others that I didn't know. For some reason, without the regulars that I knew so well, Allen's felt less cozy, less like home. Was there a chill in the air? I pulled my cardigan sweater closer around my chest.

On camera, Cronkite reminded us that aside from being a Miss America runner-up, Anita Bryant was best known as spokeswoman for Florida orange juice commercials. Bryant had gotten famous for telling the television audience, "A day without Florida orange juice is a day without sunshine."

Now, I thought to myself, she'd switched to selling something else. Something dark. I could hear aggravated murmurs from Cecil and the other guys sitting at his table. I drew in a ragged breath. Keeping up my camouflage was harder with Anita Bryant stirring things up. Where was my drink? I glanced at Les; he was moving in slow motion.

Cronkite went to a film clip of Bryant at a Midwestern news conference. A newsman asked about her motives for the campaign. Surrounded by microphones, the dark-haired, former beauty queen beamed at the camera and opened her mouth to oblige.

"Since homosexuals cannot reproduce," she said, striking a tone of both sincerity and loathing, "they must recruit children to freshen their ranks. We must not allow them to continue."

I clinched my fist, furious, thinking: *How can she get away with saying a pure lie like that?*

Somebody, a woman's voice, growled: "One of them mess wit my baby and he gonna get his ass kicked!"

I blew out a frustrated breath. What Bryant was saying boiled down to a load of crap. You didn't choose or get recruited like you were joining the army or some kind of club. You were born the way you were born.

I thought about Stacey and rubbed the palm of my hand across my lips. Nobody had recruited me into being attracted to women. Nobody had forced me to love her. That admission woke up The Corners, the place, at the back of my mind, where I'd vaulted my secrets. Like autumn leaves, they began to crackle and rustle. Which served to unnerve me even more than Anita Bryant. Mostly, I could keep them quiet and still as a tomb.

On screen, you could see the reporters scribbling furiously on their pads. Bryant was gabbing away, talking like she'd made some kind of a scientific study and was releasing the results.

It pissed me off that people put the rap on us for what pedophiles did. If you paid attention to your stats, or to what the neighborhood grapevine whispered about the husband down the street, you'd know that damn near all pedophiles were heterosexuals. To cover that up, folks muddied the water so that people would confuse pedophiles with homosexuals. But they weren't the same at all.

I paid attention to the screen again. Why wasn't somebody questioning Anita Bryant's claims? The reporters were just standing there, eating it up like starving animals. That was the scary part. I lit a cigarette and I dragged my hand across my lips again. When Les put my drink down in front of me, I almost knocked it over grabbing for it.

One reporter finally asked Bryant a question. He wanted to know how she chose the name for her campaign. She put one white hand to her neck and looked earnestly into the camera's eye.

"We chose the name because we want to save our children by stopping these homosexuals. They're predators!"

"Lock em all up!" Shouted an angry, male voice behind me.

I jumped involuntarily, taken aback by the fury in it.

Bryant continued in a tone filled with piety: "What they're doing is immoral and goes against God's wishes!"

I flushed with anger. *What a self-righteous ass! How can she claim to know what God wanted?*

"Damn sissies!" Said another voice filled with disgust.

Cronkite switched to a sidebar news report that caught my attention. Last week, in a city where Anita Bryant had drawn a huge, unruly crowd, a teenaged boy believed to be a homosexual had been hospitalized after receiving a severe beating at his high school.

My bristling anger melted down into alarm, then, gradually, into dismay.

Yesterday, Cronkite continued, shortly after a local community rally in a different city where Bryant had been the speaker, two women thought to be Lesbians had been assaulted near a downtown bar by a group of men. But, Cronkite hastened to add, there was no direct evidence linking these acts of violence to Bryant's campaign against homosexuals.

By the time the sidebar ended, I felt like prey, trembling and ready to fly. Around the room, mutterings thickened the air. There was a mean edge in them.

"Serves they asses right!" Somebody near me said.

Cringing, I looked around to identify the voice. It was Nance. He'd come up behind me, and was leaning on the bar. I was suddenly, sharply aware that other people had come up to see the television better, and were standing close to me. Their nearness pressed down on my chest.

Standing next to me, Cecil growled, "Goddamn punks!" He decided to stir the pot. "Somebody oughta do us all a favor and wipe em all out!"

Predators

His tone made my hair stand on end. I could hear the mutterings in the room boiling up to higher temperatures. I'd never felt anything like this in Allen's before. Anita Bryant had raked up a kind of meanness, a kind of glad rush to violence that lay hidden underneath these people, like my friend who'd changed from Dr. Jekyll to Mr. Hyde.

Suddenly, a chorus of voices rang out.

"Fags! I ain't got no use for'm!"

"A punk ain't worth shit!"

"Freaks!"

The venom in their voices shredded something inside me. The bar was humming with murmurs and curses. Near panic had me drain my glass and I held it up for Les to see I wanted another.

Cecil's pecan-colored face had gone shades darker with anger. "If I ever catch one around me again," he said in a deadly tone, "I'll cut his balls off!"

My armpits felt sweaty. With shaky fingers, I stubbed out my cigarette, remembering what I'd heard about Cecil. Rumor said that he'd beat the shit out of this harmless, little neighborhood guy that people said *looked like* he could be "that way." Supposedly, the little guy had said something that Cecil took as a come-on. Carrying a couple of hundred pounds and six feet of muscle, Cecil had the body to put a hurtin on you, and he'd fucked up the little guy really bad. Then, he'd bragged about it in Allen's for a week. He was a stony-hearted bastard if there ever was one.

Sonny, always an ass-hole, decided to jump in. He pitched his voice to get the attention of the crowd. "Man, what about those bull daggers? If you ask me, all those women need is a real man that knows how to lay the pipe right!" He laughed loud and hard. So did the other phallic egos standing around.

Fury sliced into my brain. I slammed my glass down on the bar and opened my mouth to speak, but a voice in my head whispered: *You'd better keep your mouth shut. Did you hear how they sounded? What do you think they'd do if they knew you were one of the freaks?*

That shut me down. I lit another cigarette and listened to the voice.

Frankie Lennon

If you tell them who you are, you won't belong in here anymore. You won't belong anywhere in Evansville. Then what'll you do?

While I thought about that, at the back of my eyes, I could see myself standing in the yard of the loneliest place on earth. Just for a moment, I was a kid, back again at the Alcoa House, waiting and desperately hoping for my parents to come and get me, waiting and listening to the sound of evening crickets—a sound to hollow out a place in your heart and fill it with stinging tears.

The voice spoke again: *You won't belong. Then what'll you do?*

I tasted bile on my tongue, but I swallowed it. Swallowed and pressed my lips together. Shivers touched my shoulders like icy fingertips. I couldn't imagine. Didn't dare imagine the loneliness of not belonging. Cold dread burrowed into me and found a home. For warmth, I hunched over my empty glass. Looking down into it, I saw myself there, and saw, rising up before me, a coiling, twisting mass of shadows, swaying as if it would strike.

Around the room, edges of evening darkness had stolen quietly through Allen's windows while angry, clamoring voices filled the air with gathering clouds. Near my hand, a weak, ragged patch of November light lay dying on the bar. It was autumn's end.

Closing Acts

"You sat at the crossroads for the appointed time. That means you need to learn something. What is it?" from "She'd Make a Dead Man Crawl," Gerald Houarner

1. A Fly in Molasses

Noon traffic moved slowly toward downtown Evansville. In front of me was a junkyard dog of a station wagon—faded brown, sporting so many rusted-out dents that a body shop would be hard pressed to straighten them all out. Its impatient driver kept revving the motor, frustrated that he could only get so far in the line of cars waiting their turn at the intersection.

I was on my way to a lunch meeting with Ray, the editor of *The Evansville Courier,* at his newspaper office. A couple of years ago, someone had recommended to him that I write a feature column from the Black perspective. When Ray had offered, I'd jumped at the chance. Once I began to do the column, I'd discovered, for the first time, what it meant to me—writing and seeing what I'd written in print. Capturing the words to express things swirling around inside of me was magical. Like spinning straw into gold. It didn't matter that it didn't pay. At least, not in money. The payoff was a reason for me to keep on breathing. Especially in the last ten months. The thought of those months shot me back, for a moment, to the icy-sharp edges of depression. I didn't want to fall back into that. Better to concentrate on something else.

Like: Why had Ray asked me for lunch? Since I mailed my articles every six weeks or so, it wasn't our habit to meet at all. In the back of my head, my Monkeys were at play—chattering in whispers, churning up anxious feelings inside me. That wasn't the only thing they were churning up anxiety about. My paying job as a life insurance salesperson at The Prudential was on their agenda, too.

My boss had decided, a few months ago, that I should be certified to sell auto insurance, and, this morning, I had taken the test for it. Or rather it had taken me. Even though I'd studied for it, the information hadn't come together for me. Right from the start of the test, it had been a fight to keep my mind from floating away every few minutes. They'd called time when I was six questions from the end, and I'd used the *eeny-meeny-miney-mo* strategy, randomly marking answers, just to finish up. The Monkeys were laying bets now about my not passing the thing. Did I care? Yes. No. Maybe. I wasn't sure. If I hadn't passed, I knew that my boss wasn't going to be happy.

The junkyard station wagon in front of me gained about a foot before the light turned red again. The driver blew his horn to tell everybody he was unhappy about the whole thing. A chorus of horn-blowing joined him. I glanced at my watch, muttering. I was stuck like a fly in molasses.

I didn't want to keep thinking about the test thing, but The Monkeys kept niggling with it. Would my boss be unhappy enough with my test score to show me the door? He might. In the last ten months, you could rightly say I hadn't been pulling my weight. My sales volume, never something to brag about, had been dying a slow death. Harold, the agency manager, who'd hired me, had finally called me in to talk about resurrecting my sales.

2.   Death and Resurrection

Harold was a silver-haired, White man who impressed me as a throw-back to Ozzie Nelson's 1950's suburban America. He took pride in two things as far as I could tell: Being the lead tenor of his church choir, and in his agency's sales record as one of the top five in the region. When I'd gone in to see what he wanted, it was near the tail end of the afternoon. I sat as he gestured at the hard, armless chair facing his desk.

Closing Acts

"You know, Frankie, we've understood how difficult these past months have been for you. We understand it takes time to grieve."

My mind had cut out then. *Click* went the lens behind my eyes. It pulled up a picture that I didn't want to see: Jay lying in the casket in the funeral home, his hands holding the two red roses I'd brought. The quiet of the darkened viewing room had been spooky. As I'd walked toward the casket, it had felt like I was watching myself in a movie scene. Watching death play out. It was so unreal that I could barely grasp it. Except that there was Jay, in death as handsome as ever. I examined his face. His thick eyelashes lay on his brown cheeks perfectly, as if he was wearing mascara. And he had a mole that looked like a beauty mark on his cheek. People had said he was maybe a bit too good looking, that his features were almost feminine although his hairy chest and strong arms had screamed masculinity.

As I'd gazed at him, the voices of The Monkeys rose up in a deafening volume. What was I going to do without Jay? They wailed. How would I block out those things I didn't want to face without him? They sang viciously. I knew I was on the edge so I'd bent over his body in the casket and talked to him. Talked because I was about to fold up. Collapse like a wind-up toy. I'd scolded him: "When I saw you last Friday, I told you about my premonition, the nightmare, and I asked you to come home with me for the weekend. But you said no. So I told you to be careful. *Careful.* Why weren't you careful?" Foolish as I felt doing it, I'd kept talking to him. Talking to him had been my survival instinct taking over. "Why did you try to jump your sister's crazy-ass boyfriend like that?"

William, the boyfriend, had shot him, later claiming he'd been afraid Jay was going to pull a gun. I'd stared down at Jay, trying to see where the killing bullet had torn at his neck, splashing blood and severing the carotid artery. But his shirt collar covered the wound and I could find no telltale mark that declared that he was never going to open his eyes again.

Harold's voice, rattling on and on, in a show of what he thought was righteous compassion, dragged me back into the present. I'd shut down the memory of Jay in the casket.

Harold had said: "After I lost my father, I told myself 'When life gets tough, the tough get going.'"

His skills in bereavement counseling, I'd noted, left much to be desired. I'd tried to keep my attention on what he was saying, but my mind took me away again. Back to last spring, that unbelievable time when—not even two months after Jay—Daddy, my last anchor, had collapsed and died.

Click. There was Daddy in his casket at Jarnigan's Funeral Home in Knoxville. And there we were standing over him: me, Sylvia, my stepmother, and Aunt Avice, Daddy's sister-in-law.

Daddy's face had been shockingly ugly to me—so unlike the sweet Hershey Bar face I'd loved. In life, his full lips had often curved into a teasing smile while his eyes twinkled under his thick, dark eyebrows. In death, his features had been contorted by the funeral home people who'd molded, stretched, and flattened Daddy's face so that it looked like a grotesque circus clown. I still wished I hadn't gone in to look at him. As it was, I had only been able to look at him for a few seconds before I began to tremble so violently that Aunt Avice had to catch me up in her arms to keep me from falling.

Harold was still yammering. Now, I couldn't breathe.

It got like that ever so often now. Some days, during these last ten months, shrouds of fear and misery lay on my lungs in black, smothering layers. If only I could erase all of it—wave a wand, make Daddy and Jay come back. But I didn't have the power to change reality. So it hung there above my horizon. And there was no running from it.

Harold fixed me with a deeply serious stare and said: "This insurance agency has sales goals that it has to reach, Frankie. And those goals take priority even in the face of tragedy," he paused.

I could tell he thought himself generous for acknowledging the two deaths that had slammed me back so far that even my friends weren't sure I could come back in one piece.

"I need you to do your part. Put your shoulder to it. Try. Even when it's hard." He smiled sympathetically, having given me some fatherly advice.

At the end of the meeting, I'd given him the assurance he wanted: Make a course correction and resurrect my sales. Get off my ass and go sell lots and lots of life insurance.

Today was a little more than six months later and my sales were still dead as a doornail. And so my performance on the test this morning was probably crucial. I sighed. If I lost this job....

At last, the red light changed again. The cars ahead of me took off and, switching my foot from the brake to the gas pedal, I followed suit, heading for *The Evansville Courier*.

3. The Offer

Ray met me at the elevator, smiling. He was a big White man—six feet. Middle age flab had worked its way around his chest and stomach. He rocked back on his heels and stuck out his hand. We exchanged greetings and he escorted me to his glassed-in office.

"I've ordered in lunch for us while we talk. I hope that's all right?"

I smiled. "Of course."

We walked back, past typewriters, copiers, reporters in ties and shirt sleeves, where lunch waited. Exchanging pleasantries, we sat down, uncovered the plates, and dived into the delivered-in rib eye steak and tossed salad.

This was not a deli or hot dog menu, and given that we'd never ever had lunch before, some warning bells went off in my brain. Whatever this lunch was about, I figured it had to be about the last three feature pieces I'd written for the Op-Ed page— "Baptism," "A Dream Called Eden," and "Black Phoenix." They were not at all like what I had been writing for the paper before. My Monkeys had gone ape-shit when I'd written those pieces. They had a point. "Eden" stepped on White toes and took an unapologetic tone. "Phoenix" could be read as a scary warning to White America. "Baptism" was a coming-of-age piece focusing on how I'd changed during Black America's struggle for equality in the Sixties. When I'd gone into the post office to mail the essays in a big yellow envelope, one of The Monkeys had screamed, *Are you completely crazy?* so loudly in my ear that I dropped the envelope before I could get it into the mail slot. My hands were trembling with pride and excitement when I pushed it in. "Baptism" had been published two weeks after. But not the other two yet.

Between bites of food, I looked at Ray. "This is very good. Thanks for asking me."

Ray nodded. Then he threw me a zinger. "Frankie, what would you say to an offer to come here to work?"

I stopped chewing and looked directly at him. Silence. I was thrown completely off. I knew that what I'd written was different. Disturbing, even. So I expected something. But not this. In the silence, I looked out at the busy newsroom.

A newspaper job. It's what I'd dreamed of doing when I'd entered college and declared a major in Journalism. After my first couple of months in college, I'd even worked up the nerve to go into the campus newspaper office to volunteer. Their newsroom had been busy that day, too. Like what I was seeing now: People on the phone, or typing, or editing, or talking to the person at the next desk. I looked at Ray, remembering that nobody in the busy college newsroom had looked my way that day. I'd been told by a red-headed boy with a pimply face to have a seat to wait for senior staff person to come talk to me. Nobody ever did. I'd sat at the newsroom entrance for more than an hour before I finally took off and never went back. I gotten the message: You're not wanted here. Shortly after, I'd changed my major to English. But that romantic idea of being a reporter had never really left my heart.

Lately, I had gotten a taste of how it felt to be writing what I wanted to write, not what somebody else told me to write. That taste had been a deep thrill—despite The Monkeys trying to scare me, especially when I'd pushed through their bullying to finish the pieces I'd mailed in. The feeling at that moment was so new that I couldn't find a way to put it into words for myself. All I knew was the feeling was better than getting high on Mother scotch. Did I want to give that up? Hell, no.

"What about my other two pieces? Are you going to run them?"

Ray put his fork down and fixed me with a serious stare. I felt my throat close up on the piece of steak in my mouth.

"We can't run them, Frankie." He paused, then shook his head. "They're too... too militant."

Well, there it was. *The* worst word White people could use to characterize us Black folk these days.

My conspiratorial inner voice, Vee, jeered in her best Butterfly McQueen-*Gone With the Wind* voice: *Lordy, Miss Scarlet, you got to save us from those riled-up, militant darkies out there.*

Shit. What a bitch this was. I was disappointed. More than that really. Much more. And I didn't know what to say.

Ray picked up a sheaf of typed papers atop a yellow envelope. My articles. I could see my handwriting on the envelope. "This is radical stuff for Evansville readers to swallow. 'Baptism,' they could read and feel pretty much okay about. It shows that you wrote it from where your writer soul lives. That makes it work for them."

Them, of course, was White folks, the majority in the city. Us Black folks were about nine percent of the population, probably less in newspaper readership.

"The other two you wrote..." Ray let out a breath as his cheeks turned rosy pink. "You were pretty rough and what you said, true or not, doesn't go down smoothly." He peered at me. "You haven't answered my offer yet."

"Why do you want me to come here to work? I mean, in light of what I wrote."

"You're a good writer. I can use you on my team."

"What exactly would I be doing... reporting?"

He dropped his glance a little too fast. And his face changed. Just a bit. "We'll decide on your responsibilities once you get here." He looked up at me again. "And did I mention the salary?

The money would be far better than what you're likely to be making at The Prudential."

"You said 'we.' Don't you run the paper?"

"I answer to an executive board. I have a boss, too." He smiled broadly. A little too broadly I thought.

"Would I still be able to do the features?" I thought I knew the answer but I wanted to be sure.

His eyes went stone serious as he shook his head. "You'd be too busy for that."

I wanted to frown but I kept my face in neutral. "I need some time to think."

"Sure. Give me a call." He stuffed the typed papers back into my yellow envelope and handed it to me, smiling again. "Make your call soon. For now, let's finish our lunch. I've got deadlines."

At the elevator, I said my goodbyes to Ray, promising to call him in a few days. The wait for the elevator gave me a chance to think, to try to get back my bearings. *Militant*, Ray had called my writing. When he'd said that, I saw the last door to my salvation in Evansville slam shut in my face. The Monkeys shrieked and shouted in my head: *Well, you sure blew it! We told you not to! We told you!*

And they had. Damn near drove me crazy telling me not to write those pieces, but deep down I'd known that it was really, really important for me to go ahead. The more I wrote, the more I'd felt sure that I was *supposed* to do it.

Ray's offer stood before me, waiting. What was I going to do?

The elevator doors swooshed open. A couple of secretary-types scooted in ahead of me. In age, they were about decade behind me, in their twenties, I judged. They gossiped and giggled together—fresh-faced blondes, with roses blooming in their cheeks. They reminded me of some of the long-legged foxes at Keller Crescent who had worked as administrative assistants to the account executives. I used to have lunch with them from time to time. What had been striking to me was their uncomplicated, all's-right-with-the-world perspective. It seemed to me that women like that, who understood and accepted where men had placed them in the world, had it easy as pie. Accepting your role in the chorus line meant you always had a place. Because you knew your steps and performed them without complaint. For a second or two, I envied them. Wished I was like that. In my soul, though, I knew I never could be.

The lights above the elevator doors lit up floor numbers as we descended. There was tightness in my chest about Ray's offer and I curled my hands into hard fists to try to relieve the tension weighing me down. If I took the offer, I'd have a job making a helluva lot more money than selling insurance on commission, and that was really tempting. So what was I waiting for? My parents, if they were alive, would have frowned at my hesitation because a good job meant I'd have enough money to live comfortably, not paycheck to paycheck like I was now.

Paycheck to paycheck. A rippling resentment at Keller Crescent spread in my chest for that. If I was still there, I wouldn't be living paycheck to paycheck or selling insurance. It had been six years ago that Keller Crescent had laid me off. Things had spiraled down from there. Maybe I should have left town then. But Jay was still alive. And Daddy. So I didn't want to. Still, losing the only job I'd ever really loved here, courtesy of Nixon's recession, had been a crippling blow. Confidence in my love for writing, in my ability to make my living from it had been steadily building; thanks to Keller. Then, the universe played a cosmic joke—jerked the rug out from under me; and *Poof!* It had all disappeared.

Poof, poof, poof! Chanted my Monkeys.

They loved for me to remember bad times, so they could tell an even grimmer story. After Keller, money had been tight.

Tight as Dick's hatband, they sang happily.

Between drawing unemployment, living on frozen, chicken pot pies, and working weekends waiting tables at Allen's, I'd managed to stretch money while I looked for work. Which had been embarrassing and frustrating because people had looked at me like *I'd* done something to lose the damn job. Soon I'd found out that companies didn't like the idea of hiring a Black woman at entry level with that kind of experience. Those days had been tough and scary. Worse than when I'd run back here from New York in 1970.

Tough and scary, tough and scary, tough and scary, repeated my Monkeys.

I thought about the two jobs I'd had before Prudential: at Community Action Program's Housing Program, a job only funded for a year, and at Colonial National Bank in the Bookkeeping department, where I dealt with people forever mystified about why their personal checking accounts were always overdrawn. The bank job barely paid enough to make rent and groceries. So I took to raking through the classifieds daily. Which was how I got to Prudential.

Once upon a time, I would've gladly grabbed Ray's offer. It was like the Calvary come to rescue my raggedy wagon train. If I got fired at Prudential—but even if I didn't—I should've been happy about it. But I wasn't.

The elevator doors slid open at the first floor. A crush of people coming back from lunch flowed in as I stepped out.

4. Take Me to the River

Without an inkling I was going to do it, I turned the steering wheel toward The Ohio River levee. On River Street, lined with nineteen century, gingerbread houses, there was a little parking area overlooking the broad breast of the river. I turned into it and parked, feeling the gray, February sky pressing down.

I lit a cigarette and acknowledged silently that I was smoking more and enjoying it less, yet the act of smoking brought some kind of comfort. Which I needed because, so far, the day had rolled out like a gremlin's revenge. Once out of the car, I headed for one of the empty benches and sat, staring at the far shore across the river.

Most of the time now, except when I was writing, I felt like I was slipping and sliding, always trying to find solid ground. I peered up at thick, steel-gray clouds, hiding the blue sky that I hoped was up there somewhere. These days, the only time I felt alive was when I was writing. Truth be told, the only time that I *wanted to be alive* was when I was writing.

I blew out smoke and watched flocks of birds gliding, banking, and swooping against the canvass of the sky. For some reason, watching them and listening to their screeching brought back dark memories of my premonition nightmare, whispering at evil things. Just then, a car pulled up onto the paved area and stopped beside mine. I was surprised to see the driver, Nellie, who was a friend. She waved and got out.

Nellie was about seven years younger than me. Heavy-set with a pretty face, she was genuinely sweet- natured. I counted her as one of my handful of true friends in Evansville.

"Saw you sitting here, Frankie, and stopped to say hi. Not working today?"

I threw my cigarette butt on the ground and mashed it out. "I'm duckin out on work for the moment. Had a lunch date with the editor from *The Courier*."

"Yeah? What was that about?" She sat beside me on the bench.

Her presence soothed the ball of jumbled up feelings sitting in my stomach. "They don't want to publish my writings anymore. The pieces I just turned in are too *militant*, Ray said."

Nellie shook her head. "Umm, too bad. I liked what you've been writing. You musta hit a nerve or two."

"Three or four, I guess."

"Maybe somebody else could publish what you write."

"Who?" That question hung like a storm cloud in the air. We both knew there was nobody.

She shrugged and gave me a measured look before she said: "Is that why you look so down and out?"

I nodded. "He did offer me a job though."

"You don't look like you're glad about it."

"No, I'm not."

"Why do you want to stay at Prudential?"

I shook my head. "You know I didn't like the idea of going into sales from jump street, but I promised myself that I'd do the best I could. Help Black people buy the best life insurance for reasonable prices. I tried to look at it kind of like a mission." I sighed. "It's not cutting it for me anymore though." *If it ever really had*, I admitted to myself.

"That was a good mission," she said "and you did your best. I can vouch for that."

One of the things I liked about Nellie was her attitude. You could count on her to give you an encouraging word.

She looked me full in the face. "Mind telling me why you're not excited about the job offer Wouldn't you be a reporter?"

"See, that's something I don't know. He was vague about what I'd be doing, but he said I wouldn't have time to write my articles anymore."

"You didn't take the offer?"

"No. I told him I had to think about it."

We were silent for some long seconds. Mentally, I tried to confront what had happened today—flunking the insurance test and my column being cancelled, but my emotions wouldn't let me. I felt uneasy. As if I had come to the edge of something where there was no place ahead to put my foot.

Finally, Nellie fixed me with a penetrating look. "Girl, when are you going to get out of here?"

"Huh? What do you mean?"

"Leave. Leave Evansville. Have you thought about it at all?"

Off and on, thoughts of leaving had skittered across my mind since Jay and Daddy had died. "Not seriously."

"Maybe you should. What's Evansville doing for you?"

My mind didn't want to delve into that. Didn't want to face that snaky tangle. Sounds of cawing birds overhead nudged me to look up. In perfect formation, the black birds—were they ravens or crows?—flapped their wings in time with each other. Some birds broke the formation and looped around the others, as if to check that the whole group was moving as one. They then rejoined the others, flying in unison again. Where were they going? They seemed so sure of their direction.

I dropped my eyes, frowning about what Nellie had asked me. To leave town, I'd have to know where I was going, what direction to take. I looked up at the birds again. How did they figure out where they were going? Where would I go if I left Evansville?

Nellie said: "Gotta be going. You alright here?"

"Yeah. I am. Thanks." I stood up. "I need to get outta here myself... get back to work."

We walked to our cars together. She took off as I stepped into my car, still thinking about the birds. I took a deep breath and turned the key in the ignition.

5. The Third Act

I was standing, smoking, in the wooded area behind the red brick, Prudential office where I worked. There was a nice thatch of woods here. On a little rise a few feet from me, a cluster of bare trees huddled together, branch-arms held up and out like graceful ballerinas. It pleased me to meet with them—the tree goddesses I called them—while I tried to clear my mind and work up some enthusiasm for the way I was living my life.

Of course, Harold was pissed off at me for flunking the test and though he hadn't said so, it was clear he expected me to take it again. The thunderbolts dancing in his eyes said that if I wanted my job, I'd better.

And do you? asked Vee.

Grimacing, I kicked up some dirt from the ground with the toe of my black boot. I just didn't have the heart for this insurance stuff anymore. But if I didn't stay at Prudential, where? My job prospects in Evansville were bleak enough to make me want to scream and beg for mercy.

Are you going to go to work for Ray then? Vee pressed.

At that moment, the answer to her question was as complicated to me as Mr. Miller's high school Geometry homework had been.

The thing was, even if I took Ray's offer to work at the newspaper, it wouldn't be the same as writing my own stuff. I could keep writing on my own. But who would publish it? And wasn't getting published as important as writing my stuff? Nothing would be the same.

Of course, it wouldn't, said Vee, *because you would have let them shut you down. Put you and your typewriter in moth balls.*

Moth balls? It had taken me so long to start writing like this. Why, I didn't know. Only that when it had come, it was like finding a cool drink of water in the middle of the desert.

How are you going to stand living here without writing anymore? Whispered Vee.

The thought of not doing it anymore brought sudden tears to my eyes. I couldn't give it up, could I?

Do you trust Ray about the kind of job he's offering? Vee asked me.

Something inside me didn't like it. It felt like a deal with the devil.

Nellie's face materialized in front of mine. Another friend, Ron Glass, had told me years ago that I needed to get the hell out of Evansviile. Were they right about me leaving? Honestly, those thoughts had been weaving through my mind for a couple of years. What *was* holding me here now? Ten years ago, when I'd come back from New York, it had been for Jay. All the years following, I'd been busy spinning illusions about him and, like Sleeping Beauty, had fallen into an irresistible slumber. But the bullet fired into Jay's neck had finally jarred me awake.

Glancing at the cluster of tree goddesses again, I whispered: "Oh, wise women, tell me what to do."

Peep down the road at your future in Evansville, I heard.

I did. There was nothing to see. Nothing. If I stayed, my life was going to be a dried up piece of shit. A shiver ran from my throat to my toes. I had to face it. There was just no way to hide any more. I'd stuck around and played it safe. Used excuses. Leaned on crutches. Now it was time-out for that. Daddy was gone. Jay was gone. And I was at the end of it.

I lifted my eyes. Up there, flat, gray clouds drifted through February's dead-white sky. If I wanted to go, where *could* I go? For a second, I allowed myself to step into the dark shadows of The Corners to think about Stacey. I touched that tender place, wondering whether I should move to the city where she lived. Would she want me there? Should I call her and ask?

Closing Acts

She wouldn't want you around, whispered The Monkeys, sounding just like Auntie, who'd told me long ago that nobody wanted me.

I strangled a sob in my chest and stepped away from the place where my Stacey-memories lived.

"Where could I go?" I whispered to myself.

An outlined shape that vaguely reminded me of the United States materialized in front of my eyes. There was North where I'd tried before. North was New York to me. That hadn't worked. There was South... I could go home to Tennessee. I shook my head. That would be leaping out of the frying pan into the fire. So that left west—California.

Trying to stampede me back in line, The Flying Monkeys screamed: *You can't go! Are you crazy? You can't. You don't have any money to go anywhere!*

So what? I told them.

I looked at my watch, thinking of Ron Glass out in Hollywood. He'd probably be at the studio taping "Barney Miller" about now, but I could phone him there. I knew he'd help me if I asked him. And I had to ask him. It was time. Because the third act was over, and the theater, at last, was closed.

Exotic

"We have all come to earth for a reason—to learn the lessons that the earth has to teach and to bless the world through sharing what we have learned."
Alan Cohen, author

"You attract to you the events, persons and experiences required for your growth"
Alan Cohen, author

Where's Hollywood?

"Hollywood—it's big as the sky."
From Frankie's first impressions

1. Ready, Set, Go

On the tarmac sat the sleek, silvery jumbo jet, sunlight bouncing off its finish. The thing looked like a huge bird... predatory and hungry to me.

"Flight 124 to Los Angeles, now boarding," said a male voice over the terminal loudspeaker.

Los Angeles, I thought, anxiously, *might as well be the moon.* I clutched my purse in a sweaty fist. Other passengers walked toward the glass exit doors, laughing and talking; some commented on the unseasonably warm, spring weather. My insides shrank back from following them out... from walking toward the plane and going up the boarding steps. Automatically, I began to take small, panicky breaths—shallow and tight. That was enough to bring out The Flying Monkeys.

What are you doing? They screamed, sensing my extreme vulnerability. *Better go back now before it's too late!* They cautioned, implying unthinkable horrors waiting if I disobeyed them.

Sondra, a friend since college, had driven me to the airport. She was a self-styled Black nationalist who'd come back home ten years ago, vowing to make her mark on Evansville. About my moving to Los Angeles, she was ambivalent at best. It was not the most reassuring attitude from a friend. What I needed, at the moment, was more like a squad of cheerleaders yelling me across the last ten yards to the goal post.

She turned now and gathered me into a loose embrace. "Good luck out there," she offered with a slight frown of disapproval.

"Thanks," I mumbled. "I'll write you." She nodded and I walked out the exit.

Outside, I turned and took a last look at Evansville. Its landscape was still farmlands flat, without far-off mountains to lend it majestic thrust; it was without the skyscraping drama of tall buildings. My mind recorded it to remember. There was nothing memorable. Not really. A tremor in the middle of my chest belied that. It reminded me that I did have memories, deep and lasting. Since I'd finished grad school, Evansville had filled a need—kept me feeling snug and secure. But it had filled that need at a very high price. For too long, I had dismissed that price as unimportant. Then, death had pushed me to a fork in the road, and I'd been forced to throw the dice for my future in another direction. So now, I was moving away. And I had no idea what was going to become of me.

Time to get on with it, I thought. Before fear took over and robbed me of my nerve, I took myself in hand and pushed forward. A gathering of tears touched the corners of my eyes, and I pressed my lips together, forcing myself to take measured breaths so I wouldn't cry. As I climbed up the boarding steps, a smiling stewardess dressed in navy blue stood at the entrance. Without another look backwards, I stepped toward her, smiling back.

Inside, I found my assigned seat and sat on the edge. The sign overhead told me to fasten my seat belt. I did—with shaky fingers. My nerves were a raw piece of meat. The Flying Monkeys swooped down and ranted at a pitch so nerve-bending that I was sure the other passengers could hear them.

You're nuts, going to some strange place!
You don't even have a job!
And no place to live!

They were right. Who did I think I was riding off into the badlands alone? The Lone Ranger? At least he'd had sense

Where's Hollywood

enough to have Tonto by his side. How had I worked up enough nerve to make this move?

Ron Glass' face drifted out of memory. He'd been a friend of mine since I'd first moved to Evansville and after when he'd moved to Hollywood to pursue acting. Home for a visit a few years back, he'd met me at Club Paradise for drinks, and as we laughed and talked, he'd said: "You need to get out of Evansville, Frankie. It's not your kind of place."

That, of course, wasn't news to me. It was news, however, that another person could see it. "Right." I looked at him sheepishly. "I know I should, it's just that …."

As my words trailed away, he'd given me a penetrating look. "You're not ready to do it yet, huh?"

I'd shaken my head, and he'd dropped the subject.

Three months ago when I'd called him at the studio where he was taping his show, "Barney Miller," I'd said: "Ron, I'm going to leave Evansville."

"About time," he'd said in that mellow voice of his.

"I want to move to Los Angeles. Will you help me—adjust, find my way around?"

"Of course," he'd said.

Later, he'd called back to tell me his sister, Gerrie would meet me at the airport and let me stay with her until I found a place of my own. His support had given me extra gas to get going. But I was going to need money and because I wasn't working at a job that had let me save money, I was going to have to figure out how to scrape some dollars together. The Monkeys had screamed and bitched night and day. I'd had to make a massive effort to ignore them because I'd decided to go. Which meant I had to keep on moving forward. I was too scared to pay them any mind anyhow.

Selling my stuff was the key to getting some money, I'd reasoned. My apartment became a street fair marketplace where people could come in, look, and buy. And come they did. I spread it all out: jewelry, plants, my pots and pans, iron skillets, kitchen utensils, place mats, matching cloth napkins, serving bowls, platters, stemware, and the pewter flatware. It was hard to give up my treasured, orange and gold complete table setting for four which I'd saved up for months to buy. And my antique furniture. Just before a buyer came one day to make an offer, I looked around one more time at all of my golden oak pieces: the dining table and chairs that I'd had refinished, the pie safe, the china cabinet—things that I'd searched out in old barns and dilapidated sheds to collect. Things I'd bought to make a life of my own. After I'd sold it all, my apartment looked like a hollow shell—empty and spent, and although I couldn't verbalize it then, I'd known that I was letting go of something more than furniture and household things.

On the plane, the steady flow of passengers through the aisle had slowed to a trickle. I looked at my watch. It was ten in the morning on May 5, 1981. Almost time to go.

What are you doing? Stop! Oh, stop! The panicky Monkeys screamed at me.

I took their warning to heart. For a very bad moment, I wanted, more than anything else, to lunge for the door and run down the steps. *I could*, I told myself. *I could.* They hadn't closed the doors yet. Breathing deeply again to steady myself, I clutched the arms of my seat for dear life until the stewardess closed the doors.

2. Hello, L.A.

At baggage claim, equal parts anxiety and excitement pumped up my heartbeat as I retrieved my luggage. Some of my things had flown with me; the rest were packed in my car which I'd paid to have driven across country. Feeling a little lost, I waited amid all the bustle of arriving passengers and watched the honking cars, like horses on a carousel, going round and round the airport. Waiting at curbside for my ride, I blinked in the brilliant, bright California sunshine. It was unbelievable that I was really here. How in the world had I managed not to lose my nerve?

Soon, a slender, honey-skinned woman with sandy hair, jumped out of a car driven by a dark-skinned man. I was more

Where's Hollywood

than a little relieved to see that it was Gerrie; she made a beeline to me, giving me a big, welcoming smile while her tall, wiry man-friend, who was wearing a Dodgers baseball cap, scooped up my luggage and piled it in the trunk of his car. Then, off we went.

As we drove out of LAX, my head swiveled from left to right, breathlessly taking the sights in. Gerrie chattered about this and that, but I was only half-listening. My mind was full of questions about what I was seeing. Where was the desert landscape I'd seen in the movies? Where were those funny-shaped mounds of rock, and the mountains whose tops were flat like tables? Where was the sand? The cactus? The tumbleweed? I'd really expected Los Angeles to look like a John Ford western. Instead, I saw big pink, flowering bushes preening by the roadside. I saw trees wearing lavender blossoms on their branches. I saw Spanish style homes, landscaped green lawns, flowers that were like bursts of flame, and rows of island palm trees. The reality of the Los Angeles landscape was disorienting to me. As we crested a hill, I gaped at a field of cows grazing near pumping oil derricks which stood yards from the street on which we were driving. Cows? Oil? Was I in California or Texas? Ahead, on the horizon, I spied the famous Hollywood sign; behind it, sat rows of blue-gray mountains, like cutouts against the sky.

"Those are the Santa Monica Mountains behind the Hollywood sign," said the man. I'd forgotten his name already.

Being a lifelong fan of the movies, I felt like I'd died and gone to heaven. Now that I was here, I was agog with heart-skipping excitement. "Yes. Okay. Where's Hollywood?" I asked.

Gerrie tilted her head toward the mountains. "That way."

I stared at the sign, transfixed; scenes from old movies starring Elizabeth Taylor, Rita Hayworth, and Ava Gardner ran through my head. Here I was in the place where people conjured dreams that had entranced me when I was growing up. Hollywood's magic lantern had been my secret primer in matters of sex and desire. It had shown me luminous images of screen goddesses that watered my woman dreams. A trembling thought of Stacey floated up from The Corners. Those dreams still slept, like seeds underground, in my soul.

My watch said that we'd been driving for more than ten minutes. I had no idea where I was. In Evansville, we'd have been at our destination by now, but I could see that compared to Evansville, this place was as big as the sky. I was thrilled and intimidated by that thought.

What are you doing? The Monkeys kept saying, trying to unnerve me with a load of misgivings. But I finally managed to gag and cage them, thank you, Jesus. I didn't need them stirring up their nasty pot of Black Widow spiders, slimy toads, and squiggly snakes to scare me back to Indiana.

We passed a sign that said: La Cienega Boulevard. I mumbled the name to myself, trying to sound out the pronunciation.

But Gerrie heard me: "You'll have to get used to the Spanish names. That's not La Sa-*knee*-ga. It's La See-*ana*-ga."

"La See-*ana*-ga," I repeated. I'd spent a number of years in Evansville trying to figure out how to pronounce German street names. Now, I was going to have to stumble through Spanish pronunciation.

We drove on. At a stop light, there was an intersection with two shopping centers facing each other on opposite sides of the street. Black people were all over the place. Big ones. Little ones. Fat and skinny. All colors of our rainbow. Knots of teenagers, books in arms, sashayed down the street, hooting and laughing together. One brother dressed in a suit and bow tie had a pink cake box in his hand. He was trying to sell whatever was in the box to the passersby. At a bus bench, women—some sitting down, others standing—waited with impatience written all over their faces. I wasn't used to seeing that many of us out and about, doing everyday business. It seemed a seven-day wonder to me.

"Are we in Watts?" I asked. That name was my sole frame of reference for where Black people lived in L.A., thanks to coverage by television news of the riots in the sixties.

Gerrie craned her neck around at me. "Hell no!"

"Oh." I gathered from her tone that I'd said the wrong thing.

Where's Hollywood

"Watts is way south of here," said Gerrie's companion, chuckling.

She watched me watching people coming and going this way and that. "Sorry," she said, "I forgot you don't know *where* you are. Look, you have to understand that it'll be a little rough figuring out L.A.—where you are and how to get where you want to go. It's complicated compared to Evansville. But you'll figure it out."

"Let's give her a little tour," said what's-his-name, pulling over into the right lane. "This is the Crenshaw District. And this street we're on is Santa Barbara Boulevard."

I saw rows of apartments on either side of the street. There was a sign in front of one group of apartments saying "Gloria Homes." The apartments looked like tiny houses. Further down, around the other apartments, the landscape became downright lush with tropical looking plants and trees dressing up the yards around the buildings.

"This is 'The Jungle'," Gerrie said, pointing. "Used to be where up and coming Black people wanted to live. Now, they want to live in Fox Hills."

Gerrie's friend said: "Since this is Frankie's first night in town, we can stop at Roscoe's for takeout food and get something to drink—make it a celebration." Gerrie gave him a look. "I'm buyin," he reassured her.

"What do you think, Frankie?" Gerrie asked.

"Sounds good to me. Especially the drink part. Can we get either scotch or gin?"

"That's a bet," he said.

I smiled, allowing myself to relax for the first time. And beginning to feel right at home.

A Day in L.A.

"This town's so spread out, no one would hear you if you shout."
Shannon McNally, singer and songwriter

1. Fired

Emma crossed a slim brown leg and sat back on her couch, jiggling an ice-laden glass of whiskey. She took a sip and sighed.

"Rough day at the office?" I inquired, enjoying the gin martini I'd brought to her apartment. Since she lived in the apartment upstairs from me, sometimes we had a drink together at the end of the day.

Emma worked as a manager of some department at the UCLA campus. She squinted her brown eyes with displeasure. "Thank God it's Friday! This grind is getting on my last nerve." She set the whiskey bottle on the end table next to her. "How's the typing and filing?"

Since I'd gotten here, almost a year ago, I'd been doing secretarial work in a real estate development office. It made sense to do something for a paycheck while I figured out things... like how to get around in Los Angeles and where to find a job that used my writing talent. My typing skills were decent enough to get the job, and getting better. Filing, though, was a horse of a different color.

"They fired me today."

"Whaaat? Why?"

"Tina says—"

"Who's Tina?"

"The office manager and she..."

While I explained, I pictured the June day, a month ago, that Tina had dropped several letters on my desk, and proceeded to point out my problems.

"You misfiled these, Frankie," Tina had said.

I looked at the letters marked with a red date stamp of several months ago which meant they'd been logged in as "received" by the office. "Damn," I said. "I thought I was getting better at filing things."

"Guess not," Tina said. "Mr. Cohen was looking for these letters and couldn't find them." She shrugged. "I dug them out."

"I do the filing. Why didn't he ask me to find them?"

Tina rolled her eyes. "You know how he is."

What I knew was that the both the partners smiled and laughed a lot when they were around Tina, a twenty-something, blonde Mexican with translucent skin and long legs. I'd passed twenty-something more than ten years ago, and my legs, while more than decent, had never been long.

"Is he mad?"

Tina shrugged again and made a face. "Since the dates show they're kind of old, I told him that we might have received them right after you came here and were still learning the system."

I thought that was nice of Tina, trying to save my butt. She knew, from my past filing mistakes, that I'd been struggling with how the partners wanted things filed. It wasn't a standard filing system like other places used. In some cases, theirs was based on the city where the partners planned to build a shopping center. Or on the big company they were wooing to do future business with. Sometimes on the name of a newspaper located in another city, or maybe on a client's name. There was no consistency that I could see and there was no chart key to use. Even though I'd been on the job for over 6 months, it all seemed like a giant jigsaw puzzle—or, more accurately, a dart board. Some days, I'd hit the bull's eye; most days, apparently, I didn't.

I asked: "Did he buy that story?"

"Maybe." She took a breath.

I watched her face, noting that something in it translated "maybe" into "no." The main partner, old man Cohen, never seemed comfortable around me. I'd caught him frowning at my spending down time reading the office real estate magazines, or daily newspapers. Pretty soon, I'd learned to hide whatever I was

A Day In L.A.

reading when he was in the office. Although I really didn't understand why reading—which signaled you had a brain you wanted to use—would be frowned on by an employer as long as you had completed your work and stayed attentive to do whatever was needed. What was wrong with trying to learn something about the business? I'd noted that they never frowned at Tina being on the phone yakking on her down time. Of course, she wasn't the one who was misfiling things. I was.

She said: "He wants me to supervise you more closely, from now on; I'll look at the mail after you open and stamp it, and then I'll mark what file the letter should go into. But you've got to be very careful."

"Thanks, I will." I'd felt embarrassed that I was struggling with their dumb filing system, but I'd welcomed her help although a sinking feeling in my stomach had hinted that my days were probably numbered.

"Anyway, Emma," I said, "today, the bosses told Tina that the office needed another kind of girl... one that's 'experienced' in working in an office like theirs." I shook my head and took a sip of my martini.

Emma said: "Damn. I'm sorry about that. Probably office politics. Cause I know you ain't no dummy."

To acknowledge her compliment, I raised my martini in salute; it helped cover my embarrassment. I really hated being fired because I couldn't catch on to a office filing system. It made me feel stupid. Feeling stupid always started a burning sensation tracing its way to the middle of my chest. To ease the burning, I took a couple of swallows of the gin.

You've been having a streak of bad luck lately. First, the robbery last month, now the job."

"Yeah. Bad luck," I agreed, nodding.

"What'll you do? About the job, I mean." Emma asked.

"Find another job, I hope. I mean, I'd better... find one, I mean."

If I could help it, another job would not be as a secretary. When I'd first gotten to L.A., I'd raked through the unbelievably thick classifieds in *The Los Angeles Times*. Day after day, no college teaching positions listed. No copywriters advertised. That was bad enough, but it got clearer and clearer that I was also going to have to cope with the extra added hurdle of not knowing my way around. Or even understanding where things were located, and how far away they were from where I lived. An hour? Thirty minutes? Around the corner? How was I going to figure this out? I'd started to feel desperation inching its way through my chest. The easy answer seemed to be employment agencies. They knew where things were located and they had lots and lots of office jobs. And they'd do the footwork—make the inquiries, sell my skills, and tell me how to get where I needed to go. That was how I'd gotten hired in the real estate office. The big disadvantage now was that I'd have to do all the footwork myself. The agencies didn't deal with the kinds of jobs I was interested in.

I opened my mouth to say more, but Emma's brother, Walter, a skinny, dark shadow, glided into the small room that Emma had turned into a television den. It was obvious that he'd already had his evening cocktail. Something about him didn't sit right with me. Maybe because he watched me like I was something ripe on a tree and dangling just out of arm's reach. I'd seen that look before on men's faces and my ego usually found it flattering. With him, it made my skin crawl.

"I thought you had a job, Frankie," he said.

Emma gave him the story. I sipped and thought about Walter. He didn't work and I wondered why Emma didn't throw him out, instead of supporting him. He seemed to be both a servant and a child to her. What did he do all day while she was a work? Wash dishes? Cook an occasional meal? Do the laundry? Walter didn't seem to be very useful around the house.

He gave me a lazy smile, showing missing teeth. "So you gotta find a job, huh?"

"Yep." I took a sip to avoid his eyes.

"What do we have for dinner, Walter?" Emma asked. Her tone said I'm the lady of the house here and you'd better jump to it.

A Day In L.A.

Looking sheepish, he gave a weird chuckle. "I ain't cooked nuthin."

Emma sighed in exasperation. "Okay. Guess we'll order out tonight."

"Hey, Emma," I said, "Come over to The Beachcomber Restaurant with me. You can order take out and we can have a drink.

She gave Walter a withering glance. "Good idea."

Standing, I said: "I'll get my purse. Meet me at my apartment."

"Give me about ten minutes and I'll be down," she called as I went out her door.

2. My Woman-Jones

At the bottom of the steps, I saw Linda, who lived with her aunt in the apartment a couple of doors from mine.

"Hey, how's it going?" She asked. Linda always wore her long, graying hair in a ponytail. I wondered if she was Indian or Black or Mexican. Her looks were flavored with a little of each. That was something else I still found a little disconcerting about Los Angeles. Unlike the other cities I'd lived in, you couldn't tell who was what. Like New York, this was an international city with a rainbow of people in its streets.

I put a smile on my face and answered: "Everything's cool. How's your aunt today?" She was taking care of her aunt, so her aunt's income could take care of her. It wasn't a load of money, I gathered, but it was enough for Linda to avoid a regular nine to five every day.

"She's feeling good."

I nodded and made a slight movement toward the door of my apartment, signaling an end to the conversation. But I hesitated. Linda's expression indicated that she had something more on her mind. "Say," she said, "when are you going to come with me to the temple?" Before I could think of an answer to put her off, she gave me another option. "If you don't want to try temple, what about coming with me Wednesday night to a meeting in a member's home in Beverly Hills? After I bed down my aunt, you can drive us over."

Car-less Linda was trying to recruit me for her Baha'i religion. And something else. I was pretty sure I was picking up sexual feelers from her. I told Linda: "You go ahead. I don't want to promise right now."

"Sure." She nodded and moved off.

I beat myself up for sounding like I might change my mind later because I knew I wouldn't. Although I wasn't attracted to Linda, for some months now, I'd been uncomfortably aware that my woman-jones was peeking its head out to check the lay of the land. Maybe it was even sending out vibes because, not long ago, a guy I'd just met had asked if he could watch while a woman he knew had sex with me. After I picked my jaw up off the floor, I gave him a decisive *no*.

Right then, I knew that L.A. offered me uncharted territory where you could do what you wanted with whomever you wanted, whenever you wanted—and be anonymous. Whatever my sexual urges led me to do wouldn't be on the five o'clock cocktail hour circuit because nobody gave a damn. Even if I let my woman-jones out, I could stay in the shadows here. *Why don't you?* Vee asked. I couldn't answer her because I didn't know why.

I watched Linda saunter toward the street. She was a hustler and I knew she'd give me the pitch again. There seemed to be a million hustlers in Los Angeles. I thought of what Gerrie had said to me the first day in L.A. "Look, I can see Evansville all over you. Since I'm from there, I know what people like you mean to street people in L.A. Let me give you a piece of advice. Keep your eyes open and stay sharp. You're fresh, just-got-to-town meat. And these people are hungry. They'll be trying to get what they can, anyway they can. From *you*. Remember that."

As soon as I turned the key in my door, I could hear loud music coming from one of the apartments. Tina Marie was belting out how much she needed lovin. Somebody was always playing their music loud enough to rouse the heavenly host. You could hear everybody's music around here because the apartment

A Day In L.A.

buildings were so close together. When I'd first gotten here, I'd liked listening to someone else's music. Especially on Saturday and Sunday mornings. But now that the shiny newness of Los Angeles was wearing off, it got on my nerves.

Inside, I put down my martini glass. My place was nothing to brag about. A bachelor with an ugly coffee table placed in front of an equally ugly, yellow plaid sleeper sofa, sitting on a thin brown carpet. No kitchen, just a counter with a small refrigerator behind it, on top of which sat a two-eyed burner. Off the living room, there was a full bathroom and a dressing room where you could hang clothes and make up your face.

I glanced at the huge picture window set low in the wall and went over to pull the curtains shut. That picture window was the only thing I had liked about the apartment when the property manager first showed it to me. It was the only thing that made the place bearable even though the view was nothing since it looked out on the concrete side of an apartment. Without the window, this tiny place resembled a dark cave. But the window had betrayed me by beckoning the robbers to come inside one day while I was at work; and when they'd left, my fur coat, rings and television had gone with them. The apartment manager had replaced the window and I'd replaced the television. The diamond ring Uncle Frank had given me for high school graduation was gone forever, as were the other rings and fur coat I'd saved for two years to buy. All I could do was grin and bear it. I'd mourned the loss, but it was all a part of living in a big city.

My typewriter sat on a squat little stool since I had no table for it. Beside it, sheets of paper lay scattered on the rug. I picked up one sheet and looked it over. I'd been writing poetry since I'd gotten here. Some of my imagery was good, I thought. Not that poetry had ever been my forte; yet here I was using it to record some of my impressions of Los Angeles. When I got anxious, nervous, or a little depressed about feeling like a fish out of water here, writing helped because it refocused my feelings away from all that.

What would come of my wanting to write? I had no clue. The day I'd gotten here, I'd asked Gerrie, "Where's Hollywood?"

And she'd pointed north. Since then, I'd begun to understand that Hollywood was more of an idea… an illusion, rather than a place. A dream of glamour and fame and fortune. Hollywood was a city—a part of Los Angeles, but I didn't find glamour or beauty there. Its shops, eateries, and even the sidewalks looked cheap, dingy, and rundown. Technically, the whole of the entertainment industry wasn't even located in Hollywood. I'd hoped to get into the entertainment business as a writer and had asked Ron if he had those kinds of connections. He didn't and I had no idea of how to break in. Down the line, maybe, I'd figure all that out. Meanwhile, I was writing something every day. I smiled to myself at that. Before I knew anything, Emma was knocking, and we took off.

3.   Bars

The Beachcomber was split into two sections—the bar and the restaurant. As we entered, I gestured for Emma to follow me into the bar section to the left of the restaurant. The décor was—what else?—beach. Fish nets hung from the ceiling. Behind the bar, golden, red, black, silver fish swam to and fro in a beautiful, large aquarium. Shells of every shape and size decorated everything. Of course, there was a big television behind the bar at an angle so most everybody could see the news or sports event of the moment.

Emma and I sat down at the bar and the bartender came over to get our drink orders. We nodded at each other. He was a swarthy man that looked to be in his thirties. Life in L.A., I had learned, often included the sacred, daily workout. His sculpted muscles said he was a believer. I was becoming one, too, courtesy of Bally's Fitness Centers.

"Gin martini," I said. I'd taken to drinking martinis for the last month when I was out at a bar.

Emma gave him her order and asked for the menu. The bartender put the menu, napkins and our drinks in front of us, then went off to tend other customers. She took a sip of her Jack Daniels and looked around. "How'd you find this place?"

A Day In L.A.

"Stumbled on it by accident."

There was a hint of intimate elegance in the atmosphere. Low lighting flattered quiet customers tucked into booths along the wall. "This place is okay. You come here often?"

"Yeah. I do. Neighborhood bar and all. You ought to start coming with me."

"Maybe I will."

I doubted it. Unlike me, Emma seemed to do all of her drinking at home. I missed drinking with my Evansville drinking buddies at Allen's. Emma was nice enough, but she wasn't really a friend, just a neighbor I had an occasional drink with. At the moment, The Beachcomber was my usual daily stop. Here, I might see Lisa and her husband in the evenings. They were the only people I really knew who stopped in here.

In a few moments, the bartender came back to get Emma's food order. I listened while she ordered a couple of Chinese dishes and several sides. I should have been hungry myself but worry was setting up shop in my head. Where to find a job? If I could just figure out where the colleges were located, teaching could be a fallback plan.

When I'd gotten to L.A. and settled in with Gerrie, I'd noticed that there was a map printed on the back of an unbelievably thick phone book. I'd taken to studying it, trying to make some sense of where I was and how all those places—Hollywood, Beverly Hills, Culver City, Westwood—connected. I kept looking for a coherent whole. Something like what I was used to back in Knoxville or Evansville or even Bloomington. I couldn't find it. Metropolitan Los Angeles appeared to be a bunch of neighborhoods, communities, and cities stitched together like a quilt. Monstrously confusing.

Job hunting was going to be tricky. Thinking about that made me feel dog tired. Like I'd been climbing up a very steep mountain for a very long time. L.A. had thrown fast balls and slow balls my way. Some of them I hit; other times, I'd struck out. Like today. The thing was, I was weary of always being at bat—of having to constantly adjust to whatever was being thrown at me. Of feeling like I could never relax.

Emma said: "So have you got any job leads yet?"

"You must be reading my mind. I was just thinking that I've got two hurdles with this: Find a job and find out where it's located. After a year, I still don't know my way around."

"Pull out your Thomas Guide Map because L.A. *is* complicated," she agreed.

"I do have a possible lead though. It's at California State Northridge."

"CSUN? That's The Valley."

"Well, I'm going to call Monday to try to get an interview. Then, I'll find out how to get there."

"To get there, you'll need to take the 405 freeway."

A waiter brought Emma's order and she asked: "Are you staying?"

"Yep." I pulled my martini closer to me.

"See ya, then." She downed her drink and left.

Twirling the stick of olives in my martini, I glanced around at the people in the room. Not many here today. Down at the far end of the bar, a middle-aged man in a three piece suit was glumly studying the contents of his whiskey glass. His expression said he wasn't in the market for conversation. In one of the wall booths, two blondes, smoking and nursing glasses of white wine, talked in hushed tones. Unlike Black bars, there was no music playing; the customers here preferred the Lakers game or whatever sports event was being televised, or the news. I wasn't a sports fan, but coming here was better than staying in my apartment alone.

I sighed. It was hard adjusting to Los Angeles although there were enough clubs to make my head spin. At first, having so many to choose from was like being a kid in a candy store because I was used to only handful of clubs. I'd searched out bar after bar. The Page Four, The Flying Fox, The Executive Club, Roscoe's Chicken and Waffles—all of them, neighborhood bars in the Crenshaw District. After a while, I realized that there was a drawback: I didn't know anybody to drink with when I got there, and people out here were not small town friendly. Whatever it was I was looking for—my niche, a comfortable place to curl up, whatever—I hadn't found it yet.

A Day In L.A.

Los Angeles was a big city. Huge and sprawling. It was hard, almost impossible, to make any connections. Unlike New York, I could see the sky, grass, trees, flowers, mountains. But like New York, it left me feeling isolated and disconnected. Those feelings floated around in the pit of my stomach every day. At night, they played out that unhappiness in my dreams. I took a sip of my martini. These were the same kind of feelings I'd had at Auntie's Alcoa house where I could never find a place that felt like I fit. And these were the same kind that had run me out of New York with The Flying Monkeys screaming behind me. I'd struggled hard to leave Evansville, and, now, I was struggling to make it here in a place so big that you could get good and lost, and nobody would ever know it. Scary. But, I was staying.

As if on cue, Lisa and her Scotsman husband, Ian, came in and took their usual seats at the far end of the bar. I raised my glass in salute to them and Lisa gestured for me to move close to them. I climbed down from the barstool and asked the bartender to move my drink.

"What's new with you?" Lisa asked as I sat down next to her.

I lit a cigarette and opened my mouth to tell them about my day.

Exotic

Exotic: "Strange or different in a way that is striking or fascinating; strangely beautiful or enticing."
Webster's Dictionary

"I knew you were exotic," said Page, as she flipped the sheet off her shapely, high yellow, smoothly-muscled legs.

I stretched, beside her, to loosen my morning kinks. "What d'you mean, *exotic*?" She had a way with words, I'd noticed, choosing quirky expressions to fit her ideas. Sometimes I could follow her; sometimes, not. This was not.

"Hold on," she said, springing up from the bed and rounding the corner leading to my bathroom.

When the door clicked shut, I sat up and let out a long breath while my fuzzy brain tried to get a grip on last night. Last night and the lusty, bed games I'd indulged in. In bed with a woman? What was going on with me, for God's sake? Had I tumbled down a rabbit hole into topsy-turvy Wonderland where White rabbits talked and Cheshire cats disappeared into thin air? Memories of college and Stacey zipped through my head, heating up my soul and, at the same time, prickling me with annoyance that her fire could still touch me. I shook my head. What was I doing? Why had I gone down this path with Page? Sighing, I fell back on the bed, my confused head warning me to run for the hills while my body tingled with desire for more.

Random noises from my apartment building—a woman hollering at somebody, a kid crying—tugged me back into Saturday morning. Page came back and bent down to pick up her bra and bikini panties which we'd tossed onto the floor.

I sat up again and asked: "What is *exotic*?"

Sitting on the edge of the bed, she smiled. I was intrigued by that smile. It twinkled; it seemed to hint that she was in on a huge joke, so funny, that, any second, she'd have to burst out laughing.

"Exotic is you—and this." She patted the bed "You know... what we did last night." Her jiggling, brown-nippled breasts winked at me as she fixed the clasps on her lavender bra.

"Oh." I thought about it for a beat or two. "And I'm exotic?"

"Sure you are." She pulled her arms through the bra, then slipped on her panties.

My eyes roamed over the contours of her hourglass figure. I admired the smooth, roundness of her thighs... the luscious curve of hip, blossoming into a waistline that—I slapped back my rising libido, tempting me to reach out and pull her back into bed. She was twenty years younger than me and I needed to quit this! Before I couldn't.

Page padded on bare feet into my tiny kitchen. I lived in a single—one big room with a counter dividing the kitchen from a living room doubling as a bedroom. "Got coffee?" She asked, rummaging around in the cabinets.

"Instant. Cups and coffee, first cabinet to your left. Teapot's on the stove. Sugar and milk in the fridge."

While she put water into the teapot, my mind repeated the word she'd used. *Exotic.* The soft sound of it nuzzled in my ear, conjuring images of ancient, desert caravans bearing fabulous silks of blue and green, red and gold, caravans laden with spice jars scented with roses and honeysuckle. *Exotic.* I had to consider the word because it was such a wonderfully gorgeous description, so unlike the shrill words like *Bulldagger!* And *Freak!* that I'd heard time and time again. *Exotic?* I thought it was weird and fascinating, that particular word. Because it implied something beautiful. Something unusual... maybe even precious. Was I unusual? Was what we'd done in bed beautiful?

The teapot whistled and I left those questions hanging in my mind. Page lifted it off of the burner and poured hot water into the cups and put them on the table. "How do you want your coffee?"

Exotic

I grabbed for my red robe which was draped, for some reason, on the lamp shade. "Black. Nothing in it." I put on the robe but left it hanging loose because I didn't know where the belt was. "Take the doughnuts out of the fridge so we can have some." I'd bought them yesterday morning. Which was, it seemed, a million years ago. In the Before Time when I hadn't yet stepped over the line. When I hadn't yet violated my own golden rule that read: Don't Mess Around with Any More *Women.*

Page plunked the instant coffee and doughnuts on the glass top dining table before she sat. As I slid into one of the chairs, I, suddenly, felt shy. I still couldn't really get my head around how last night had happened.

"What're you thinking about, Frankie... last night?"

I spooned coffee into my cup, stirred, and mumbled, "Yeah. Last night. Wondering how it happened." I hadn't meant for that last part to come out.

"I know we were drinking, but don't you remember?"

"Yeah, I... I'm just—"

"What?" She interrupted, sounding a little distressed.

"—surprised." My words drifted off. I deliberately avoided her luminous, dark eyes.

What could I say? That I didn't mean to sleep with her... that I'd only slept with men starting with when I crossed over with Danny. And how many years ago was that? Eighteen, nineteen? In my mind's eye, I could still see the sunlight bouncing off of Danny's blond, Beatle-style haircut. What I'd wanted from him was to turn me... make me a female permanently wedded to males. Surely, he had done that. Between him and Jay and the other men. That's what I'd thought—what I'd convinced myself of: That my woman dreams had only been a phase. That, in college, Stacey's golden fire—hypnotizing me, drawing me to her—had only been a bump in the road. That I'd gotten past that. Outgrown it. That's what I told myself, what I'd talked myself into believing.

Page fixed her own coffee and took up the one-sided conversation again. "I've been looking at you... for a long time… when I'd go out of my way to deliver something from Dean Ashton to you in your classroom, and when you'd come into Dean's office for something, I—"she cut herself off. Then: "You didn't pick it up?"

There was silence while she waited for some word from me. Something. But I couldn't say that a long time ago I'd shut off things inside myself like picking up on woman vibes. All I could do was stare at her short, curly, black hair and her pixie eyes. Stare blankly, feeling stupid. Feeling self-conscious. Feeling all mixed up.

Page said: "So tell me this, if you didn't pick it up, why did you say yes when I asked you yesterday to come out for a drink? What did you think was going to happen?"

Finally, questions I could answer. I said:"I thought it would be fun." At work, she always amused me with her wit, her quips, her snap-crackle-and-pop talk."Because you make me laugh."

Reminds you of Stacey, doesn't she? Whispered Vee in my brain. The truth startled me and I gritted my teeth against it.

She nodded. "It was great being with you." Her eyes were penny bright as she looked directly at me. "Did you have fun?"

Nodding, I gave her a smile.

"You think we can see each other again?" She asked, and without waiting for that answer, she added: "I was thinking, if you'd like to go out again, we can go to Jewel's Catch One tonight. It's Saturday night and there'll be a crowd. What do you think?"

Before I could ask her what Jewel's Catch One was, there was a knock on the door. I wrinkled my nose, puzzled. "Who could this be?"I asked myself aloud while I walked over to the closed door "Who is it?" I asked, clutching my robe together to hide my naked body.

"Hey Frankie, it's Blue. Let me in." He hollered.

Willie Blue? We'd broken off our thing last spring and I hadn't seen him since. God! I definitely didn't want to be bothered with Blue."And what the hell you doin here?"

"Open the door, Frankie. I want to talk to you."

Exotic

I cracked the door open and said: "I gotta put on some clothes, Blue. Walk to the bench down there and sit." I closed the door quickly and walked back to Page who was hovering around the bed, straightening out the bedcovers. "Blue's a man I used to date," I told her. "Look, I'm not gonna throw you out. Just let me see what this fool wants and we can keep talkin over coffee." She looked uncertain. I tried to reassure her. "Why don't you take a shower? Towels are already in the bathroom."

"Okay." Page nodded and headed for the shower.

I pulled on some pants and a bra, remembering Willie Blue. He was one of the men I'd messed with since coming to Los Angeles four years ago. He'd hooked into me back in '82, the day I started teaching at California State Northridge. I'd been in the Learning Center, desperately trying to make sense of the mess of student records that my boss, Rosentene, had assigned me to straighten out before the Center opened. As I'd been sorting and sifting through mounds of paper, Blue had sidled up to me, grinning. He'd introduced himself and presented six, red, long-stemmed roses, saying, "These are for the lovely, new addition to the Pan African Studies Department. Welcome." I'd blushed at his charming gesture like a country-bumpkin. For the next few weeks, he was like a fast and furious tide coming straight at me. Rosentene, having checked out Blue's moves on me, had tried to warn me away from him. But had I listened? Uh, uh. No. Short on looks, Blue could put on the charm, but it was the two-penny hustler kind, I'd realized later.

What did I ever see in him? I asked myself, buttoning up my shirt. I stared at myself in the mirror and pulled my fingers through my mussed-up hair. Talk about bad timing. What the fuck did *he* want? I wasn't looking forward to this. Our parting had not been pleasant after he'd told me that he was engaged to an African princess. Though I figured he was exaggerating about the princess part, I'd still felt like an old dishrag being tossed into the corner. I smoothed down my clothes, pulled open my door and stepped out. The air smelled dry and warm.

The first floor of The San Vicente Garden Apartments was open to the October sky. It was landscaped with winding, gravel paths, blonde desert grasses, and flowering bushes. Benches had been placed here and there. Blue was leaned back on one, arms casually draped over the back. As I walked toward him, I took a deep breath.

Still thin as a rail, he was wearing his usual sunglasses pulled down on his nose. With a broad smile, Blue said: "Hey, what's doin, girl?" He scooted over on the bench and gestured that I should sit next to him.

I didn't. "What're you doin here, Blue?" I asked, folding my arms across my chest.

"Oouch. Don't give me the chillies, baby... after all the trouble I took finding you." He glanced around. "Nice place you moved to."

"You got me outta bed, Blue, and I do not have time for the bullshit. What's goin on?"

"Bed?" He made a show of checking his watch. "You still in bed at 11:30? A manin there with you, baby?" He smiled lazily. "Bet he ain't good as I am."

I let that pass. It wasn't sex that had kept me with Blue. It was loneliness. He was like the rest of the men I'd been to bed with over the years... no sexual fireworks. Except for Jay. Jay had been good, but I had to admit, after last night, that being with a woman was a one hundred percent improvement. That was a disturbing realization. Quickly, I dismissed it and focused on Blue.

Stepping closer to him, I said: "Blue, you still haven't told me what you want. Why are you here?"

For a second, his expression went sheepish. Then I saw him change it into the familiar one—high-handed, bold, arrogant. He stood up and bent toward me. "Say, let's you and me go out tonight, baby. I'm a little short on the ducats, but you can kick in something so we can have a good time, right?"

Blue was always short a few ducats, and always a half of a step ahead of his creditors—whether drug dealer, car payment, or the landlord. Which was why, when he told me he was engaged, I'd understood that he had found another, a better money hookup.

Exotic

I sat down. "What happened to your princess? Aren't you still engaged to her?"

"She's around." His tone implied the princess hookup wasn't working out. He sat down again and tried to put his arms around me. "I miss you; you know we had some good times, remember?"

I remembered that I'd shelled out the dollars on the three or four things we'd done together—a trip to San Francisco, one movie date, one dinner date to Black Angus. The rest of our two years together was spent in his tiny apartment, with me drinking scotch while he sold cocaine or pills or weed to people who tramped in and out. And I remembered him huddling in his walk-in closet, smoking coke in between running to the window and peeping through the blinds to check in case his drug supplier was out there waiting to be paid.

I scooted out of his arms. "I don't think it's a good idea, Blue."

"Sure, it is."

It was more than a little weird and deeply ironic, Blue showing up here this morning. As if the universe was telling me to take a careful look at the men I'd fooled around with here in L.A. What did it all amount to? Why had I gotten tangled up with Blue?

He was one of those men you settled for, whispered Vee.

That was no lie. Sharp claws of shame raked through my guts. Always settling for whoever I could get. Always figuring I couldn't do any better... even in Evansville. Especially in Evansville.

"Come on, what about tonight?" Blue pressed.

He stood there, waiting.

I thought about Page waiting inside, and I felt a thrum. A vibration. "No, Blue. Go back to the princess. I'm busy."

"Can I call you later on this week?"

Something was looming on my horizon. I could feel it inside: Some important thing. A decision? A direction?

"You don't have my number," I said, avoiding his question, feeling this thing that was coming... trying to brace myself for its coming. Or was it already here?

He came back at me with, "I've got your number."

Inside, I felt antsy—jittery, and I shifted my weight from one foot to the other. "Look, Blue, you need to get on outta here."

"So can I call?" He stood there, not letting me off the hook… waiting for me to answer. Like Page was waiting.

"I can't stop you," I said, turning away.

"Okay, then. Stay cool." I watched him take a few steps toward the entrance gate before he turned. "I'll get back to you." He tipped me a wave and I nodded as he disappeared around the corner.

At my door, I hesitated. What was I going to do about Page? In truth, last night, she'd brought me back home to the place where I truly lived. She'd led me to the hidden door that I'd padlocked and walked away from years ago. Now that I was back to it, what would I do? Walk away again when Blue called? Or leave it open and walk through it?

I had a feeling that today would tell. A glance at my watch told me it was noon. As I stepped back through my door, the day was already feeling like a Christmas box waiting to be unwrapped. I smiled.

Tribes

Tribe: a family, esp. a large one.
Webster's Dictionary

"...and chile, they say he's telling everybody he's Gay!" Declared a man's voice dripping with scandal and reproach.

My head swiveled to the left and I stared at the three young, Black guys hunched over drinks at the corner of the bar. I could clearly hear every word they were saying because it was always relatively empty in Jewel's Room on Saturday afternoons. Only a handful of people were at tables that sat at the edge of the dance floor.

"You tellin tales, Miss Thing. Ain't no way one of our Black preachers gonna admit to that!" Said a second voice, clearly shocked and tickled pink about it.

They sounded like women gossiping over the back fence although they didn't look like it; all three looked like poster boys for football's hall of fame.

"Well, he is! Can you believe it, a preacher saying he's Gay? From the pulpit?" Asked Scandalized, his voice rising for the sake of drama.

Like most bars, Jewel's Room was the site of much gossip, intrigue, and signifying. It was the main Black Gay bar in Los Angeles and what you heard here was usually provocative.

The third man in the trio, whose body language told you he was straight as an arrow, said: "I'm appalled. How could you admit to being Gay in public these days? This is 1987. It's getting ugly out there with people saying we're spreading some kind of disease. Who the hell is this man?"

One of the bartenders on duty, a teeny-tiny woman who always seemed to know more dirt than a Hollywood gossip columnist, was huddled with them. "I know Carl," she confided while she polished shot glasses. "Knew em back in New York when he was with The Bradford Singers on Broadway"

"Huhn! One of those Broadway divas, I might have known," said Tickled Pink. He had a Hollywood handsome face.

"Tell us more, dear!" said Straight As An Arrow.

The bartender moved closer and dropped her voice to comply, so I couldn't hear the rest. News about what was going on, "in the life" and otherwise, in L.A. came through Jewel's faster than a speeding bullet. Since I'd been living here, I'd learned that unless you're plugged into some kind of network in Los Angeles, you don't know what's going on in this giant beehive. In the last six years that I'd struggled to make a nest here, I'd been out of the loop, disconnected until seven months ago when I'd found Jewel's.

"Psst, Henry!" I called to the other bartender, the one closest to me. He switched over. The color of butternut squash and slender as a willow, Henry didn't have the come-hither body of an Adonis, but he loved to roll his hips as if he did when he walked. The walk, he'd told me in all sincerity with a bit of drama thrown in for effect, was an essential part of his "glorious personae as a queen." I had figured out that Henry wasn't what they called flaming, but he was close enough so that he couldn't pass for straight even if he'd wanted to. It was clear, however, that he did not.

"Another scotch?" Henry asked when he was facing me.

"Not now. I want to know who they're talkin about down there." I nodded in the three musketeers' direction.

"The new Black preacher in town. He's Gay and he's out. They say he's starting a church named Unity Fellowship of Christ especially for The Children, and he's telling them when they come, they don't have to be in the closet."

"Whaat?" I was momentarily silenced by such daring. And fatally intrigued. A move like that smacked of bold non-conformity. A thing dear to my heart.

"What's his name, Henry?"

"They said it's Reverend Carl Bean."

Tribes

In Black talk, whether Gay or not, when you heard somebody referencing the almighty *they*, you knew it was shorthand for The Grapevine, the fastest messaging system in the known world. Sometimes, what *they* said was gospel truth; sometimes, it was straight-up lies. Sometimes, it fell somewhere in between.

Before I knew it was going to happen, a string of questions popped out of my mouth. "Where's the church? What street? What time?"

Henry was wiping the bar. "I don't know. Let me check with the girls down there." He grinned devilishly at the label he'd given them.

I goggled at him, a little shocked at his calling them girls outright. Wasn't that an insult? Some gay men didn't like it if you implied they were feminine in any way. Since I was still new on the block, so to speak, I wasn't quite sure about how to take things people said at Jewel's. Coded language, I was used to. Black folks had always used coded language so that White people couldn't understand what we were talking about, but The Children spoke code that was even more cryptic. This was a different world. And I was still learning my A B C's.

Suddenly, music blasted out of the jukebox as Jimmy Jam and his partner, Terry, hit the opening licks for Janet Jackson's "Control." It brought back memories of the first night I'd come to Jewel's. Bass rhythms had been rolling through the room like tidal waves. A flickering strobe light caught the exaggerated poses of the dancers, so that they resembled a still life study as they moved like metronomes to the music's pulse—heads bobbing, bodies swaying, arms dipping in perfect sync to Janet's beat.

And I'd been dazzled. Not by the dancers, mind you, or the music. But by the same-sex couples everywhere I looked: On the lighted stairway going up to the next level, lolling against the rose-colored walls, roosting on barstools, vibrating on the dance floor. Women with women. Men with men. I'd been dazzled because I'd never been in a public space before where you could congregate and be who you were without fear of discovery. A girl-girl couple passed by, stopping, for a moment, to kiss each other full on the lips. Their open intimacy with each other had me gaping. Near me, at a table, a quartet of men eyed each other outright as they laughed and shouted over the music. As if on cue, I heard Janet declare: *I do what's right for me,* while the percussionist steadily kept the backbeat. I felt dumbstruck and in awe of these people. Never had I seen anything like this.

I ordered a drink and, out of the shadows, a woman emerged. The sharp contrast of her precisely cut, white pants suit against her skin's soft blackness drew my eyes to her. As she flowed through the crowd, something about her beckoned other women, and they positioned themselves, like sweet temptations, in her path. When she neared, they stepped close, smiled, touched her arm, and leaned provocatively into her space. I watched, fascinated. She was a lodestone woman. A magnet. *Like Stacey,* something in me whispered. Eventually, the woman in white stopped at an empty bar stool next to mine and ordered a beer. While she stood waiting for it, I desperately wanted to ask her name, but shyness kept me silent.

I smiled remembering that night. I'd never found out who the woman in white was. And though I always looked for her when I came, I'd never seen her again. If I ever did, maybe, I'd have the nerve to speak to her.

I'm in control, Janet sang. *Control... control... control....* The word echoed again and again as the song ended.

I glanced down the bar at Henry. He was busy cackling with the musketeers. I took a sip of scotch and lit a cigarette as the jukebox came to life again. *Ohh, I wanna dance with somebody,* Whitney Houston wailed, and two guys wearing running suits followed each other to the dance floor. For a few minutes, they had the spotlight to themselves, dancing with racing energy, as if they were sprinters going for the finish line. Then, a tall, busty woman, dressed in jeans, escorted a woman in a skirt and boots to the floor.

The women began to do a smooth, updated version of the Jitterbug, and as they did, my mind kicked backwards to my obsession, in the tenth grade, with Dick Clark's *American Bandstand*; it was the television show I'd raced home every day to see. I'd call Judy and we'd talk as we watched blonde Justine, dark-haired Mike, the two Carols, and all the rest of the regulars take to the dance floor. Our conversation was all about who danced the best, the outfits the girls were wearing, which couple was the cutest, the records we liked, and all the other things teenagers talk about. Growing up things.

On Jewel's dance floor, the guys were doing The Snake like keyed up dynamos while Whitney insisted that she wanted to feel the heat with somebody. The Snake was a dance I hadn't managed to master, so I watched them, trying to figure out what I was doing wrong. As I did, I flashed back to seventh grade and teaching myself how to do the Jitterbug by watching Acey Boy's dance show for local Black kids on television. It had been hard to teach myself, but I'd managed it because I'd watched other people for a long time. It was important to me to be able to fit in, to be able to dance when the d.j. played "Rockin Robin" or "Jim Dandy to the Rescue" at the dances in Vine Junior High's gym after basketball games.

When you're growing up, that's the way you learn. By imitating others, like you, in public places. You watch. You copy them. You learn how to dance. How to act. I was watching the couples on Jewel's dance floor, but in my mind's eye, I saw myself in Vine Junior's gym with Russell, Sammie, Bernie, Calvin, and all the sweating boys standing in a bunch on one side while, on the other side, us nervous girls waited for one of them to take that long walk across the floor, hold out a hand, and ask one of us for a dance. It was the same ritual every time. One boy broke the ice, then the rest followed suit.

Following suit is one way you get schooled about the rules of engagement with the opposite sex. I put my cigarette out, thinking back. In Evansville, at Allen's bar, where I was busy blending in with the crowd, I'd been bold because I knew the moves in the boy-meets-girl game. And I'd played the game to keep my camouflage tight. To survive. Here at Jewel's, the moves were new to me and I'd been shy with the woman in white because I'd felt like a know-nothing. Like I was back at Vine Junior in the shoes of the sweating boys, trying to figure out what to do next. Whatever the moves for girl-meets-girl were, I didn't know because I hadn't been schooled for it. Even though, I'd been with Stacey and a few other women before I'd found Jewel's, it had all been secret. That meant the moves were different—indirect and obscure, not like the ones you'd make in a place where you could be open. You danced a different dance in secret.

On the floor, Busty woman and her partner moved together like Fred and Ginger, weaving The Jitterbug into The Walk in sure-footed patterns that made it all look easy as pie. The guys doing The Snake were good, too, but there was something about the way they moved that reminded me of two puppets being jerked up and down by an unseen hand.

I thought about Stacey and me. Years had passed since those days in college. Together in secret, we'd lived in a bottle. Adrift. Without a tribe to give us aid and comfort. For us, there'd been nobody to compare notes with. Nobody to ask advice from. Nobody to teach us. No way to learn how to be who we were without shame. *Was that why we didn't make it?* I wondered. *Why fear had gotten a toehold and eaten us up?* All of a sudden, I felt cheated because, I realized, that in all of my life, there'd been no public spaces where it was safe to take off my camouflage, where it was safe to watch and learn. Straight people took those things for granted, but we were deprived of them. Something heavy settled on my shoulders as I thought about what we had missed. What we were denied. And what that had cost us. Cost me.

I looked over at Henry again, thinking about what he'd told me about this new church. Would it be a safe space, too, like Jewel's? Some place warm where you gathered for comfort with others like you around the campfire? Maybe. But there was a strange reluctance in me to find out.

Henry was hip-rolling his way back to me. He looked like Mae West. Or Lucy Ricardo imitating Mae West. I couldn't decide which. Either way it was hilarious. I chuckled to myself.

When he reached me he rolled his eyes toward the musketeers and said, "I asked the girls. Church starts at 11:30 at the Ebony Showcase over on Washington, near Rimpau. You going?"

I shrugged. "Might." And I stared down into my empty glass, trying to make up my mind. Curiosity nudged me to go. After all, I wasn't doing a damn thing on Sunday mornings except pouring myself a glass of mother scotch while I watched Terri Cole Whittaker preach wealth and abundance.

The cynic in me put in a word. *Why bother?* It asked. *This church won't be any different than the rest you've tried.*

Nobody knew but me that after years of searching, I'd finally given up on finding a church and a preacher that could move something inside me. Resigned to that, I was reluctant to get my hopes up again for nothing.

I watched Henry moving about. He was in his glory. No camouflage for him. I wondered how he'd managed to survive like that. Camouflaging had been the only way I'd known. The first maxim had been: Stay in the shadows. And don't show yourself to other people—not even to others like you. This new preacher was going against all that. Like Henry, he was putting himself out there for everybody to see. Which was why he intrigued me. He was breaking all the rules, going against all I'd learned to do. And that was fascinating. Exciting.

The little rebel that lived inside me peeked out, right then, and tugged at my sleeve.

What the hell, it whispered. *Let's go see what this preacher is about.*

And that's all it took.

Sanctuary

Sanctuary: A building set aside for worship. A holy place. Asylum of safety and security. Place of refuge or protection. A Christian church. Reservation where animals or birds are sheltered and may not be hunted or trapped.
Webster's Dictionary

1. The Ebony Showcase

My first time going to church at Unity Fellowship Church of Christ was in 1987 when services were being held at the Ebony Showcase Theater; the Ebony was an old girl whose days of glitz and glamour had passed. She sat on Washington Boulevard, near the corner of Rimpau; I found her without any trouble because she sported an old-fashioned marquee, topped off with a vertical sign announcing her name in fancy letters. When you walked into the lobby, you could tell she had been a queen, but her reign had ended and that she had fallen on hard times. In the theater, the seats had been upholstered in a rich, red; now, you had to be careful of which seat you chose because, on some seats, the faded, red upholstery was so worn that the nails might snag your clothes. In bygone days, the wall color, now faint and dull, had been a deep, rich hue, accented with gilded wall sconces that, over the years, had tarnished. The roof must have had holes in it because, overhead, I could hear the sound of bird wings. Pigeons had somehow gotten in and were roosting there in the rafters. We could hear them cooing and could see them flapping around the ceiling. On either side of the stage, red velvet curtains hung, showing threadbare patches here and there. There was a small podium and although somebody had rolled a piano on stage, there was no choir. Back then, there wasn't even a person to play the piano.

Frankie Lennon

I'd come out of curiosity. Fascination, really, with what I'd heard about the man who'd had the nerve, the courage, to be a minister as an openly Gay man in the heart of the Black Los Angeles. Reverend Carl Bean had put the word out that he was starting a church where you didn't have to be in the closet. Where you could be out. Be openly who you were. Doing that went against the social grain in a very big way and I sensed a sea change in that message. Sensed the presence of something that I'd looked for in a church and had never found. And so, I came.

The first time I went I saw about two dozen people, some of whom I recognized from Jewel's Room. There was a tentative feel about being in this new church. As if we were all waiting for some dramatic something to jump off. Which was not surprising since a lot of us drew breath, I'd noticed, as if we were living our lives inside a soap opera. But there was nothing dramatic that occurred. Only a quiet sense, for me, of coming home. A feeling that would draw me back again and again.

On Sundays, I'd always sit in the back, a vantage point that let me see the others coming in. Sitting in the back also gave me full view of whoever got up to speak during Testimony. Which took place before the service actually began. The same woman usually led it each Sunday. It was pretty informal. She'd simply stand down in front of the stage and ask who wanted to talk about what was happening with them. During Testimony, Reverend Bean would stand near the stage's left wing, listening to what the people were saying. A short, stocky man with luminous eyes in a walnut brown face, he always wore a plain, black robe that looked more like a graduation gown than one of those fancy, big-sleeved, velvet-trimmed outfits that preachers usually favored.

I had to get used to Testimony over time. The first Sunday I'd come, this part of the service had completely taken me aback. People standing up and talking about very personal things like: "I lost my job," or "My lover left me," or "My rent money is runnin funny"—that kind of honesty went directly against the ironclad rule I'd been taught back home in Knoxville. "Never tell your business. Especially to strangers." Those rules, I began to understand, didn't apply at Unity. Camouflaging and making

Sanctuary

myself invisible were old ways that I'd learned to survive, but I'd paid a high price to use them. Here, it was about finding common ground to build on. About telling the truth. About talk that reveals rather than hides. It was about learning to trust the connection you were building with other people. It was about something entirely different than what I'd experienced at other churches.

2. Affirmation

Having been told over and over again that we had been excommunicated, not just from church, but from God, most of us came into Unity feeling trapped. Threatened. Lost. Like animals being hunted into extinction. Or untouchables banished into the artic wilderness.

Reverend Bean understood that and so, at the beginning of Unity's service every Sunday morning, he spoke words of Affirmation. It was, I began to understand, after a time, a ritual act of healing with words. He would dim the lights and ask us to close our eyes. Then he would say:

"Wherever you identify yourself sexually along God's rainbow, know that you are not in error. You are God's creation. You are not a mistake. Homosexual, Lesbian, Transgender, Heterosexual, Bisexual. God made you the way you are. And God loves you just the way you are. So love yourself and know that you are very special!"

It was so strange to hear it. To take it in. To let it become a part of us. Because we'd been told, over and over again, that we were freaks of nature, an abomination, the snot in God's nostrils. They had preached at us that God, and all good people who loved God, hated us. But now, now, someone had come to tell us the opposite.

"God loves you just the way you are."

Having someone affirm me out loud Sunday after Sunday gradually began to change the shape and substance of reality for me.

"You are not in error."

Listening to those words, to that Affirmation, changed not only the mirror that I looked into, but what I saw there.

"You are not a mistake. You are God's creation. So love yourself."

In West Africa, the Dogon people of Mali have an expression which means the mighty power of the word: *Nommo*. They believe in the magic power of the word. The power of words to transform. *Nommo*.

Sunday after Sunday, I listened to the Affirmation. The words were healing me. Changing me. Sunday after Sunday, its power worked. *Nommo*. The mighty power of the word. One day, I looked into the mirror and found it was no longer cracked. One day, I looked into the mirror and the image it showed me was whole. *Nommo*.

3. The Welcome Table

Sometimes, during Unity's service, I thought about Auntie's version of God. When she was babysitting me, she would listen to radio services, sitting in her rocking chair in her living room, with the *Bible* open on her lap. I was required to sit with her and listen. On the radio, the southern White preachers would rant and rave about sin and sinners, sounding like maniacs possessed.

"Come to Jee-suz!" They would suddenly holler, scaring me half to death. "He'll wash away your sinss-zuh!"

These preachers and others, my own included, seemed to be practicing a religion awash with sinners who were always being threatened, judged, and condemned, and who were constantly being exhorted and cajoled into following a path to salvation. Nobody seemed to want to follow it; you had to be pushed into it, like a stubborn mule. Which, to me, made their path to salvation seem a depressing prison sentence, something to be served out and endured, or, worse, a grim torment that required you to suffer in guilt-ridden martyrdom. There was a catch to this kind of religion though. You had to "prove" you were worthy to be saved. Preachers and church saints made it clear that not everybody was worthy. Only some got chosen. *Does God discriminate?* I wondered back then. Now, I knew it was people who did that. Did it and put the rap on God.

At Unity, the motto that "God is Love and Love is for Everyone" attracted a lot of folks, not just Black people and not just Gay people. Reverend Bean had chosen that motto because God, according a verse in scripture, has no respect of persons. In other words, you didn't have to prove you were worthy since everybody has an open invitation to the welcome table. God, I learned at Unity, wasn't into the discriminating business.

Unfortunately, that was not so for people, by and large. By the late 1980's, there was a new kind of discrimination. And a new kind of oppression brought on by a virus. AIDS. In the beginning, it ravaged Gay men, becoming the mark of Cain and a new kind of leprosy. You were shunned if you had it. You languished alone in hospital beds, mostly unattended by frightened nurses and bewildered doctors. Or you suffered alone at home—too devastated to tell anybody, too ashamed to admit that you'd got it. And chances were, you died alone, in the grip of a merciless affliction that wasted you to skin and bones.

AIDS. No communities of color stepped up, in the beginning, to fight it and no Black churches would touch it. Reverend Bean was the first to take it on with Unity, and its outreach arm, Minority AIDS Project to welcome, hug, kiss, and help those who were ill. We advocated. Demonstrated. Educated. Visited. Shopped. Cooked. Nursed. Cleaned. We stayed to hold their hands. Right through to the end. Stayed to bury, to remember. To celebrate the going home. Because others wouldn't.

AIDS. It would set Unity apart. And it would change my life.

4. The Bible

By 1989, Unity had moved to 5149 Jefferson Boulevard, into the big space that, during the week, became the lobby of Minority AIDS Project. The word had gotten out and, most Sundays, it was Standing Room Only at church. If you came late, there'd be no more seats and you'd be standing around the walls, or listening out in the hallway which led back to the offices. In the area that served as a pulpit, there were proper chairs and a podium for Reverend Bean and our assistant pastor, Reverend Zach and about two dozen folding chairs to seat our choir, the Voices of Unity, officially robed in wine and rose. Near them, and almost out of sight, there was a piano in the corner. This one, our choir director, Darren McCarroll-Jones, played like nobody's business each Sunday.

Song was an old African and, eventually, African-American way of healing. Of unbinding. Song freed us from the worries, the uncertainties, the torments. You could fly away home on a song. Every Sunday, the choir sang and we joined in, singing to lift our wings. And fly.

I don't know what you came to do, the lead singer's voice would ring out.

And the other choir voices would answer: *I came to shout for Jesus.*

They would gather the song in their throats and hurl it out to the rest of us and we would stand to catch it, mold it, sanctify it with hands clapping, heads nodding, bodies swaying under its galvanizing power. As Darren's fingers flew across the piano keys, waves of emotion, tidal and mighty, would rush through the church, building until the church moved, alive with what Reverend Bean called the Holy Ghost. Song was deliverance. Unshackling in its power. Suddenly, you'd see a man leap out of his seat, crashing over chairs, pushing aside people's confining hands, so he could sprint around the aisles. Then, across the room, the Holy Spirit, like a whirling tornado, would catch hold of a Transgender woman and she would hop out of the front row holy-dancing in spike heels all the way to the back of the church. Some would rock and weep; some would dance in place, stiffen, and topple straight back, like felled trees, into waiting arms. Others just jumped for joy while male and female ushers would rush hither and thither, passing out Kleenex and wooden-handled fans.

After the music ministry, it was "study time," as Reverend Bean would call his sermons. He'd tell us to get out our *Bibles* so we could go to work. We were all, in our own individual ways, captives. In chains. Beaten up and terrorized. But Reverend Bean told us we couldn't really be free of oppression's chains just through dancing and singing. We had to, he showed us, confront the thing that preachers had used to terrorize us: *The Bible.*

It didn't matter whether some of us had been Methodists, like me, or Baptist, like Reverend Bean, or Apostolic, or A.M.E. or Presbyterian or Catholic. We'd all been bullied, brainwashed, and beaten up. And the *Bible* had been the tool people had used to demonize us, scare us to death, and keep us under control—no matter whether it was because we were people of color, or women, or same gender attracted.

We'd been clueless that its books had been compiled, censored, and used by people who wanted to control and exclude folks from the welcome table. A case in point, Reverend Bean reminded us, was how certain verses in the *Bible* were used to justify keeping us Black people as slaves. "Like anything else," he said, "you can use things in the *Bible* for good or ill.

"Don't be intimidated by this book," Rev would say to us, holding up his *Bible,* realizing that we were clearly terrified of it. "It's sixty-six books all written by different people who saw and understood the world within the limited knowledge of their own cultures and time."

Well. That was an eye-opener. Different people? Not God? I could see Auntie spinning in her fundamentalist grave.

In one of his teaching sermons, Reverend Bean tackled the two creation stories in Genesis which, he showed us, had obviously been written by two different authors who wrote in two different styles. We were amazed as he went through them and pointed out the differences.

Using the *Bible* to further bigotry and oppression had started a long time ago, we found out. With red ink, margin notes scribbled all over his *Bible,* Rev would come out from behind the podium and walk between the rows of chairs where we sat. He wasn't just preaching; he was teaching, giving us permission to really think about the book that we were studying.

"You have to read the *Bible* for yourself," he'd admonish us. "You have to think," he'd say. "You have the right to interpret, to ask questions."

When Rev turned to the story of "Sodom and Gomorrah," everybody trembled in their boots. This was the tale most used by preachers to put us Gay folks on trial and condemn us to the torments of hell. Reverend Bean deconstructed the story and dispatched our fear of it, going through the verses, line by line, careful to include historical and cultural information for clarification. He emphasized that the word "know" in that story is typically translated using a connotative interpretation that implies sexual intimacy and he told us that it wasn't uncommon for words in the Bible to be misinterpreted in translation. Perhaps deliberately. For "Sodom and Gomorrah" is, basically, not a story about homosexuals on the rampage, but a story about the importance of hospitality in desert cultures, about their xenophobic suspicion of strangers, and about how women were commonly used as placating sex objects.

Reverend Bean's gifts as a teacher and forthright boldness in the pulpit was a wonder to me. What Reverend Bean was doing on Sundays was waking us up—liberating us from double-tongued ideas that had oppressed us, then put us to sleep. But then oppression can only work on the sleepers. On people who don't know or don't want to know what's going on.

Week after week, I kept coming back, thirsty to learn, ready to go beyond the limits and boundaries that Auntie's kind of religion imposed. Study time at Unity was about Liberation Theology. About freeing people from oppression and injustice. About giving you new wine in new bottles. Not about follow-the-leader, without thinking on your own.

Jesus of Nazareth, that radical thinker and liberationist, had done the same when he'd questioned the "Hebrew Scriptures." He'd gone around fighting oppression and injustice, wandered about giving people new ideas, gone about changing water into new wine and putting it in new bottles. That new wine, eventually, became some of the books of the "New Testament."

5. The Pigeons

When I think back to those days at the Ebony, I always remember the sound of flapping wings. The wings of pigeons flying overhead. They'd gotten in somehow and there they'd be—flapping frantically against the ceiling, bewildered at being trapped inside.

The pigeons. Maybe they were a sign. Because, in a way, we were like them—bewildered and desperate. Trapped inside a sexual identity that others despised. Each of us came to Unity looking for something. For asylum. For refuge. For deliverance. Like the pigeons, we had been flying frantically here and there—for all of our lives, really—flapping and bumping, lost and looking for a place we could simply be free. Like the pigeons over our heads, searching to get out, we, too, came searching. But our search was for a way in—to freedom, to peace. A way in: To sanctuary.

Skirmishes

The noon meeting of Alcoholics Anonymous in South Central Los Angeles was bedlam, as usual. As you came up the steps, noise greeted you first. The rising and falling babble, the heavy, shuffling footfalls, the clicking, castanet sound of high heels, the scuffing and scraping of metal chairs on the wooden floor. Noise. And then, you waded into a shifting kaleidoscope of people, Black, Brown, White. They were everywhere—so many that they threatened to overflow the walls of the mid-sized, second-floor room. People lingered at the entrance; people talked in bunches near the door; people stood inside; people sat in rows of folding chairs; they were smoking, eating doughnuts, and drinking coffee, waiting for the meeting to start. Overhead, cigarette smoke swirled thick as fog. Young mothers scrambled after screaming toddlers, men trudged to the back, headed for the super-sized coffee pot on the counter, and groups of newcomers, seated on the front row, whispered to each other and their sponsors.

In front of a picture window, up front, sat the leader's desk and beside it stood a podium, edged with small, white, Christmas lights that blinked on and off. In a corner, there was a small evergreen tree, waiting to be dressed.

Today, as I weaved through the moving people toward the front row, anxiety and confusion reigned supreme in my head. Cup of coffee in hand, I took my seat and tucked my legs under me before glancing up at the podium. A woman in glittering earrings was there reading. Instead of focusing on her, my mind raced this way and that, gnawing, like a dog with a bone, on my undoing a couple of hours ago. *How could this have happened?* My mind worried. *What am I gonna do?*

I tugged my focus back to the woman reading at the podium and part of a sentence filtered through my brain. "—admitted we were alcoholic," I heard her say.

And a memory burst into my field of view. I saw me, six months ago, standing in this room, admitting myself an alcoholic out aloud. That June day when I'd said those words, I'd felt as if a cloak of iron had suddenly fallen away from my shoulders. Almost immediately, everything brightened, just as if someone had turned on a light behind my eyes or thrown back thick curtains blocking my view. That was then. Right now, things didn't look so bright to me.

A screaming howl from somebody's baby startled me. I looked around and saw the baby's young mother a couple of rows away from me. Frazzled-looking as I felt, she rocked and bounced the howling bundle frantically, then shoved a bottle into the baby's mouth. If you didn't have a babysitter, you dragged your kid to the meeting. "Take yourself to meetings," they told us, "like you took yourself to the bar and to the liquor store." Meetings had to come first, before anything and everything else. I didn't want to drink again, so I followed the suggestions. But sometimes, things happened. Like today. Things that, meetings or no meetings, made you want to take a drink.

I glanced the faces around me. I knew I was like them: An alcoholic, desperately struggling to stay sober, but plagued by an allergy and an obsession to drink my way into the grave.

"Why can't you just stop?" Nita had asked me back in Evansville after watching me drink myself under the table one afternoon. "Why can't you make up your mind to just stop after five or six drinks?" Her brown eyes were earnest and full of concern. "Sip some water. Eat some Beer Nuts." She'd suggested, making it all sound so simple.

And I had tried. More than once. After drink number five, the first time. After drink number two, the next. Neither experiment worked. I figured it was what I was drinking that got me in trouble. And so, the third time, I'd tried with one glass of white wine. One glass of wine. Not one glass of scotch. Not one martini. Just wine. How hard could it be? Harder, I found out, than I could imagine. As hard as crossing the Sahara without water. One glass led to another, and another, which, then, led to a scotch or three, and before I knew it, I was blasted. *Why?* I'd asked myself in despair. *Why can't I do what Nita suggested?* I'd asked myself so many times after that.

The first week in these rooms, Sam's pitch had told me why. "It's the first one," he'd said. "That's the one that got me drunk. That's the one that gets us all drunk. For us, one is one too many."

Nobody understood that saying the way another alcoholic did. Nobody. If you listened to our stories for the similarities, not the differences, you'd discover that the road we'd all traveled had come out the same: First, it was fun, the drinking. Then, it began to sour and you found yourself on the chase, looking to reach the perfect high again, the one that you thought you'd reached once before, the one that would fix it all, forever and ever. The thing was, you never found it again if you'd ever found it in the first place, and the chase was becoming a grind now, something that was more work than fun. Then, came the day that you wanted to be shut of it all. Hang up your drinking glass, so to speak, and retire to a little coffee and tea with maybe a beer or a cocktail every now and then. And you tried to do it, but, by now, alcohol was on you like Tar Baby, and you couldn't shake it. The more you strained to break free, the tighter alcohol bound you. Until, one day, you knew. You knew it was not going to let you go. Not ever. And you figured you'd die that way, holding on to the bottle and the bottle holding on to you. Sometimes, I still wasn't all that sure that I wouldn't end up that way even though I was in twelve step now. Staying sober—learning how to live without liquor, without the reflex habit of it, without its false sense of protection—was monstrously hard. Billy had said so fifteen years ago in Allen's Lounge. He hadn't lied.

The woman with the glittering earrings had finished reading and the leader, a silver-haired White man, whose eyes said-don't-mess-with-me-today, looked around before calling somebody to come up next. I tried to shrink in my seat, praying he wouldn't call on me. Sharing at the podium scared me; so far, I'd never put my hand up on my own, and I'd never volunteered to share although, a couple of times, I'd been called on to do it. The leader pointed at a young brother seated a couple of rows back from me; the brother got up, making his way, in slow time, to the front.

Relieved, I lit a cigarette just as, out of the blue, an ambush thought dropped into my head: *A drink would be just the ticket right about now, wouldn't it? A scotch on the rocks to take the edge off, or a cold, three-olive, very-dry martini sliding down your throat would...*

Reluctantly, I pushed the half-finished thought away. Rear action thoughts like that scared me shitless. Sometimes they bombarded me like a blitz. Other times, they scaled my walls and sniped at me. I never knew when the hell the skirmishes would start. Or end. I looked down at my fingers. Temptation had them trembling, ever so slightly, like autumn leaves shiver when a cold breeze slithers by. I looked at the coffee in my hand, half-wishing that it was scotch or gin, and took a sip. It tasted like Mississippi mud.

At the podium, the young brother kept his head down. It was no wonder. His face looked like somebody had tossed him out of a window last night. I wondered if somebody had. His reading voice scaled up peaks, but mostly dropped down into valleys. I could barely hear him. "—is the desire to stay sober," he croaked.

Wanting to stay sober is one thing, I thought to myself as I listened to him. *Living it is another.*

True enough, nobody had promised a rose garden, but they didn't say anything about the part where everything, big and small, made me feel like I was hanging by my fingernails. Which kept me overwhelmed, tense, and tired. It was no walk in the park, this sobriety thing. Land mines were buried beneath the soil everywhere. Step wrong and you'd blow yourself up. Even your own thoughts were out to ambush you. I sighed. Why was it so hard?

My chest quivered as I breathed out. Alcohol had dulled my feelings most of the time. Had kept them mostly numb and asleep. Now, fears of every stripe and hue dogged me each and every second. Getting through the day sober was like inching forward in thick fog while I fought for balance on a rickety bridge that stretched across a deep gorge. Every waking moment, I kept blindly grabbing and clutching for a hold, kept sticking out my toe to feel the way, and always, always being terrified of losing my balance, of falling head over heel into the shadows below. Right now, the shadows felt very close—just a breath away. This morning, I'd gotten fired from my teaching job.

A rising hum of conversation coming from the back of the room threatened to drown out the ragged pitch of the brother's reading voice. The leader banged sharply on the desk for quiet and some people lowered their voices; others shut up altogether.

My head cranked out some the film of this morning's demoralizing calamity. Mortified about being fired and not wanting to be seen by anybody at the school, I'd hurried out of the building to the parking lot on Fifth Street.

At my car door, I'd heard a seductive thought whispering in my left ear: *You could go to Roscoe's have some chicken, have some waffles, and while you're waiting for the food, have a scotch on the rocks to calm your nerves. You deserve it!*

On the tail end of it, the sober part of my brain had gotten an SOS through: *Call your sponsor!* It had screamed and kept nagging me until I'd found a pay phone and dialed her up.

She had listened patiently to my hysterical ranting, then told me: "Don't drink. Get to the noon meeting. I'll be late getting there but wait for me."

So here I was. Following her orders. Though part of my mind kept longing for a cozy restaurant where they served waffles, fried chicken, and mother scotch, if you wanted it, on the side.

There was another woman, dressed in red sweats, at the podium now. I knew her. She'd relapsed and, two weeks ago, made it back to the rooms. The wear and tear of five months out there showed on her: Eyes puffy, tufts of dry, broken-off hair slicked down with too much hair grease, a sickly sheen to her walnut skin, the red sweats just a wee bit soiled and tattered. Looking at her, at any of the relapsers, gave me the willies.

They'd gone out and had one more for the road. *Would I? Could I?* I wondered now.

One of the monkeys whispered: *It would be so easy. Such a simple thing, just get up. Go around the corner to The Flying Fox. It's easy enough to order up one for the road.* Mesmerized with the idea, my butt was a couple of inches off the seat when I thought about Marcie. That's when I caught myself and sat down.

Marcie was an old-timer who liked to remind everybody that she had more than twenty years sober, and that she'd seen a lot of folks go out, but precious few come back. Marcie—a petite redhead with freckles—had a savagely amusing way of describing the relapsers who made it back. She called them scouts. "Scouts," she'd say, in a tone spiked with irony, "go out and check the lay of the land. They be thinkin they can go back out there, and come out on top."

Each time I'd heard her say it, my head drew a picture of a horse with the relapser astride it dressed in buckskin and a cowboy hat, galloping out into the barren landscape, liquor bottle in hand, ready to do ferocious battle.

Fully enjoying her own spiel calculated to warn us against even thinking about going out, Marcie would say: "When alcohol finish whuppin they asses, they crawl back in here, if they lucky, with a butt full of arrows. You better know alcohol out there seriously kickin some ass." She'd paused for a moment, giving us a hard scowl. Then, she'd go back at it: "You go on out there if you want to. Just go on! Me? I'll be sittin right here! I got my ass kicked enough the first time around. Out there, alcohol be stone waitin on us to come on back for another round. And it ain't takin no prisoners."

At that, the room would laugh. But there was an uneasiness beneath it. What Marcie said was funny because she had a way with words, but there was nothing funny about the message. It was a straight-up warning. Any one of us could go out. We knew that. And we knew that if we did go, we might not make it back. A whole lot of us had died out there having one more. And that was plain scary.

Skirmishes

Just like my drinking dreams were scary. Where, once, scotch had been my Linus blanket, now it was my own personal boogey man who had the leading role in my nightmares. In them, I watched myself putting the glass of mother scotch to my lips, smelling its fumes, struggling not to, but finally surrendering as I tipped the glass up, and let the scotch fall into my mouth.

The first time I had the dream, I woke in a cold sweat and called my sponsor, panicked. What did it mean? Was I going to drink again? She'd assured me that almost everybody has the dreams at first.

"Relax," she'd said. "They can't tell you your future."

But I wasn't convinced. Alone at night without a shield to ward off the nightmares, the fear of drinking sank its teeth deep into my neck and I worried: Was I fighting a losing battle?

The relapser at the podium opened her pitch by saying: "I'm glad I know now I have a committee in my head that's out to get me." Tears gleamed in her eyes and her face crumpled. Someone walked forward and handed her a tissue. She took a few moments to get hold of herself.

Some people called alcoholism's run-amuck, booby-hatch thinking "The Committee." I'd named mine "The Twelve Monkeys." The monkeys were a treacherous lot. Always chattering. Always up to no good. Since this morning's catastrophe, they'd slipped out of their cage and I couldn't catch them. They'd been nattering at me so much that I'd smoked more than half a pack of cigarettes already, wishing I could shut them up. Right now, they were determined that I would pay attention to them and only them, so they'd turned their shrill voices up to fever pitch. Five of them stepped forward.

The first one screamed: *You should have known better!*

You quit that job at Minority AIDS Project to lose this one at a half-ass college downtown? The second roared.

Where was your brain? The third yelled

The fact that I'd had my doubts going in for the job interview only made me feel worse now. It had been plain, at the time, that this was one of those johnny-jump-up business colleges that usually don't last. I'd brushed my doubts aside though, thinking I was being paranoid. Twenty-seven years of drinking had effectively stamped out my confidence in my own judgment. Now, I was paying the price for not listening to my instincts.

You're stupid, Frankie, I berated myself.

Stupid, stupid, stupid! Repeated the fourth monkey.

Couldn't you see that student was hell bent on getting you fired? Why did you let her take your job? Screeched the fifth one.

I sighed. From the start, that student had wanted to take over. Wanted to show the class she was running things. She found out I wasn't going to let her when she and I had some minor showdowns. Then, she trumped me by running to the college dean with her eyes full of tears and a story about how I picked on her. The dean—not wanting to lose the dollars the student would take with her if she dropped out—opted to side with the student. Without warning or discussion, this morning, the dean had handed me a pink slip and the one week's pay I had coming. Shame and anger had seeped into my belly as I rose to my feet in her office. Panic had clawed into my back as I'd rushed out to my car.

Those feelings had made me want the bottle. Really bad. And I still did. Remembering now stoked the wanting. Put a high flame under what was already simmering. What was I gonna do for a job?

Have a drink, suggested another monkey in a civilized tone. *A martini lunch would do you good, you know.* Its tone of voice was quite rational. *Can't you just see it?*

Indeed, I could. A long-stemmed, frosted glass. Green olives floating in crystal-clear liquor. I licked my dry lips, remembering the stinging, saltiness of gin and vermouth on my tongue. It would cool the bonfire in my brain that the monkeys had set.

I shook myself away from those thoughts and concentrated on the relapser. She had recovered herself. "What I have to remember," she was saying, "is not to listen to The Committee." Her somber eyes told a story full of grief.

What made her give up? I asked myself. Something big, I was sure. Illness. Somebody died. *Or maybe,* I shivered, *she got fired, like I did.*

Skirmishes

The reality of losing my job reared up like a one-eyed giant then. Fired. No job. Unemployed. What was I going to do for money? I didn't have anything saved. Fear unthawed inside me, and a chunk of it rolled down into my chest. *Am I gonna go out, like she did, and get my butt shot full of arrows because I got fired?* The question made me want to run. Run to mother scotch, like I always did when the going got tough. But I had to hang on because you weren't supposed to drink. No matter what. That's what they said. You weren't supposed to drink. No matter what. *So why did she?* I wondered.

As if she'd been reading my mind, she said to us, "I guess you're want to know what it was that sent me out."

The silent room waited. I waited, stiff with anxiety.

"Nothing," she declared in a flat tone of voice.

I frowned at her. What did she mean, nothing? The newcomers in the seats to my left, squirmed. Behind me, I could hear someone strike a match. Some mother's little kid belched. Confused, thinking I misheard her, I leaned forward. The room leaned with me.

Her expression screamed defiance for a moment; then, it changed into something else. Regret? Disappointment? Anguish? "What I mean is," she continued, "I never really thought I was a alcoholic, like you people. And The Committee in my head kept on me, kept saying why not have a drink?"

Yeah. Why not? Two of my monkeys echoed in utter sincerity.

"I ain't had a good reason to go out that door; just didn't think I had a good reason not to." She stopped and looked us over. I could tell by the woman's eyes that she was remembering something. "The Committee asked me 'Why not have one?' and I just picked up. Wasn't nothing in particular sent me out." Her voice broke on the last.

Shockwaves rolled over me. *Nothing? Nothing sent her out?*

We told you, all this A.A. stuff ain't about nothing! Yelled the monkeys, delighted. *We told you so!*

Like a tidal wave, hopelessness crashed down on my head. Then it swept me up like a tsunami and shook me like rags.

Christ, what was the use? I asked myself. *If nothing in particular could take you out, what was the use in beating my head against the wall? What was the use in struggling every, single day?*

Tears gathered in my throat while the monkeys sang like maniacs: *What's the use? What's the use? What's the use?*

Before I knew it, I was on my feet, and heading in the direction of the coffee pot at the back of the room. Defeat seeped into my heart like the spill of sewer water. *Nothing,* she had said. *Nothing took her out.* I couldn't get my head around it! At the counter, I stuck my cup under the coffee pot spigot. Hot, black liquid spilled out into my cup.

Why should I keep hanging on by my fingernails? I fumed resentfully. *Why?*

A headache decided to skirt around the back of my skull as I thought about the thirty dollars in my bank account, and the three hundred dollar paycheck in my purse. My four-hundred-fifty-dollar rent was due in three days. What the hell was I gonna do? How was I gonna pay my rent?

Maybe you should just let go of the whole thing, said one of my monkeys.

Go ahead, throw in the towel. Who could blame you? Sympathized another.

In response to that I heard my sponsor's voice in my head, saying: "We don't drink, no matter what."

I smiled to myself bitterly. *Well, at least, I would have a good excuse for going out. Not like that relapser woman.* When they asked me why, I wouldn't be saying it was nothing that took *me* out.

Leonard ambled up to the counter and gave me a smile.

I glared at him. *This is too hard!* I wanted to scream at him, scream and then run out and find a martini.

Why not go get one? The monkeys sang. *Why not? Why not? Why not?*

Like the relapser, I realized, at that moment, that I had no answer. None at all. Suddenly, my feet began to move, heading for the door.

Skirmishes

"Take off your running shoes and stay a while," said a new voice from the podium. It was Sam.

I stopped, frozen, in my tracks and peeked back over my shoulder. Leonard, who was spooning a ton of sugar into his cup, checked me out, grinned again, and gave me a thumbs-up sign. Though I wasn't feeling it, I acknowledged his support with a weak smile. It was the best I could manage.

"Don't leave five minutes before the miracle," Sam said.

People in A.A. had a million slogans, a litany of code talk for every crazy impulse you had, for every half-baked idea you came up with, for each and every misery you thought you'd die of. This was a new one I hadn't heard before. It intrigued me in spite of myself and I backed up.

"If you think you've got a reason to drink," Sam said, "think again."

He definitely got my attention with that one. I decided to go back to my chair.

The monkeys didn't like that. Their jabber had pushed me toward the door. I wasn't supposed to come back and sit down. But they weren't going to give up. They chanted at me like a tone deaf choir. *No-job-no-money. No-job-no-money. No-job-no-money. What're-you-gonna-do-what're-you-gonna-do-what're-you-gonna-doooooo?*

In counterpoint, Sam said: "You can find a lot of excuses to take one. Money worries for one."

As I sat down, I looked at Sam mystified. How did he know? That was a real mystery to me, how the old timers always seemed to know what was going on in your head.

Sam looked at me and said: "But we don't have to drink, even if we want to." With twenty-two years in, Sam, who always wore his salt and pepper hair in a ponytail, had a load of wisdom and experience to offer. I listened to him because he came from the heart.

"Everything is a test, you know. Whatever the problem is, this, too, will pass." He paused, his eyes shifting from me to the other newcomers in the front row. "Stuff happens. It's called life. We used to try to find relief from it in a bottle. But I'm here to tell you, you can get relief from problems by talking about them. Talk to your sponsor. Talk to other A.A. people. Raise your hand and come to the podium."

The monkeys clamored for my attention. Screaming like mad things, they were doing their best to turn my insides into a boiling volcano. *You really screwed up! Really, really screwed up!*

I ground my teeth and wrenched my attention away from the sound of their voices. I wanted to hear what Sam was saying.

"There is a tremendous amount of hope in these rooms. It's where I found mine," he said. "This program is an inside job. Just like a caterpillar changes inside its cocoon, we change inside when we work this program. Do the footwork and the change will come, I guarantee you. One day you'll look up and the obsession will be gone. You'll be free."

Free, I said to myself, feeling something warm spread its soft wings into my chest. Butterflies—blue, white, purple, orange, and gold—rose in a glorious cloud before my eyes.

"Hang on. Stay with us and remember: We don't drink. No matter what because it's the first one that gets us drunk. One is one too many."

"And a thousand ain't enough," a male voice hollered out, finishing the well-known saying.

As Sam left the podium, the room rumbled with laughter, acknowledging the pure truth of that declaration.

Inside my head, the monkeys yammered: *How you gonna pay your rent? How? How?*

Finally fed up, I knew it was time for me to turn the tables on the monkeys. No more skirmishes with them like this one if I could help it. When the monkeys saw what I intended, they fought and kicked frantically, but I reached out anyway, grabbed them by their scruffy necks, slapped them into their cage, and turned the lock. For good measure, I dropped a blanket over them to muffle their screaming voices. The last thing I heard was: *How you gonna pay....?*

I didn't know how the rent would get paid, but I knew one thing. I wasn't gonna drink. Not today. Not tomorrow either, God willing. I wasn't gonna drink, one day at a time. What's more, it was time for me to do some things to make sure of it. After taking a deep breath, I looked at the leader and, for the first time ever, I raised my hand. The leader pointed to me.

I stood. "I'm Frankie and I'm an alcoholic," I said, then walked, without hesitation, straight to the podium.

Roger

1. Shadow of Death

I looked into Roger's eyes and saw that he was going to die. That thought filled me with a well of tears that threatened, any second, to spill over and drown us. Drown Roger, me, drown Lauren and Mike who were standing beside me at the foot of Roger's bed at Chris Brownley Hospice. He lay unmoving on his back, his arms, small as twigs, folded atop the sheet covering him.

You'd think with me working at Minority AIDS Project for the last two years that I'd be used to it by now, used to seeing AIDS come round, lay its scabby, ruinous hands on folk and then slowly and with great care lay them waste. But I wasn't. Nobody was. You didn't, you couldn't get used to it. And some days you wondered just how long you could take it, looking on as people you'd grown to admire and love fought to live as the virus sucked them in like quicksand. Every day. Until it took them under.

Tears stood visibly in my eyes, and by concentrating all of my will, I held on to them. Just barely. All three of us were struggling not to fall apart. Which was why we'd come together during lunch to help each other hold the fort. And there was another reason. One we couldn't bear to say aloud. Coming together was better because none of us wanted to be alone when we saw what we didn't want to see: That pale horse on the horizon, its rider galloping steadily on, coming to gather another, a beloved, into its bony arms.

Nobody spoke. We hadn't seen Roger for three weeks, not since that last time at church; what we were witnessing had, momentarily, paralyzed us, wiped our minds clean and rendered us mute. Mike's cocoa-smooth face looked mottled, as if someone had punched him in the stomach. Even Lauren, ordinarily unruffled and calm, looked shaken. Casting about frantically for something to say, I opened my mouth and closed it several times before I could speak.

"Roger," I finally said. It was obvious that Roger was too weak to talk and I stood there, anxiously wringing my hands. He looked over at me, trying to focus, trying to smile. "Lindsay and I are getting married in September. We expect you to be there with Darrell, you know." As soon as the words were out of my mouth, I felt like an idiot. What was I thinking? This was June. My wedding was a lifetime away for Roger. Wondering why I had I started this, I stumbled on. "So, so you've got to rally and get home in time for it."

We were all floundering, trying to find something to hang a thread of conversation on. Mike glanced about and I followed his line of sight, really noticing the room for the first time. Cards of every color, flowers, and teddy bears were everywhere. A huge, bright banner with inky, well-wishing messages from Unity Fellowship Church hung from the ceiling. I'd signed it myself two weeks ago.

"I'm going to brush your hair, Roger," Lauren said into the silence. "Would you like that?" Her voice was soft and soothing, like a cat purring.

It took some effort on his part—turning his head, dragging his eyes slowly, very slowly to her face—but he managed it and gave her a nod. Lauren picked up the brush from the little table beside his bed. The paint of her long fingernails, red as blood drops, caught and held my eye as she stroked his hair in smooth, even movements. Before, Roger's hair had been a thicket of soft, tight, little curls that would have resisted the pull of the brush; now the hair was sheer threads of wavy silk, lying close against his scalp and the brush seemed to glide over the hairs on his head.

My eyes slipped down from Roger's hair to his coffee skin. It lay on his bones as dusty-dry as the leaves of fall. Even his skull seemed to have shrunk and the pillow behind his head billowed like an enormous white sail. The look of him sent shockwaves through my brain. I blinked, hoping that blinking would clear away this scene, somehow make it all instantly disappear like

Jeannie used to do in that old television series. But nothing changed. I was still standing there staring at Roger. Who was dying, after all.

Thoughts scrambled in my head. Was it just seven months ago, at the Halloween party he and his lover, Darrell, had thrown, that I'd watched him hugging people, dancing every dance, laughing loud and hard at somebody's joke? Was it just seven months ago that I'd been sure he would beat this thing and live forever?

But how could he not? For the two years I'd know him, he'd looked so good that the heads of both women and men swiveled to follow him when he walked by. I'd seen it firsthand when Roger volunteered to go with me as one of MAP's HIV Prevention speakers. I'd watch people's eyes squint in disbelief or their expressions melt into dismay when he told them he had the virus. I'd been there when they looked him over, their eyes slowly caressing the bulging muscles of his arms or the sculpted chest, molded from hours of hard work at the gym.

"You'd never guess," they'd say, almost licking their lips as their eyes moved down to his slender waist, his flat stomach, and the cupcake roundness of his butt.

"Not him. He looks so...so healthy," they'd say, their confused brains, trying to match the vision of Roger's young, handsome, smiling face and his athlete's body with the revelation that he was carrying HIV.

Yes, I could understand why they didn't believe it. He didn't look sick. Not then. But now, now, the disease had plundered and pillaged his body like an invader taking the spoils of war. It had shriveled him like a dried out melon; it had shrunk him down to a shell of himself as if all the water had run out of his body. It had made him an old man in the blink of an eye.

The enormity of the ravage staggered me.

Lauren, serene as the Madonna, still quietly brushed. My mind, shocked and jumbled, did a topsy-turvy flip, drifted away, and down-spiraled.

Roger's not the only one sick and dying, said the voice inside my head. *What about the others you know?*

Frankie Lennon

I counted them, the ones that I knew. My neighbor, Ronald; James, the photographer; Poncie, who was in the choir; Gerald, who was going to be in our wedding; Steve, Charles, Robert, George, and.... Others lined up in my mind. I could see their faces there, but, suddenly, they wavered; my windpipe closed up and I couldn't breathe. Couldn't bear to count. Was I going to have to see them all waste away? Was anybody going to be left? In my head, a line of flower-banked caskets stretched away, receding into the distant, empty horizon.

Each Sunday, there'd be somebody new showing up at Unity: Men whose skin was now the color of ashes; men whose skin had been bronze, red-boned, high-yella, panther-black; men whittled down to no bigger than a minute by the knife of the virus; men coming, sick and hanging on by their fingertips, coming with canes to help them walk, coming clutching pillows to cushion their sore, frail bottoms. Men coming. Looking for sanctuary. Waiting for a touch. Needing to be loved. Not judged. Loved. Not shunned.

My head reeled under the assault of my own thoughts. At some point, Mike had opened his mouth and a stream of words fell out. Something or another about work. It didn't matter what he said. The words were a bulwark for us. Something to hang sanity on. While he chattered, I noticed that Roger's eyes had that look that the dying get—remote, glimpsing a thing, or a place, or a time that our eyes can't see. I wished I hadn't caught that look in Roger's eyes. It bumped hard against hurt spots inside me, still unhealed, that I didn't want to mess with. It reminded me of seeing that look for the first time in my beloved Uncle Madison's eyes as he lay in the hospital, dying of cancer. It reminded me of seeing it in Daddy's eyes, ten years ago. Seeing it and understanding that he'd caught a glimmer of the landing across the water and wanted to go. I hated knowing that he wanted to go, wanted to let cancer and alcohol float him across Jordan on board that old ship of Zion. I hated it because I didn't want him to go.

I shifted my eyes away from Roger's. After Daddy, and because he was the last of my blood family, I'd thought I was through with all this. For a while, at least. Through with having to go through hospital corridors that smelled of stale sheets and piss and rot. Through with seeing disease reduce people to frail and faltering shadows of themselves.

The last time I'd seen Mama was in a room like this one. Pain rippled behind my eyes at that memory. After all these years, the claws of guilt still tore into me when I thought of her. The beginning for her had been losing her breast.

"Don't worry, Frankie," she'd assured me on the phone, in 1962, after the operation. "It's all over now."

But it turned out that it wasn't. Three years after, I could see that she was getting weaker though I'd never really believed, couldn't believe that cancer would get her, like it did Grandmama. Couldn't believe it because I didn't know of anyway to get ready for that. That Thanksgiving weekend of 1965, with Mama lying in that hospital bed, I could see things I hadn't wanted to see before. That her hair, always shining black, was now very white at the edges. That her face, always bright and alive, was now haggard and pale as smoke. I could see things in her eyes that I hadn't seen before either. Things telling me what I didn't want to hear. The worse part was that I didn't have the guts to face it, say things that I should've said, do things that I should've done. At her bedside, I saw her eyes slide away, more often than not, to gaze beyond, out into a distance further than time and deeper than space. And I felt, in the depths of my heart, that she was poised at the edge, that I wouldn't be able to hold her back. That, in the end, I would have to give her up to Death. Forever.

And here I was again. At a hospital, at a place where Death hung around like a hungry hyena.

You thought you were safe for a while, but Death came and found you. Said the voice that lived inside my head. *Now what are you going to do?*

It was as if I'd come full circle in a nightmare from which there was no escape. The landscape of Death was different this time—uncharted, unmapped. But it was Death all the same. What was I doing here?

Shaken, I gripped the railing at the foot of the hospital bed while a pool of unspent tears, somewhere deep inside, strained slowly into my lungs; they were turning into a cry, into a shriek that was crawling up my throat. I turned my back and walked toward a window, struggling to catch the shriek and stuff it down. I squeezed my hands together as if to crush, once and for all, the thick overflow of feelings welling up in my chest; without warning, anger suddenly surged forward and crowded out all else. Its fierceness stung me and I raged silently.

This virus had robbed us of a passage of time in our lives that ought to have been free of fears about a fatal disease, free of Death. Age, that brought close the stink of the grave, was still in the distance. Why was this was happening to us?

I turned back. For just a moment, the room and the people—Roger, Lauren, and Mike—seemed frozen in time, outlined in a strange starkness that chilled my heart. As I looked at Roger's face, puckered with age come too soon, the anger boiled away, evaporated into grief. We were far too young for the shadow of Death to be at our shoulders. Far too young to be burdened with this weight. But, young or not, Death was here anyway. I could see his pale outline standing there beside Roger's head.

2. 5149 West Jefferson

He died a week later. His memorial was the Saturday following in the Minority AIDS Project building. Just before his service, I stood at the door leading into the big room that served as Unity's sanctuary on Sundays and for memorials. In a daze, I stared at one of the MAP-Unity posters tacked to the hallway door. It pictured Roger, Steve, and Reverend Bean, all of them smiling broadly at the camera. Rev, dressed in his white pulpit robe, had his hands on their shoulders. I gazed at Roger for a long time, wells of sadness filling me up, remembering that last time at the hospice.

A tear broke away and coursed down my cheek.

No blubbering today, Frankie, I told myself. *Tears are a luxury you can't afford.*

Roger

But tears aren't a luxury when you need to grieve, are they? Said my voice.

I ignored it, too afraid to think about that. I was already wrestling with questions that I'd been lugging around: How long could I keep on being around dead men walking? At church on Sundays and at work everyday. How long?

It had dawned on me the other day that I had been spending a good deal of my life in 5149 Jefferson for the last three years. I was here at least six days a week. Sometimes, seven if something was going on, like a meeting, or a training session. Or a memorial. With that realization, a worrisome question had popped up that begged for an answer: What in the world was I doing working at a place where we looked into the jaws of Death everyday?

I was the one who ran from things for most of her life. Running from college down the road a piece to hide out in Evansville, Indiana for thirteen years, drinking everyday, passing for straight, scared to live my life. Running in place and going nowhere until a double dose of Death rousted me out of my hidey-hole and ran me clear across country to Los Angeles.

Yeah and a good run is better than a bad stand, right, Frankie? Said my voice.

Damn straight, I agreed.

So how did you run yourself up in here? It asked.

I had no answer to that, but I thought about it. Here I was working at a place where desperate, frightened people came in every day. People always in need, people despised for crossing borders or sneered at for not fitting in; people held cheap for being poor, and banished for the sickness inside them. Sometimes, working here made me feel like that mythical king, Sisyphus. The one condemned to forever push that huge rock up a steep, mountain incline to the crest, only to have it roll back down every time, forcing him to start pushing all over again. In doing HIV Prevention, I had to deal with all those things that spread the virus as much as blood and cum: The sexual attractions all tangled up with shame and self-hate; the self-sacrifice, poverty, and oppression tied into being a woman; the greed for power that fed racism; and the homophobia that bloomed everywhere like lilies of the field. Like that king, soon as I'd roll that damn rock up to the top and leave it there, I'd turn around to see the thing rushing back down the mountain ready to mow me down. Jesus! What was I doing at a place where everyday was a fight to get money from the city, the county, the state, the feds—from bureaucrats and politicians that guarded it, but didn't want to give it up to help people survive? A place where it was always a fight to just to keep enough food in the pantry for people who came in needing a package of dried beans, a can of fruit, some meat and bread. People who came in with eyes telling us they needed much more than food. Needed things like hope. A hug. And a bit of love. If we could spare it.

Noises from the back hall jerked me out of my reverie. I sighed, put my hand on the doorknob, and turned as the big, red letters at the top of the Roger-Rev-and-Steve poster loomed up at me: *Love is for Everyone,* the words said. A load of gnawing feelings that I didn't want to deal with dropped into my stomach as I went inside the sanctuary.

Somebody had placed a large vase of pink, yellow and purple gladiolas on the table up front. In the corner near the pulpit, the choir had taken their seats, waiting for their musical cue from Darren, the Music Director. The room was nearly filled with people sitting quietly in the gray, metal, fold-up chairs that had been carefully lined up in neat rows by church volunteers. There was no bier, no coffin, and this was not a traditional funeral. It was a memorial. A remembrance. A home-going celebration. But I didn't feel like celebrating. No sir. Not one little bit.

The beige, paneled walls that I knew so well now seemed a bit too close for comfort. Silently fighting the urge to run out, go somewhere else, anywhere else, I sank into an end row seat near the front and saved the one next to me for Lindsay. As I sat there, listening to Darren play a hymn softly on the piano, Reverend Bean and Reverend Zach, both robed in white, walked into the pulpit while Darrell, Roger's lover, entered, escorted by the ushers, Christine and Ana. They seated him in the front row, just as Lindsay hurried in and took the seat beside me. She took a look at my face and squeezed my hand.

I scanned the room. Looked at the brown, black, and yellow faces. The men, young, mostly in their twenties, looked strained, heart-heavy, and careworn. The women, somber, dispirited, pensive. There were no signs on our chests, but we were the scapegoats. They'd stamped us misfits, labeled us depraved, branded us an abomination—all because we were born same sex attracted, or both sex attracted, or trapped in bodies of the wrong gender. And with the advent of this disease, we had been cast out into the wilderness and left there. As what? A sacrifice? An appeasement? An offering? No one cared that we would die. They were all afraid. The preachers had turned their backs. The doctors had slammed their doors. And so here we were, an ancient clan trudging this wasteland, blistered, bone weary, and alone.

Darren's fingers touched the keys, signaling the first song from the choir. They rose, and a tenor voice offered encouragement. *They, that wait on the Lord,* the voice told us in slow measures and with great tenderness, *shall be renewed in strength....*

I looked at Reverend Zach. He sat with his bronze hands gripping the arms of the pulpit chair, his young, lean face transfixed as if he had discovered some great treasure hidden within the music.

The lead singer went on in a voice that was full with tears and hope. As he sang, I recognized this song as a verse from the book of Isaiah. He was the prophet, I remembered, that told the Hebrews if you had patience and if you put your hope and trust in God, things would turn out all right in the end. The song went on while I silently mused about that. I had my doubts. Where was the end anyway? This road we were walking ran off so far into the distance that you couldn't even see the end. I looked from Reverend Zach to Reverend Bean whose walnut-brown face was in repose, his head nodding in time with each piano chord. He'd started it, this walk we were on. He was leading us. What could he see? Did he know where we were going, where we'd end up?

Anguish settled over me like a heavy veil. Just what, in God's name, were any of us doing at MAP, taking on Death as our adversary in a battle that surely we were going to lose? What good was it doing? We were dying anyway. A tiny little virus had hurled us, blind and lost—God help us—into the mouth of the wilderness, into an endless desert, into a fearsome, unknown country without compass or canteen. How were we going to survive it? Death was taking us down in double-quick time. And I didn't want to be here watching at the end. It was going to be too painful.

Teach me, Lord, how to wait, the choir sung in perfect harmony, responding to the lead singer's call.

Wait? My head responded. *Wait? Uh-huh. No. I had to get out of here. Wait for what? You can't outwait Death. It came out the winner every time.*

I'd fooled myself into believing I'd made peace with it. But I hadn't. Death was the Gorgon. Medusa. The Reaper. The sum of all fears. And I didn't want any parts of it. Not again.

Though I was struggling to keep them at bay, memories took a scalpel and sliced into my brain, exposing wounds still alive, still pulsing with grief. I was four years old and back at East Vine Methodist Church, screaming while Mama was taking me away from Grandmama, rigid and unmoving, in the casket. I was twenty-one years old, dry-eyed and swaying in agony, as I leaned over Mama's rose-covered casket, hoisted above the freshly dug grave. I was thirty-six years old, standing in an Evansville mortuary, one April morning, looking down at Jay, silenced once and for all by a bullet that tore into his neck. Two months later, I was trembling in a Knoxville mortuary, looking down at Daddy—whose sweet Hershey bar face had become a grotesque Death mask, barely recognizable to me.

Now, the choir had swung into the song in full measure. *Be of good courage,* they sang. *Wait on the Lord,* they said. And before I knew what was happening, something had come undone inside me. Like rocks breaking free of a mountainside, there were tears. Tears, suddenly, here on my face. Embarrassed, I wiped at them with the back of my hand, trying to stop them before someone saw me. But they kept coming. And coming. Without warning, they had become a cascade.

Lindsay put her arm around me and Ana brought me tissues from a Kleenex box. Why couldn't I stop? The tears bewildered me Where were they coming from? The harder I tried to stop them, the more I could feel things breaking apart inside me. Breaking apart and rolling downhill becoming a rockslide. Tears loosening the load that I was carrying, had been carrying for so many years. The guilt, the fears, and the doubts binding me were giving way under the gentle assault of tears. They felt like mountain rain on a hot summer afternoon. Tears, like a balm. Soothing. Mending. Restoring. I couldn't stop them, couldn't fight them. So I gave in and let them do their work.

At the end of it, we went outside, standing in clumps and pairs, there in MAP's parking lot, waiting for Reverend Bean to finish it, finish the memorial by giving us words to let go of Roger, so he could be on his way. We'd replaced the tradition of going to the cemetery to see someone's body put into the ground with the ritual of the balloon release. A rainbow bouquet of balloons symbolized the spirit of the one who had died; releasing the balloons into the sky signified the journey homeward. Christine and Ana came round handing out balloons to everyone. I took a red one. Lindsay took green. As soon as everyone had a balloon, the final litany began.

Above us, I watched clouds, looking like pearls that someone had scattered, floating lazily on a backdrop of ocean-blue; it was bright and clear and warm, instead of the usual, June-gloom, gray day. Before I knew it, the balloons were going up, rising heavenward. Their upward flight reminded me of an old spiritual and I hummed it under my breath, silently reciting the words.

We are climbing Jacob's ladder. We are climbing Jacob's ladder. We are climbing Jacob's ladder. Soldiers of the cross. At the end of the stanza, I finally let go of my red balloon and watched it—watched Roger—make his way, riding up and up into the deep and endless sky. Going home.

After the benediction, Lindsay drifted away to talk to someone. But I still watched the red balloon on the tail end of the others, all of them disappearing, one by one, into the soft blanket of blue. Paul, my colleague at MAP, came over and stood beside me, smoking quietly for a few moments. We both watched until they'd all gone.

"See you Monday for the 8:30 meeting, Frankie, right?" He asked.

I looked at him, and opened my mouth to say: *No.* To say: *I've had enough and I'm not coming back to MAP and all this death.* I'm sure that's what I was going to say.

But what I said was: "Yeah, I'll be here, Paul. Bright and early."

The Throwaways

1. Prologue: Misfits

It was probably going to be one of those days at Minority AIDS Project. The weather inside the agency felt rocky. Storm clouds hovered closely overhead. People looked grim and sounded snappish, and that had started about three weeks ago, after Roger died. For the past four days, there'd been flare-ups every morning—threats, arguments, nasty bouts of profanity and name-calling. Doing today's training was going to be a challenge. But that wasn't unusual because our staff was The Walking Wounded, and when our wounds ached, we showed it. All morning, I had been hearing arguments, like Fourth of July firecrackers, popping off up and down the halls. Easily irritated, people were taking their fractured feelings out on whoever was nearest. All of which meant I had to stay loose and roll with the unexpected. And, I had to be willing to let them show me how to teach them.

Not easy. All of our lives we'd been told we were the misfits of society—the throwaway people. The work of the Health Education Department was to do HIV prevention with the people of color communities nobody else wanted to work with. MAP hired throwaways to educate throwaways: Gays, Transgender women, Lesbians, gangbangers who'd done time in juvenile detention hall, school dropouts, the homeless, dope addicts, and alcoholics. And we had to learn to work with each other. Every. Day. It was a trip because a classist hierarchy emerged that mirrored larger society. It was a hierarchy that divided, of course. It pushed us to judge each other. Which group was the scariest? Which group was better than the other? The gang boys looked down on the queens. The gay boys looked down on the transgender girls and the lesbians. The lesbians were hung up on playing roles; you were either femme or butch... and butch was always better. The dope addicts thought they were better than alcoholics. The dropouts were intimidated by anybody who'd finished school. If you'd done time or been in juvie hall, you were hipper, slicker, and cooler than anybody else because you'd gotten your own special brand of education. Like larger society, judging was always about identifying somebody that you could you put down in order to feel better about your own miserable self.

2. Trouble

I was sitting in front of the training class beginning to explain how the retrovirus, HIV, makes copies of itself in a cell when I noticed Danny whispering in Kevin's ear. Because Danny was always starving for attention, even though he looked like a little angel, you could depend on him to stir up trouble. Especially if he and Kevin put their heads together. As he listened to Danny, Kevin shut the gold compact he carried to endlessly admire his flawless, black skin and he raised his eyebrows in exaggerated surprise.

Pointing at Little John, Kevin suddenly let out a hearty guffaw—such a surprising, manly sound, and if there was one thing Kevin never claimed, it was manliness. Everything about him announced that he was a chocolate bonbon. A queen, to use correct term in community vernacular. And queens are, more often that not, difficult—the original divas. Some I love. Others I'd happily push off the face of the earth.

Little John, a muscled, ex-gangbanger who prized his masculinity above all else, growled, "What's so goddamn funny, Kevin?"

"You, Johnny boy. Danny told me about your gang initiations. Sounds like you gang boys had some bootycall goin." He snickered.

Kevin yelled: "Trrrade!" He exaggerated the word, drawing out the syllables.

The Throwaways

It was a deliberate insult. Being called "trade" meant you did sexual business with a gay man or a transgendered woman. Trade meant you were a pound of flesh used for pleasure. Something for play. A sex toy. Homophobes and men on the down-low would cringe at this kind of name-calling exposure. As far as they were concerned, having sex with somebody who had the same equipment put you beyond the pale of manhood. Not acceptable in their minds. It messed with their idea of macho. Of whatever it was that made men think they were supposed to rule the world.

"Who you callin trade?" Little John's face had gone red.

"Yeah, who the fuck you callin that?" Echoed T-Baby, sitting beside Little John. The two of them were like twins.

"Ooh, no she didn't say that!" Krystal, a transgendered woman who was wearing an almost real-looking auburn wig, tossed her locks and giggled. Kyrstal loved to egg things on.

I thought I'd better intervene before things got out of hand. "Okay, folks, let's can it." It was a futile gesture.

"At least I *know* who I am!" Kevin said, voice vibrating with the knife-edged tones of a challenged snap queen. "Some of us," he sniffed, lifting his chin in a regal fashion and crossing his legs like a Las Vegas showgirl, "can't say the same." All he needed was a crown on his head to symbolize his royal personage.

Little John's head swiveled in Danny's direction. "What'd cha tell em?" He barked. "I never tole you nothing bout no trade. What'd ya say, fucker?"

All eyes in the room riveted to Danny. Who was pleased as punch to have the spotlight. Having the spotlight meant, to him, that he was, for the moment, important enough to merit attention from somebody. Anybody. Even if it might mean somebody was going to kick his ass.

Danny smirked. "I only repeated what you told me. You said that at the gang initiations, '*sometimes guys had to be with another guy and mess around*'."

Our jobs encouraged us to learn about each other's sexual appetites and vulnerabilities; here was something new about being in a gang that we didn't know. One more time, I was learning, because I was working at MAP, that you just couldn't know what people do sexually. And that's why the virus could willy-nilly travel from one person to another. Sex drew strange bedfellows. Men did all kinds things. Without a rubber. Because having a rubber on hand and using it meant you were fully aware of what you might do, and awareness added shame and took away deniability. The virus liked that. Denial was a Petri-dish that the virus loved to grow and mutate in.

In the awkward silence that followed this revelation, Krystal said: "Sounds like *trade* to me."

I loved Krystal for a lot of things, not least of which was that she'd taught me much about Transgendered women. But she could be a pain-in-the-ass. Especially if she had it in for you. And she most definitely had it in for Little John who'd told her more than once that she needed to stop wearing dresses because she was a man, not a woman. Krystal really loathed Little John. His saying things like that messed with the easily-destroyed self-image she'd carefully put together.

My head throbbed with frustration. Just as I opened my mouth to put a stop to this runaway train before it crashed, Little John, face looking like a thundercloud, leaped over at Krystal. At almost the same moment, Little John's fellow gangbanger, T-Baby, lunged at Danny. Chairs fell over and people scrambled out of the way.

"Somebody break them up!" I hollered, thoroughly at wit's end. People were standing around the walls, tittering and exclaiming over the excitement like magpies. I took a breath, put two fingers to my temple and pressed.

On one side of the room, Little John snatched the wig off Krystal's head and laughingly held it up like a trophy scalp. Krystal was screaming like a stuck pig and cursing furiously: "You mother fucka! How fucking dare you? Give me my fucking hair!"

He laughed at her fury. "This ain't no hair. This be a wig!"

Over in the corner, T-Baby had Danny by the collar up against the wall. Three people, doing their personal versions of street fight control, rushed at Little John and two others at T-Baby.

The Throwaways

Before anyone was hurt, the flare up was over. Muttering and growling, the contenders settled down and went back to their chairs. The referees went back to theirs while the room bristled with tension. We were teetering on the edge of wiping out all plans for training today.

Teaching them was like walking in the dark. I didn't know the way because I'd never taught students like them. The majority were resistant, sullen, and scared stiff of being embarrassed that the information would be too difficult to grasp. Learning is a bitch when you've been told you can't because you're too black and stupid, and you ain't worth a damn. I knew that they resisted because they were being pushed into new territory where they might fail at something. And they'd been told they were failures too many times.

They could read, but most didn't have much confidence they could master the kind of reading I was bringing in for the training. I didn't blame them for that. It was hard. I had to learn it first, without any help. So I relied on the *Being Alive* newsletter to teach me. The articles were excellent, but difficult, loaded with chemistry, biology, and general science concepts. I'd never taken those courses. Not even in high school. But I figured out that it was the terminology of the sciences that blocked my understanding. So I looked up the words and phrases. Kept a notebook to help me. It was a tough nut to crack, learning about the complexities of HIV, what it does in the body, the medicines to slow it down in trials as experiments, and the alternative treatments that people were discovering. No easy matter for me even with a couple of English degrees, so I understood it was not going to be a breeze to teach or learn.

3. Mr. Hollywood

Sometimes, like today, I was aware that I was running a never-ending race, and I was getting tired of pushing back on their resistance. So maybe I'd just ease off and take a little break today. I opened my mouth to call off today's training just as the door to the inner offices opened. Out of the corner of my eye, I saw Vera, our Chief Financial Officer and Reverend Bean's right hand, come out with a White man in tow. He sported a deep tan and silver-white hair laid and sprayed into perfect Hollywood waves. I wondered who he was. No telling. People were always trooping in here to see Reverend Bean, asking how he managed to operate an AIDS program in poverty-ridden South Central Los Angeles, wanting to know the secret of his success. What a lot of them really wanted was to find out how to make a load of money pimping folks with the virus. Later, I'd ask Vera what this one wanted.

She was moving just ahead of the man, her face tight and unreadable, stepping fast enough to let you know she was on a mission to get the man out of the door. But Mr. Hollywood foiled her scheme by stopping to gawk at the staff sitting in the semi circle of chairs. Giving us a hundred dollar smile worthy of Hollywood's Red Carpet, he bobbed his head to acknowledge the various pairs of eyes that turned his way to briefly check him over. Vera, having reached the door, looked back with her hand on the knob, and realized she'd lost him in transit. A frown of exasperation spread across her mocha-colored face while she moved back toward him.

Since he wasn't going to go away quickly, it was obvious to me that courtesies had to be observed, so I went toward him, my hand outstretched. "Hello," I said, "Frankie Lennon, Assistant Director, Health Education."

Meanwhile, Mr. Hollywood waited silently for Vera, who was standing beside me now, to introduce him. "This is Steve Farrell," she said, her voice parked carefully in neutral, "Manager of Contracts and Curriculums for the County."

At the word, 'County,' you could feel the ill-humor rising from all of us like heat from the desert's sand. *What luck,* I thought grimly, *a visit from the very folk who make our lives at MAP hell on wheels.* We all knew the County hated MAP and had tried, for years, to find something suspect in one of our programs so they could defund us.

"And what are we doing here today?" He nodded amicably in the staff's direction, his voice bright and phony.

The Throwaways

At that, people started muttering and buzzing. His tone was a bit too much like the school principal talking down to a bunch of first graders. His use of the royal "we" aggravated me, but my tone was polite.

"Training Day," I answered. "I was just doing a little review with the staff on how the HIV virus replicates."

His eyebrows lifted at that. A puzzled crease just touched his forehead while he swept the fingers of his left hand through his silver-white locks. As he did so, his hair floated up in a cloud and settled back into its perfectly combed style. It was a Hollywood gesture. Pure special effects. I wondered how often he did it. And how many people he thought he impressed with the gesture.

"I wasn't aware that we'd approved a training curriculum for Minority AIDS Project," he said.

The line was innocent-sounding enough. You had to know the lay of the land to catch what hid behind it: A threat and reminder that you weren't supposed to do anything, if you had County funds, without County approval. Doing things without approval could get you defunded. Vera's lips were pursed together as if she'd caught a stinking waft of something. Abruptly, the chattering murmur in the background stopped. The staff had caught the scent, too.

I smiled, pushing down hard on the feelings that, if I let them go, would lead me into saying things that would get the agency into deep trouble. I smiled, carefully searching for words to answer this White man who thought he owned the world, and who certainly thought he had supreme rights over a little non profit agency run by Black people that had the temerity to keep going without kissing the collective asses of the powers that be.

"We thought," I began, trying to pick my words of appeasement carefully, "that it would not be breaking the rules to announce some subjects that the County has said are appropriate for training. Your guidelines, I believe, said that would be all right. If we read it wrong, this session will certainly be cancelled. Will you give us some guidance, Mr. Farrell?" It was code for *Please, don't whip us Massa; we's tryin to do right*. It was an updated version of Steppin' Fetchin' shufflin for the White boss.

I did it, hoping to avert trouble. Because it was me, after all, as the agency's trainer, who'd scheduled this session before the curriculum had been approved.

"My sense of the issue is," The frown melted away and a hint of The Hollywood Red Carpet smile peeked out, "that it's fine to take that approach for right now." It looked like my little speech delivered in the properly humble tone of voice had been conciliatory enough for him. But until he was out of there, nothing was certain. He put his right hand to the knot of his necktie and lifted his chin as if to make an adjustment. The gesture was calculated to focus your attention to the silk, blue-gray tie that was two shades lighter than the shirt he was wearing. "I'll give you my personal permission to continue for today only," he intoned, his hand dropping to the buttons of his charcoal gray suit. It fit him like a glove. Custom-made, Italian design, I figured. Cut to emphasize his thirty-something looking body.

Right then, I made a major error by picking up the handouts from my chair that I'd already passed out to the staff, and I could see curiosity lighting up his frosty blue eyes.

He held his hand out toward me, palm up. "May I?"

I threw a helpless glance at Vera before handing them over. She rolled her eyes and hunched her shoulders ever so slightly. What was she to do? She couldn't tie a rope around him and drag him out the door though she probably wanted to.

He did a careful scan of the papers, while we waited. Finally, lifting his eyes to mine, he said, "But this information is so—*so sophisticated* for you people here!"

I shrugged at Mr. Hollywood's remark even though the blatant racism pissed me off. He was stupid to think that of us... a mistake a great many White people made. I had to admit, following his glance, that we were an unlikely looking bunch who didn't present a picture of an attentive, ready-to-learn, note-taking students.

He looked at the staff, looked back at me, then shook his head as if I was hopelessly deluded. "Good luck," he handed me the papers. Then, he turned and marched out of the agency. Vera made a face at him after she'd closed the door behind him.

One of the guys whistled and screamed, "Scrumptious butt, honey!" He sounded like Flip Wilson doing the character, Geraldine.

Everybody cracked up.

I said: "Let's take a quick break. Be back in fifteen, please."

4. Dark Horse

Out back in the parking lot, which served as our break room, I lit up a cigarette and watched the staff drifting out in twos and threes. Danny and his gossip buddy, Kevin, made for a corner, cackling like hens all the way. Had the fight Danny instigated drained the poisons out of his system for today? I sighed, hoping so. Danny was a walking testimony to what happened to gay men who fell in the clutches of religious flim-flammers, promising a miracle that would never happen. Those of us like Danny, so desperately screwed up because of the stigma surrounding our sexuality, were easy targets for those men of the cloth who swore they could get rid of the devil inside us and promised to make us blessedly heterosexual; whereupon, our families would now love us and we would qualify to avoid the fires of hell. Believing that Nature, God, or whatever Higher Power you might put faith in had made a mistake with him, Danny had dived into the false promise, twisting himself inside out, trying to remake himself anew. What it was doing to him on the inside did not reflect a pretty picture on the outside. Since he'd been baptized at his new church, he always looked angry. He'd gotten black-snake mean and taken to sneak drinking. If he'd always been a now-and-then gossiper before, now, he considered himself the daily news, reporting everybody's business with single-minded fury—which was what started the ruckus in our training. Except for Kevin, people avoided him and his nasty tales. And trouble followed him like flies on garbage.

Krystal slid over to stand beside me. "How do I look?" She patted at the wig on her head.

"Just fine." And she did. Because she took pride in her looks, Krystal's make-up, hair, and dress were always on the money. Little John had attacked her where she could be hurt the most. It was gospel that you took your life in your hands by messing with a Transgender woman's hair.

"Those mother fuckers," she pronounced each syllable distinctly. "They *ruined* our training this morning." She pulled a sad face. Krystal would never admit that she'd brought Little John's wrath on herself.

"You may be sure that I will seek and extract revenge on their persons. However, I will wait until our training is finished."

"I appreciate that. We don't need any more interruptions."

"You know I love my training class. I learn so much from you, Frankie."

"Thanks, babe." I considered this high praise. Although it hadn't been the case at first, Krystal had come to trust me to help her learn "how to write" as she put it. Her ambition was to become a consultant trainer. She had a good shot at it because Tran-trainers in AIDS work were few and far between.

She nodded her head and left me to go talk to Rosie who was Coordinator for MAP's Needle Exchange Program.

A few more puffs and I looked at my watch. Time to go in. I lifted my voice: "Okay, folks, break's over. Come on back in."

On his way to the door, Little John swung over beside me. "Frankie," he said in a near-whisper tone, "You gon ast me t' read t'day?" His expression was so serious that he almost looked angry.

"Not if you don't want to. Something wrong?"

"Naw. I was lookin at the papers you passed out before Kevin started that mess…"

"Yes?"

"Well, I been practicin readin. You know you told me to practice."

I nodded.

"Been doin that. So—hot damn!—when I looked at that one paper, I understood what it was sayin. Ain't that sumpin?" His voice was awash in wonder. He turned to face me. "Frankie, I

The Throwaways

wanna keep on readin in class. Don't matter what that White dude said bout us. I wanna keep on readin, okay?"

"Okay. You got it." I smiled as he went inside.

Before I stepped in the door, I looked back for stragglers. The parking lot was empty. They'd all gone back in without me having to round them up. That was a first.

When I got back to the room, it was quiet. Nobody teasing anybody. Nobody cursing anybody. They were sitting there waiting. You could have heard a pin drop. Another first.

I thought about Mr. Hollywood's remark about us being unsophisticated learners. We were. And so what? Most people didn't want to lay a finger on this kind of work. The public was terrified of the disease and of the stigma that went along with it. But we were here holding the line in this fight… whatever we had to learn to do it. Mr. Hollywood had nudged us. Made us remember that we were doing more than collecting a paycheck here at MAP. Maybe, probably, by tomorrow, we'd forget how he'd nudged us. Didn't matter. Something else or somebody else would nudge us forward next time. Somebody or something would give us the juice to put our backs into it… to pull, to push, to keep going—to not give up the race.

And we wouldn't because we were the throwaways—the dark horses that nobody bet on.

Pandora's Box

1. Coffee and Advice

When I told Pete, over coffee and rolls, that I was going to come out to the people back home, the force of his voice carried loud and clear above the Saturday morning sounds at the Farmer's Market .

"Are you insane?" He shouted at me from across the table. "Don't do it!"

Startled, I almost jumped out of my skin. As it was, I splashed some coffee on my pants. At the next table over, some well-to-do-looking White people turned and looked at him. Pete ducked his head apologetically at them. They gave him a blank stare for a moment before going back to their conversation.

Disapproval put a deep scowl on his nut-brown face. "Who in the world gave you that bad advice?" He asked, voice noticeably lower. The clatter of dishes and the traffic outside on Fairfax had me straining to hear him this time.

"Umm, nobody, really," I said, feeling and sounding a bit timid. His response had knocked me back a peg.

"Nobody? Well, why in the world would you, then?" Pete picked up his cup. His pinky finger stuck out in imitation of dainty delicacy.

"Because," I said, "I can't be getting married and be in the closet, Pete!"

He looked at me like I'd gone soft in the head. "Telling people is in such awful taste, dear, don't you know that?"

"I don't think honesty is in bad taste, Pete."

"But everybody will—will know," Pete sputtered, outraged at the thought, He paused and shifted gears. "You'd be cutting your own throat, Frankie."

I said nothing to that. I was still trying to recover my balance from his initial response. I'd been looking for support, not censorship. Or, at the least, understanding. Instead, I felt like a child being scolded. Maybe because Pete always sounded like a proper school marm.

I'd met him before I started working at Minority AIDS Project, at a time when we both were teaching at one of the quadrillion business colleges dotting the landscape of Los Angeles. I was teaching Proofreading, which was more English grammar than anything, and he taught Sociology, but he had Hollywood dreams of going into fashion design.

"It's working at that place, isn't it?" His tone was accusatory. "I told you not to do it," he reminded me, smug and self-satisfied.

Why had I brought this up? How could I have forgotten that, two years ago, it was Pete who'd admonished me not to work for Minority AIDS Project?

"It'll ruin your career," he'd said when I called to tell him I'd gotten a job there. "People will think you're...."

I'd finished his sentence. "A Lesbian? Queer? Gay?"

"Well, quite frankly, yes!" He'd sounded appalled. The conversation had gone downhill from there. After that, we hadn't talked for months.

Pete's glasses slipped down and he pushed them back into place. "Being around all those people has just ruined you," he lamented.

I stared at Pete. Short, just this side of plump, Pete was Gay and closeted and under the impression nobody knew simply because he worked hard to make sure nobody would guess. But however hard he tried, his slip was still showing, so to speak. The way he drank coffee or tea, holding the little finger of his hand out delicately; that was a very queenie thing to do. Straight men didn't do stuff like that. And, apparently, there were other things about him that people could clock him on. I remembered the time while we were still teaching together when one of his students had come to me, bitching about the grade she'd gotten in his class. After she'd finished venting, she'd told me that Mr. Holden—Pete—wasn't fooling anybody with his act. She'd said she knew that he was Little Richard's sister. I'd had to work hard to keep a straight face behind that.

Because he'd have been mortified, I'd never told Pete what that student had said although, at the moment, the thought was crossing my mind. *All those people?* If I hadn't just come from an eight o'clock A.A. meeting, I would've cussed him for the nasty, little queen he was. But recovery made you think twice before you did things. So I lit a cigarette and held my tongue. But I took revenge by deliberately blowing smoke in his face.

While he coughed daintily from the smoke I'd blown in his vicinity, I repeated: "All those people?" There was a dangerous edge in my voice.

"You know what I mean. Gays and Lesbians going around identifying themselves to the world! Some people don't have sense enough to keep their business to themselves," he declared, adding sugar to his coffee. "I mean, why draw attention to yourself? What's wrong with blending in? Isn't that what this country is about?" He was on his high horse and feeling really good about it.

I sipped my coffee silently. Blending? I'd had enough of that—of being a cheap imitation of straight people. Enough of forcing myself to walk their walk. It was the same as being chained in a slave coffle. And quiet as it's kept, blending took your freedom. It made you a slave. You just didn't want to see it that way.

Pete mistakenly took my closed mouth to mean he could take some liberties. "And that church you go to, some kind of cult, I heard. People say…"

"Wh-hoa! Stop right there! I'm a second away from cussin yo ass out!" I'd had enough. I wasn't going to let him diss Unity. Not by a long shot.

He closed his mouth and waited for me to cool off. Without speaking, we watched the parade of Saturday morning shoppers. They looked like they were from the neighborhood: Mostly elderly and White, along with some Hollywood industry types who drifted by, toting coffee or juice and sweet rolls.

Finally, he broke the silence. "Frankie, why open up Pandora's box?" Pete asked, genuinely mystified. "Telling people can stir up such terrible feelings. Why invite trouble?"

That was true enough. Still, there was another side to the argument. "What about my feelings?"

He shook his head. "They don't matter."

"Why not? I've been stuffing them for years, Pete. Till it hurts. And you're telling me they don't matter? Why not?"

"Here's why," he said, pushing his eyeglasses up to the bridge of his nose the way he always did before a class lecture. "Like it or not, you have to recognize that, generally speaking, people don't much like us different ones."

It was the first time I'd ever heard Pete identify as Gay, however oblique. And that sent a mild shock through me. Where was he going with this?

Pete stared into his open palms as though he were telling his own fortune. "Conformity drives the herd instinct and it demands that everybody be the same. Sameness presents no threats, you see; the herd remains safe." He paused and looked up at me suddenly. "Difference, however, makes waves which will rock the boat. And, dear, when the boat rocks, people become nervous and afraid."

"So I have to keep pretending so they won't be nervous and afraid?"

Pete picked up his coffee, tasted it, made a face, and put it back down. "Yes, you do. Because when they're afraid, they get nasty. And nastiness turns very ugly, very quickly."

"That's crazy. We're talking about people I've known all my life. Not some wild mob." I stubbed my cigarette out and anxiously lit another. What he was saying brought out my anxieties because his line of reasoning was exactly why I'd stayed in the closet all these years.

Pete sighed. "You never know how they're going to react until you open your mouth and tell them. You don't know whether they'll be friend or foe. As for family and friends, they can be nastier than a mob and uglier than Frankenstein. Take my word for it, I know."

I was taken aback, and deeply distressed at his words. My brain was working furiously to refute what he'd said, only I couldn't come up with anything.

He dabbed at his moustache with a napkin and stood. "Want more coffee? I'm getting a refill."

"Sure." I watched him go, feeling frustrated and disheartened.

At one of the market stalls, I could see customers bending over tomatoes, picking and choosing, dropping them in the brown bags that the vendors provided. Outside, car horns blared and beeped in the thick of traffic on Fairfax. I sat thinking about Pete's attitude, his advice. It had put a gray misery over my heart. I'd wanted bolstering up, not a bunch of reasons to make me change my mind. I puffed on my cigarette, completely at bay and thoroughly shaken now.

Pete put our coffees down and then sat. "Why risk it? What do you hope to gain by it? Telling people, I mean."

"The truth," I said, picking my coffee up. There was a touch of self-righteousness in my tone, and I gave myself a mental slap on the wrist for it. Self-righteousness was a nasty piece of business. Not a good thing for me to indulge in. Still, I wanted to get back at him for tearing into my carefully-built threads of confidence about what I was going to do.

"And what does truth buy you, dear?" He asked sarcastically.

"No more hiding," I said, promptly. "Which buys me my life."

"Does it? Do you think the truth will make you free?"

I blinked at him, confused and drained of confidence by his questions. "Won't it?" I asked and added feebly. "It's supposed to."

With pity in his eyes, Pete gave me his answer. "Frankie," he said, "that's only in fairy tales."

2. High Stakes

The phone sat on my desk like a green toad. I wanted to pick it up and dial Knoxville, but I was scared to. Pete's warnings, a couple of hours ago, had set up the worse kind of doubts in my head now that I was home.

When I finally reached for the phone, a voice from The Corners said: *What will you say if somebody asks you to explain Jay being your lover?*

I pulled my hand back and thought about that. About what people nowadays would call my sexual identity and how I'd played tricks with it. Worn false colors. Hoodwinked everybody. Years of tricks and trickery. How was I going to explain myself? Would I say I wasn't heterosexual though I'd masqueraded as one? Would I say I wasn't bisexual though given my sexual history, some might try to label me that way? I'd woven quite a convincing illusion. So convincing that, now, even I had to wonder about some things.

And what does the truth buy you, dear? Pete had asked.

Some relief, I hope, I answered while my thoughts catapulted back in time.

Why had I crossed over to men? First and foremost, because of what had happened with Stacey. She'd been my first lover, male or female, and she'd been my Waterloo.

I'd fared no better with the next woman. Two strikes and it seemed to me that I was out. *What's wrong with me?* I'd asked myself after the second strike and, as if I'd summoned ghosts from the past, a scene materialized: Auntie and I stood facing each other in the old Mee Street kitchen.

"Nobody wants a sassy girl like you," she said, glaring at me with her wolfie eyes. "Why, why would anybody want a girl like you?" She looked me and up and down, her lips curling back in a sneer. "Nobody wants you." She said, turning her back.

Why would anybody want you? Her voice repeated in my brain, echoing down through the corridors of time: *Nobody wants you. Nobody wants you. Nobody wants you.* Like a tape stuck in a loop, for years, her words circled round in my brain. And I believed them. Wholeheartedly.

If nobody wanted me, I'd thought, shame crawling through me like a lava flow, "*if I don't appeal to women, then, I'll cross over. I'll settle for men.* I'd reasoned, trying to salvage my sense of self-worth that had somehow gotten mortally wounded years ago. Life would be easier that way anyhow I'd thought. All I had to do was bury my woman dreams in secret corners and forget about them. And that's the way it had started with men. I'd crossed in Evansville and then, Jay had come along.

I went into the kitchen and pulled out the instant. I hated instant, but coffee had become my constant companion these years that I'd been in A. A. I'd managed to burn up the coffee pot a few days ago, so I had to do instant today. The stove's gas jet whooshed into flame and I carefully lit a cigarette from it before I put a pan of water on to boil. How would I ever be able to explain all this stuff? I stared out the kitchen window at the lemon trees, smoking and thinking back. Jay. Truth be told, our relationship had been built on lots of liquor, good sex, and no risk for marriage. From time to time, when Jay had to attend to hearth and home, I'd distract myself by doing a one-night-stand with another man though Jay had been the one I'd claimed to love.

But how, asked the voice from The Corners, *could you have loved him if you've always been a Lesbian?*

The water boiled and I poured it over the instant. Coffee cup in hand, I went back to sit at the desk across from the phone. Had I convinced myself that I loved him to distract me from being who I was afraid to be? That was a disturbing question and I took a couple of long, hard pulls on my cigarette to soothe the disturbance. Before I could speculate on that one, my brain sent another memory swooping down to rattle my cage. Had I simply used Jay as a dam to hold back the flood of my desires? And when the dam was gone—well, it was embarrassing to remember that less than six months after he'd been dead, I'd slept with a woman. *And how in the hell had that happened?* My woman dreams were supposed to have been long dead and well buried. *How could the desires have come back?* Grief over Jay alone should've kept them away. But it hadn't. And women had become the lodestar of my universe again. As if Jay had been only an interlude.

I put out my cigarette. *Stop,* I told myself. *You can't really explain all this to yourself, so how do you think you'll ever be able to explain any of it to anybody else? Just pray nobody asks.*

I looked at the phone sitting there curled up like a green viper.

Who in the world gave you the bad advice to come out? Pete's voice echoed in my head.

I did, I answered. But did I have the nerve to do it? With a stomach full of butterflies, I got up, backed away from the phone, and went to the bedroom to change into my gardening clothes. Gardening was something that I'd taken up to fill the void. To take the place of mother scotch. To keep the twelve monkeys gagged, so I couldn't hear any of their wacko suggestions. Especially when I was agitated. Like now.

I stepped outside. The August afternoon shimmered blue and California hot. From my porch, turning to face north, you could see the tops of palm trees neatly laid out in rows, running all the way back to the hills and mountains beyond. The Hollywood sign rose on the horizon like an icon from my dreams. Somewhere, in a parallel universe, it was Saturday afternoon in Knoxville, Tennessee and ten year-old me was crossing Vine Avenue at the stop light, walking up to the Gem Theater's booth, paying my ten cents, and entering the eye of Hollywood's magic lantern. Knoxville. Home. Was I going to have to give it up? Would I have to if I told them?

Why risk it? Pete's voice asked me.

This was high stakes, I knew. It was a risk to put my cards on the table. To bet everything. If I lost, I'd lose Knoxville, the place I was born, the place where I grew up, the people I loved. The whole enterprise scared me shitless. Risks scared me shitless. Because I'd been programmed never to take them.

For some reason, I stood there remembering the movie, *Indiana Jones and the Last Crusade,* remembering the risk Indiana took to save his father. Standing at the edge of a gorge, he had peered down at nothing, except a chasm, miles deep. If he turned and went back, his father would die. If he went forward, if

Pandora's Box

he stepped out, it looked as if he'd be taking a fatal plunge into the deep.

I walked around to the side of the house and got the shovel. I could hear dogs barking in the distance. As I came back into the front yard, I asked myself what was worse? Taking a chance and stepping over the edge of the gorge, like Indiana, or turning back because I was afraid? His foot had hit solid rock when he'd stepped over. There'd been a bridge there all along. He just couldn't see it. If I stepped out, would there be one for me?

I went back into the front to weed around the white, long-stemmed hybrid roses bordering the stepping stones that led from the street to the porch. As I neared them, a waft of their sweet scent touched my nose. I stuck my nose into the center of a rose and savored it for a moment. On the street, little kids were running up and down the sidewalks, screaming as they chased a rubber ball. Memories of Mee Street, of me, Evelyne, and Shirley playing at The Square, memories of Knoxville flowed into my head. I stuck the shovel into the ground to loosen the dirt around the roses. Who was I going to tell first?

Telling people is in such awful taste, dear. Why cut your own throat? Pete's words kept circling in my head.

In Knoxville, the short list was Aunt Avice, Judy, Brenda, Janice and her husband, Calvin. Janice was the first friend that I could remember having. We were in Nursery School together. And in Austin High's band together. I remembered us—the tiny tot mascots—marching behind the Drum Majorette, lifting our little legs high to the beat of the band's drum.

Smiling, I wondered: Where had time gone? Wasn't it just a few years ago that I was having my annual, junior high school sleepover parties with a dozen squealing, clowning girls? Girls all over the living room, eating popcorn and hotdogs, listening to Ruth Brown and LaVerne Baker. Janice was at most of them until she went away to school. Later, when I'd had the last one in high school, Brenda was there and Nancy and Judy and four or five others. More memory pictures spilled out of my mind and I was seeing me at Y-Teen Camp, along with Brenda, Janice, Nikki, and Nancy. I could see us swimming, hiking, and watching a star-filled, night sky as we sung around a campfire. Those were good memories. Ones that pressed on the heart strings. I stopped shoveling, for a moment, and memory's lens clicked one final time. I could see us in cap and gown at our high school graduation, lined up to march down the aisle, nervous because we knew we were about to scatter to the four corners without any idea of where we'd end up. I looked up at the Hollywood sign. Where had it gotten to, the time? In my mind's eye, I could see it, running on ahead, an invisible, flowing river, taking us on a raft to parts unknown.

I sighed and shoveled up a chunk of dirt. As I did, I saw I'd caught a worm. It wiggled desperately to get away from the light and back into the bosom of the earth.

Why draw attention to yourself? What's wrong with blending in? Pete's voice asked.

I bent down to pull out some weeds, watching the worm wiggle-waggle away as the aroma of green grass and roses drifted past my nose.

Soon, the heat of the day pressed in on me. Dropping the shovel at the foot of the porch steps, I decided to go inside for something to drink. In the kitchen, I opened the refrigerator door. On the top shelf sat a quart of Sunny Day orange juice. I stared at it, remembering the orange juice queen, Anita Bryant and her notorious media campaign. Watching her on T.V. that day at Allen's came back in full force as fragmented voices rose and fell in my head. They sounded like a radio signal almost out of broadcast range.

We have to stop these homosexuals!

Lock em all up!

What they're doing is immoral and goes against God's wishes!

They freaks of nature, man!

Tears stung my eyes. Is that what my friends back home would call me if I told them? A freak?

Pete's voice cut in. *Telling people can stir up such awful feelings, dear. Why ask for trouble?*

Pandora's Box

I took out a bottle of water and shut the refrigerator. *Maybe telling would be a mistake. Maybe I should listen to Pete.*

Aunt Avice's smiling face framed by a cloud of short-cropped, white hair, appeared in my mind. She was Uncle Frank's second wife and my only living relative. When Daddy died, ten years ago, his second wife had insisted we all go to the mortuary together to see Daddy's body. I hadn't wanted to because I wasn't good at that. At seeing somebody I loved wrapped in death's embrace. My knees had turned to jelly, when we'd gone in. And then the shakes had started. Hard and uncontrollable. I'd felt like I was going to fly apart. When Aunt Avice saw me shaking, she'd gathered me in her arms and held me tight. Since Daddy's death, we'd been very close and I treasured that. What would she think about me if she knew? Would telling cut me off from her? I didn't know. And not knowing felt the same as running out of air under water.

Back outside, I sat on the porch steps. The sun was hot and high in the sky. I wiped a droplet of sweat from my nose and drank some water, thinking about the people in Knoxville. The ones that I'd grown up with, gone to high school with. What would they say? Would telling mean I'd have to give them up? And could I?

Pete's words came back once more. *But why open up Pandora's box?*

He'd been referring to a Greek myth, an old story with two different endings. The ending you'd favor depended on your perspective about life. In one, Pandora opens the box and all the human ills of the world fly out; in the other, Pandora opens the box and all human blessings fly out, leaving only hope inside. It was obvious which one Pete favored. The question was: Which did I buy into?

Left with my own runaway imagination, I could depend upon the twelve monkeys in my head to cook up fantasies of disaster at the first sign of a problem. Given my alcoholic thinking, I was prone see the worst possible scenario just around the corner. But I'd learned by listening in A. A. that what actually comes down the pike never matches up with the disaster scenarios we make up in our heads.

Since I had concluded long ago that I was no Cassandra—that I really couldn't see around corners, now what? Was I gonna let the monkeys win out and scare me away from doing the right thing? Or was I gonna do an Indiana Jones and take the risk?

I stood up, opened the screen door, and headed for the phone. My hands shook as I reached for it. I hated this feeling. It was like the one I'd had at Y-Teen camp so many years ago as I was standing at the edge of the diving board, trying to get my nerve up to try my first dive. Anxiety had rippled up and down my stomach as I stared down into the water, nudged into tiny waves by the afternoon's gentle breeze. A tightness had circled and clinched my chest. The others had done it—glided to the end of the board, bounced up once, and dived, arching their bodies to neatly cut into the water. Now, it was my turn, but I was scared. Scared of doing a belly buster. Scared of people laughing at me. Scared of God knows what. Just like right now.

I looked at the phone again. The day in Allen's when Anita Bryant had said those awful, lying things on T.V., I didn't have the guts to speak up and tell them who I really was. Belonging, fitting in with the group was the most important thing to me, then. But now, here I was getting ready to kiss belonging and fitting in goodbye if need be.

What had happened since then?

Time. An ole tune rolled through my head and I could hear Sam Cooke's velvet-smooth voice singing: *It's been a long, long time comin, but I know, I know* change *is gonna come.* What had happened? Time bringing things to my doorstep that had changed me. Like working at Minority AIDS Project. Like going into Alcoholics Anonymous, and like finding Unity Fellowship Church. Change had come on time's coattails. A.A. had birthed it in me and Unity was breast-feeding it. As for MAP, well, Pete had been right about Miss MAP changing me, but wrong about it ruining me. Working at Miss MAP gave me backbone. And courage. I wasn't the same woman now as I was that day in Allen's.

Pandora's Box

Reverend Bean's voice spoke softly in my ear: *You are not a mistake You are God's creation, made in the image and likeness of The Creator. So, love yourself.*

Since I wasn't a mistake, why should I keep on living like I was? Acting like I was? I had to admit, it was scary, this idea of stripping off my camouflage. I thought about Henry, Jewel's bartender, living exposed, in his own "glorious personae as a queen." How would it feel to live in the world like that without camouflage? I didn't know, couldn't imagine. What I did know was that camouflage did something to you. Something toxic. Something deadly. If I let it, it would kill me, one day. Kill me deader than a doornail. And I wanted to live. That's what had really changed about me. I wanted to live.

I dialed Aunt Avice. While the phone rang, I realized I was holding my breath.

Breathe, I told myself. *Breathe. In. Out. In. Out.* My stomach twitched like a cat's tail.

"Hello," Aunt Avice said.

"It's Frankie, Aunt Avice, how are you?"

"Well, I'm fine now that I'm talkin to you, darlin." Her southern accent was as sweet as maple syrup.

"Aunt Avice," I said, standing, like Indiana Jones, at the edge of the gorge, "I have something I need to tell you about me."

And as I stepped off the edge, I saw hope rising, like a butterfly, from Pandora's box, then, felt, suddenly, the blessed assurance of something solid beneath my foot.

Discover other fine publications at:

http://www.darkoakpress.com

www.ingramcontent.com/pod-product-compliance
Lightning Source LLC
LaVergne TN
LVHW011415080426
835512LV00005B/68